T0216032

Lecture Notes in Computer Science   10544

Commenced Publication in 1973
Founding and Former Series Editors:
Gerhard Goos, Juris Hartmanis, and Jan van Leeuwen

More information about this series at http://www.springer.com/series/7409

Irene Garrigós · Manuel Wimmer (Eds.)

Current Trends in Web Engineering

ICWE 2017 International Workshops
Liquid Multi-Device Software and EnWoT,
practi-O-web, NLPIT, SoWeMine
Rome, Italy, June 5–8, 2017
Revised Selected Papers

Springer

Editors
Irene Garrigós
Universidad de Alicante
Alicante
Spain

Manuel Wimmer
Institute of Software Technology
and Interactive Systems
TU Wien
Vienna
Austria

ISSN 0302-9743   ISSN 1611-3349   (electronic)
Lecture Notes in Computer Science
ISBN 978-3-319-74432-2   ISBN 978-3-319-74433-9   (eBook)
https://doi.org/10.1007/978-3-319-74433-9

Library of Congress Control Number: Applied for

LNCS Sublibrary: SL3 – Information Systems and Applications, incl. Internet/Web, and HCI

Printed on acid-free paper

This Springer imprint is published by the registered company Springer International Publishing AG part of Springer Nature
The registered company address is: Gewerbestrasse 11, 6330 Cham, Switzerland

Preface

ICWE 2017 marked the 17th edition of the International Conference on Web Engineering and was held during June 5–8, 2017, in Rome, Italy. As in previous years, the conference main program was complemented by a number of co-located workshops, tutorials, and a doctoral consortium. All of these satellite events are designed to give researchers and practitioners an opportunity to interact in a setting that is both more informal and focused at the same time. This volume presents revised contributions to the workshops and tutorials.

Workshops have always played an important role in the ICWE community as they are a vessel both for exploring new trends and for in-depth discussions on core topics of Web engineering. This year two new workshops were presented at the conference, one focused on the Web of Things and other focused on the design and development of open data and services on the Web as well as open source. On the other hand, most of the well-established workshops broadened their focus to harbor contributions addressing novel and emerging requirements and opportunities, such as Web mining, recommendations in social media, natural language processing, or liquid software and services. At the same time, classic themes, such as Web modeling, ontology engineering, social networks, adaptivity, the Semantic Web, were also represented during the workshop program.

A total of five workshop proposals were submitted and reviewed by the workshop Program Committee with respect to topicality and chance of success. Based on their recommendations, the workshop chairs accepted the five workshops. Two of these workshops were jointly held by their organizers, and thus also have joint proceedings. The four workshops whose papers are included in this volume are:

- Liquid Multi-Device Software and EnWoT 2017: Second International Workshop on Liquid Multi-Device Software and First International Workshop on Engineering the Web of Things
- practi-O-web 2017: International Workshop on the Practice of the Open Web
- NLPIT 2017: Third International Workshop on Natural Language Processing for Informal Text
- SoWeMine 2017: Third International Workshop on Mining the Social Web

Messages from the organizers of the four workshops are presented here. In addition to the workshops, three tutorials were held at ICWE 2017. The tutorial summaries are also included in this volume:

- Liquid Web Applications: This tutorial addressed the Liquid Software concept in the context of Web applications.
- Model-Based Development of JavaScript Web Applications: This tutorial presented a model-based approach for the development of plain JavaScript Web applications.

– Big Web Data: Warehousing and Analytics – Recent Trends and Future Challenges: This tutorial explored the state of the art of big Web data warehousing and analytics as well as future challenges.

This proceedings volume would not have been possible without the work of the enthusiastic and committed workshop and tutorial organizers. Therefore, our first thank you is to all our colleagues who dedicated their time and skills to making the ICWE 2017 satellite events a success. In particular, we would like to thank the members of the workshop Selection Committee whose careful evaluations of the submitted workshop proposals were an invaluable asset in assembling the ICWE 2017 workshop program. The success of any individual workshop largely depends on the quality and quantity of submissions. Keeping this reality in mind, our thanks also go out to the researchers and practitioners who contributed their work to this volume. Finally, we would like to thank the general chair of ICWE 2017, Riccardo Torlone, and the program chairs, Jordi Cabot and Roberto De Virgilio, for their feedback and constant support.

August 2017   Irene Garrigós
                                                                                Manuel Wimmer

Organization

Workshop Selection Committee

Silvia Abrahao	Universitat Politecnica de Valencia, Spain
Cinzia Cappiello	Politecnico di Milano, Italy
Sven Casteleyn	Universitat Jaume I, Spain
Oscar Diaz	University of the Basque Country, Spain
Michael Grossniklaus	University of Konstanz, Germany
Maristella Matera	Politecnico di Milano, Italy
Gustavo Rossi	UNLP, Argentina
Elena Simperl	University of Southampton, UK
Antonio Vallecillo	Universidad de Malaga, Spain
Marco Winckler	Paul Sabatier University, France

Overcoming the Language Barrier
with BabelNet and Multilingual
Disambiguation of Text
(Keynote Talk)

Roberto Navigli

Department of Computer Science of the Sapienza
University of Rome, Italy

Abstract. Multilinguality is a key feature of todays Web, and it is this feature that we leverage and exploit in our research work at the Sapienza University of Romes Linguistic Computing Laboratory, which I am going to overview and showcase in this talk. I will start by presenting BabelNet[1], the largest multilingual encyclopedic dictionary and semantic network (now also a knowledge base), which covers 271 languages and 14 million concepts and named entities. BabelNet provides both coverage for all the open-class parts of speech, thanks to the seamless integration of WordNet, Wikipedia, Wiktionary, OmegaWiki, Wikidata and the Open Multilingual WordNet. Next, I will present Babelfy[2], a unified approach that leverages BabelNet to jointly perform word sense disambiguation and entity linking in arbitrary languages, with performance on both tasks on a par with, or surpassing, those of task-specific state-of-the-art supervised systems. Babelfy also includes a language-agnostic setting in which languages can be mixed in arbitrary ways. Finally, I will describe the most recent developments, including deep learning approaches to latent vector representations of meaning and word sense disambiguation.

---

[1] http://babelnet.org.

[2] http://babelfy.org.

Contents

ICWE 2017 Tutorials

Joint Workshop on Engineering the Web of Things and Liquid Multi-Device Software

Preface

The Web is evolving to a platform where the worlds of physical and virtual meet. The emerging Web-based services are extending human abilities for socializing and collaboration. Now, the cheap connectivity technologies foster this evolution for the rest of the things. From software development perspective, the world of computing is shifting from the era of single device computing to a new era where literally every thing is interconnected, online, and programmable.

The Joint Workshop on Engineering the Web of Things and Liquid Multi-Device Software was arranged to present the latest research and to discuss about software engineering and development in the new era of computing. The workshop was held on June 5th, 2017 in conjunction with the 17th International Conference on Web Engineering (ICWE 2017) in Rome, Italy. As the name suggests, the joint workshop focused on two themes, engineering the Internet of Things (IoT) from the perspective of Web, and on user experience from the perspective of multi device software engineering.

Web of Things is the general term used for describing all the approaches of connecting physical things to the World Wide Web. In the new era of computing the development is evolving from traditional client-server architectures to decentralized multi-device architectures in which people use various types of Web-enabled client devices, and data are stored simultaneously in numerous devices and cloud-based services. This new era will dramatically raise the expectations for device interoperability, implying significant changes for software architecture as well.

Liquid software refers to the approaches in which applications and data can seamlessly flow from one device to another, allowing the users to roam freely across all the computing devices that they have. The goal is that users of liquid software do not need to worry about data copying, manual synchronization of device settings, application installation, or other burdensome device management tasks. Rather, things should work with minimal effort. From the software development perspective, liquid software should dynamically adapt to the set of devices that are available to run it, as opposed to responsive software, which adapts to different devices, under the assumption that only one device at a time is used to run the application.

After the peer-review process, 11 papers were selected to be presented at the joint workshop. The papers covered various aspects of engineering the Web of Things and developing multi-device liquid software.

The 1st paper was "IoT Application Deployment Using Request-response Pattern with MQTT" by Antti Luoto and Kari Systä from the Tampere University of Technology. The paper describes how request-response design pattern can be implemented on top of message passing architectural style.

The 2nd paper was "Challenges when Moving from Monolith to Microservice Architecture" by Miika Kalske, Niko Mäkitalo and Tommi Mikkonen from the University of Helsinki. The paper describes what kind of organizational and technical challenges companies face while shifting from traditional monolith software architecture to decentralized microservice architecture.

The 3rd paper was "Engineering Task Automation Systems for Domain Specificity" by Carmelo Ardito, Giuseppe Desolda and Maristella Matera from the University of Bari "Aldo Moro", and from the Politecnico di Milano. The paper presents an architecture that fosters the development of Task Automation Systems that are customizable with respect to varying users and usage domains.

The 4th paper was "An adaptive formal metamodel for Semantic Complex Event Processing-driven Social Internet of Things Network" by Francesco Nocera and Angelo Parchitelli from the Polytechnic University of Bari. The paper propose a formal model for a SIoT network driven by a Semantic Complex Event Processing (CEP) where "things" are capable of establishing social relationships with respect to their owners, according to the monitoring of sensors value, changed behavioral properties, state and/or context variables and user's preference.

The 5th paper was "Towards an Acceptance Testing Approach for Internet of Things Systems" by Maurizio Leotta, Filippo Ricca, Diego Clerissi, Davide Ancona, Giorgio Delzanno, Marina Ribaudo and Luca Franceschini from the Università di Genova. The paper describes an approach for acceptance testing of IoT systems by using a realistic m-Health system composed by local sensors and actuators and a remote cloud-based healthcare system.

The 6th paper was "Semantic Discovery in the Web of Things" by Fernando Serena, María Poveda-Villalón and Raúl García-Castro from the Universidad Politécnica de Madrid. The paper presents an ontology-based approach to leverage web things discovery that is transparent to the syntax, protocols and formats used in things interfaces and propose a semantic model for describing web things and how to extract and understand the relevant information for discovery.

The 7th we had demo paper "Four key factors to design a Web of things architecture" by Francesco Bruni, Pomo Claudio and Gaetano Murgolo from the Planetek Italia SRL, from the Polytechnic University of Bari, and from the Engineering Consulting SRL. The paper presents a model for exposing electrical based measurements data over the Web to monitor consumptions, breakdown and preventing unforeseen events.

The 8th paper was "Liquid Transfer of User Identity" by Sivamani Thangavel and Kari Systä from the Tampere University of Technology. The paper presented an implementation of how the user's digital identity can follow the user while roaming from one device to another.

The 9th paper was "Wireless Brain-Computer Interface for Wheelchair Control by Using Fast Machine Learning and Real-Time Hyper-Dimensional Classification" by Valerio Francesco Annese, Giovanni Mezzina and Daniela De Venuto from the University of Glasgow, and from the Polytechnic University of Bari. The paper presents a noninvasive brain-controlled P300-based wheelchair driven by EEG signals to be used by tetraplegic and paralytic users.

The 10th paper was "Case Study: Building a Serverless Messenger Chatbot" by Jyri Lehvä, Niko Mäkitalo and Tommi Mikkonen from the University of Helsinki. The paper reported a case study where a chatbot was build for a Finish media company using Facebook Messenger platform and serverless computing.

The 11th we had a demo paper "A Homemade Pill Dispenser Prototype Supporting Elderly" by Paolo Buono, Fabio Cassano, Alessandra Legretto and Antonio Piccinno from the University of Bari "Aldo Moro". The paper descibes a device for the management of pills according to the user's therapy, with Internet of things (IoT) devices and by allowing users to manage the pill dispenser by themselves.

We are grateful to the Program Committee members for their work on the paper review and selection process. We would also like to thank all the authors and workshop participants for the interesting discussions.

Niko Mäkitalo
Marina Mongiello
Francesco Nocera
Tommaso Di Noia
Eugenio Di Sciascio
Tommi Mikkonen
Cesare Pautasso
Kari Systä
Antero Taivalsaari

Organization

Program Committee

Robert Hirschfeld	Hasso-Platter Institute, Univ. of Potsdam, Germany
Kari Systä	Tampere University of Technology, Finland
Daniele Bonetta	Oracle, USA
Hallvard Trætteberg	Norwegian Institute of Technology, Norway
Tommi Mikkonen	University of Helsinki, Finland
Michael Nebeling	University of Michigan, USA
Cesare Pautasso	University of Lugano, Switzerland
Maria Husmann	ETH Zürich, Switzerland
Antero Taivalsaari	Nokia Technologies, Finland
Jose Garcia-Alonso	University of Extremadura, Spain
Mirjana Ivanovic	University of Novi Sad, Serbia
Javier Berrocal	University of Extremadura, Spain
Niko Mäkitalo	University of Helsinki, Finland
Muhammad Ali Babar	University of Adelaide, Australia
Marco Autili	University of L'Aquila, Italy
Stefano Bistarelli	University of Perugia, Italy
Antonio Bucchiarone	Fondazione Bruno Kessler, Italy
Radu Calinescu	University of York, UK
Rafael Capilla	Universidad Rey Juan Carlos, Spain
Patricia Lago	Vrije Universiteit Amsterdam, Netherlands
Ivano Malavolta	Vrije Universiteit Amsterdam, Netherlands
Raffaela Mirandola	Politecnico di Milano, Italy
Henry Muccini	University of L'Aquila, Italy
Diego Pérez	Politecnico di Milano, Italy
Liliana Pasquale	Lero - The Irish Software Research Centre, Ireland
Azzurra Ragone	University of Milano-Bicocca, Italy
Patrizia Scandurra	University of Bergamo, Italy
Ronny Siebes	Vrije Universiteit Amsterdam, Netherlands
Romina Spalazzese	Malmö University, Sweden
Danny Weyns	Katholieke Uviversiteit Leuven, Belgium
Uwe Zdun	University of Vienna, Austria

An Adaptive Formal Metamodel for Semantic Complex Event Processing-Driven Social Internet of Things Network

Francesco Nocera[✉][iD] and Angelo Parchitelli

Department of Electrical and Information Engineering,
Polytechnic University of Bari, Via Orabona n.4, 70126 Bari, Italy
francesco.nocera@poliba.it

Abstract. Information, objects and people are the core innovation actors of human society progress. Their inner relations can be rebounded by the Internet, the Internet of Things (IoT) and social network, respectively. The integration of social networking concepts into the IoT solutions has led to the so called Social Internet of Things (SIoT) paradigm, according to the vision of a future world populated by intelligent objects that permeate the everyday life of human beings.

In this context we propose an adaptive formal model for a SIoT network driven by a Semantic Complex Event Processing where "things" are capable of establishing social relationships with respect to their owners, according to the monitoring of sensors value, changed behavioral properties, state and/or context variables and user's preference.

Keywords: Social network · Internet of Things · Social IoT
Complex Event Processing

1 Introduction

The pervasive spread of physical devices, sensors and actuators, in general objects connected to the Internet is driving an exponential growth of Internet of Things (IoT) applications. The huge amount of data flowing though IoT networks poses a big issue related to the discovery of objects that are able to provide data by executing specific services. In this context, real world applications where streams of Big Event Data are the essence, include, but are not limited to, Smart City, Smart Home, Smart Transportation, Healthcare and Industry 4.0. Several approaches for "near "real-time search have been proposed.

The Smart Home is one of the focus area of the new IoT ecosystem era, both the centrality of the house in the life of every individual, with huge potential in terms of objects and distribution services, for both the bond with some of the leading sectors. Now, must be viewed as a dream where "things", particularly all

© Springer International Publishing AG, part of Springer Nature 2018
I. Garrigós and M. Wimmer (Eds.): ICWE 2017, LNCS 10544, pp. 7–18, 2018.
https://doi.org/10.1007/978-3-319-74433-9_1

home machines and more, are intelligible, locatable, addressable or controllable through the Internet.

The evolution of existing technologies and emerging standards is increasingly oriented to optimizing the use of mobile devices. This phenomenon is related to a massive growing number of users accessing on Internet resources by a smartphone or tablet.

In parallel, the advent of the Internet and the mainstreaming of the world wide web in the early 1980s gave us the ideal technology to facilitate social networking. A social network is a community where the individuals are linked to each other by proximity, socially, by a common interest or goal. Examples of social networks include a family, a work friends and so on. When these groups connect for the purpose of communication and sharing, they are said to be "social networking".

When Social Networks meet the Internet of Things, the resulting paradigm is called *Social Internet of Things(SIoT)*. The idea to use social networking concepts in the IoT solutions to allow objects to autonomously establish social relationships is gaining popularity in the last years.

The IoT-generated data come in big amounts, are variable in terms of structure, often do not arrive at real-time, and could undermine the purpose of the services offered. This volume, speed and diversity make the storage and processing solution a very complex challenge. Traditional DBMSs, which need to store and index data before processing it, can hardly fulfill the concepts of timeliness and flow processing coming from such domains. Recently, new approach known as Complex Event Processing (CEP) emerged. CEP allows for efficient correlation, aggregation, and pattern matching of multiple distributed data streams on the fly.

In this paper we propose a Semantic CEP-driven SIoT network model to communicate and interact with smart things that humans use in daily life taking into account relevant aspects adaptation: context, users habits and profiles, information detached from external sources and sensors.

The proposed approach allows modelling and reasoning on complex adaptive architecture according to changed behavioural properties or context variables [11].

The rest of the paper is organized as follows: Sect. 2 provides a background and a review of related works, while Sect. 3 describes the proposed approach. Section 4 instantiates the model in Smart Home scenario and the last section concludes the paper and outlines future work.

2 Background and Related Work

Social Internet of Things (SIoT). The idea of applying social networking concept in the IoT solutions to allow objects to autonomously fix social relationships has gained popularity in the last few years. The driving motivations are the following: *(i)* the SIoT structure can be shaped as required to guarantee the network navigability, so as that the discovery of objects and services is performed effectively and the scalability is guaranteed like in the human social networks;

(ii) a level of trustworthiness can be established for leveraging the degree of interaction among things that are friends; *(iii)* models designed to study the social networks can be reused to address IoT related issues (intrinsically related to extensive networks of interconnected objects) [1].

Complex Event Processing (CEP). The concept of CEP was introduced by David Luckham in his seminal work [9] as a "defined set of tools and techniques for analyzing and controlling the complex series of interrelated events that drive modern distributed Information Systems (IS)."

As shown in Fig. 1, CEP systems associate a precise semantics to the information items being processed: they are notifications of events happened in the external world and observed by sources. The CEP engine provides a rich set of concepts and operators for processing events, which include the CQL-like (Continuous Query Language), queries, primitive functions (aggregation, filtering, transformation, etc.), rules, showing derived events. A CEP workflow continually processes incoming events, explore and manipulates them, and outputs derived events that are delivered to sinks, which acts as event consumers. These output regularly represent notifications about detected interest situations. The handling of events are described by Event-Condition-Actions (ECA) -based CEP rules, that combine continuous query primitives with context operators (e.g. temporal, logical, quantifiers) on received events, checking for correlations among these events, and generating complex (or composite) events [2].

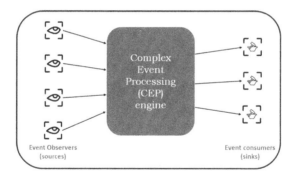

Fig. 1. The high-level view of a CEP system.

Related Work. A first idea of socialization between objects has been introduced by Holmquist et al. in their work [6], where the focus was on solutions that enable smart wireless devices, mostly wireless sensors, to establish temporary relationships. The authors also analyse how the owners of the sensor nodes should control such a process and they propose *context proximity* for selective artefacts communication, using the concept of artefacts for matchmaking. In [4] the authors propose a a platform to cluster the Internet, the IoT and social network together. With the proposed platform, most macro elements can be tracked and summarized. The research activity in [10] introduces the idea of objects able to participate in conversations. The authors propose a balanced interaction between physical, social and virtual worlds, supported by the development of a data-centric architecture based on IP-driven opportunistic communications able to make useful data available to people when and where they really need it, augmenting their social and environmental awareness. An important step has been accomplished in [8]. In this work, the authors show how to empower physical objects to share pictures, comments, and sensor data via social networks. They also discuss about the implications of the so called "socio-technical networks" in the context of the IoT. The confluence of IoT and social networks has been considered in [5]. The proposed system enables individual to share the services offered by her/his smart objects with either her/his friends or their things. Kim et al. [7] propose relevant semantic metamodels for users, devices, locations and their relationships. Their proposed semantic metamodel enable interactions between users and devices based on the rules for relationship management, for basic automation, context generation, social gamification.

3 Proposed Formal Metamodel

In this section we describe the proposed formal approach to build a Social IoT network driven by a Semantic CEP engine to support the execution of domain-specific services. Modelling relies on behavioural/contextual changes and observable properties of the user's habits and profiles. The metamodel is made up of a inference level where incoming flows of information have to be processed to timely produce new flows as outputs (Sinks). The entities that create the information flows are called Information Sources. Sources and Sinks are interpreted in the sense of the CEP metamodel definition [9]. The events to be performed are derived from high-level properties, conditions about the state, context and sensor data.

Definition 1 (Event). *Event is a thing happening in a definite time and environment, that some social entity take part in and showing some action features. An event e can be defined as the following tuple:*

$$e:: = (A, A_c, T, E, A_{ss}, L_e),$$

where A is an agent, A_c is an action, T is a time, E is an environment, A_{ss} an assertions and L_e a language expression.

Intuitively, social entity (smart object or human agent) actions are the observations of sensor data, the publishing of a post and so on.

Definition 2 (SIoTN Ontology). *Social Internet of Things Network (SIoTN) Ontology formally specifies the shared and event classes. It can be defined as a quadruple formally.*

$$SIoTNOntology =< Ec, Ei, R, e >$$

The elements in quadruples include the set of Entity classes, the set of Entity instances, the relationship $R = < Ec_i, Ei_j >$ (R includes parent-child, causal, follow and exclusion relations) and the correspondent event, respectively.

Thanks to the defined relationship between Entity instances it is possible to infer conditions between the entities, allowing the activation of a certain action.

Definition 3 (Context-aware SIoT Metamodel). *A Context-aware SIoTN Metamodel is a tuple*

$$CaSIoTNM =$$
$$< S_c, CEP, SIoTNOntology, S_k, Actions, C_x, U_m >,$$

where S_c and S_K are respectively the sources *and* sinks *according to CEP definition; CEP is an instantiation of a Complex Event Processing (CEP) engine, C_x is the Context and U_m the user's model. The Contexts model every condition of the entity adaptation can have no effect on, e.g., instance, sensors data, geographical location, nearest street address, date/time, etc. Performed Actions are based on continual query and pattern matching verifying ontological conditions.*

Figure 2 shows the metamodel of the proposed approach.

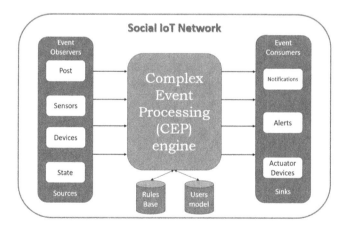

Fig. 2. The proposed metamodel.

3.1 Personalized Action Selection: Fuzzy *ECA* Rules

In this section we present a set of definitions useful for characterize the selection of actions to be performed at runtime according to *(i)* changes in requirements, *(ii)* changes in state-context/environment, and *(iii)* user's habits and needs.

In most cases, a perfect match between the actual state and context and the ones required in the condition is not to be expected [3]. Given an *ECA* rule and a state-context $\tilde{S}$, *(i)* we need to evaluate if the state-context is "similar" enough to the one specified in the Condition (C part of ECA rule); *(ii)* we want to execute the Action (A part of ECA rule) whose condition C are more similar to $\tilde{S}$. Moreover, it would be advisable that the selection procedure by the Rule Manager behaves in a personalized way. That is, given $\tilde{S}$, the selection of the action to be executed may change depending on the user. Hence, when evaluating the condition C_i of an action A_i, most comparisons in C_i are evaluated as *fuzzy conditions* in Fuzzy Logic [12], an approach to computing based on "degree of truth "rather then the usual "true or false "boolean logic values.

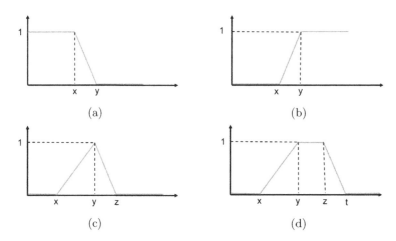

Fig. 3. Fuzzy Membership functions. (a) Left Shoulder function $ls(x,y)$, (b) Right Shoulder function $rs(x,y)$, (c) Triangular function $tri(x,y,z)$, and (d) Trapezoidal function $tra(x,y,z,t)$.

This approach offer remarkable advantages when the set of conditions is huge. In fact, we can use this logic, based on the idea that the elements of the set are defined by degrees of membership in the set of values. The basic idea is that a physical quantity can assume not only boolean values, such as true or false, but a set of values indicating the degree of truth of a certain expression.

Definition 4 (Crisp Set). *A crisp set A is a collection of objects O_i taken into a universal set U.*

Definition 5 (Characteristic Function). *A characteristic function is a function that declares what elements of U belong to the set and which are not according to the following expression:*

$$\mu_A : x \in A \rightarrow \{0,1\}$$
$$if \ x \in A \rightarrow \mu_A = 1$$
$$if \ x \notin A \rightarrow \mu_A = 0$$

Give a fuzzy set A, the proposition "x is a member of A" is not necessarily true or false but if it can be only partially true. The proposition is true with a degree of certainty which ranges between 0 and 1.

Definition 6 (Fuzzy Set). *Let U be a space elements of x. A fuzzy set A is defined as the set of pairs:*

$$A = \{(x, \mu_A(x)) | x \in U, \mu_A(x) : U[0,1]\}$$

A fuzzy logic has the aim to shape the real world no more as a binary world but in a more nuanced logic. The fuzzy logic is an alternative logic than to Aristotelica. In fact this logic rejects the Aristotelian principle of the excluded middle: if A is A, then A can not be not-A. The principle of excluded drastically defines the boundaries between opposites: high and low, good and bad, black and white, etc. In practice, the reality is less clear: not everything is high and not everything is low. For example, with the classic definition, once defined the hot temperature to above $18\,^{\circ}C$, the temperature of $17.9\,^{\circ}C$ is defined as cold and not hot.

In literature exist several membership functions as depicted in Fig. 3: the Left Shoulder function $ls(x, y)$, the Right Shoulder function $rs(x, y)$, the Triangular function $tri(x, y, z)$ and the Trapezoidal function $tra(x, y, z, t)$. The choice of the appropriate function is associated to a fuzzy set.

In this way, we can represents a general Fuzzy condition C based on *state* and *Context* information according to the following definitions.

Definition 7 (States). *Given a set of State Variables $SVars = \{v_1, \ldots, v_n\}$, and a set of corresponding domain values $\{V_1, \ldots, V_n\}$, a State is an assignment $s : v_i \mapsto d \in V_i$ that for each $i = 1, \ldots, n$ maps each state variable v_i to its current value $s(v_i) \in V_i$.*

An *Action* can change a state s to a state $\tilde{s}$, by changing the value of any number of state variables.

For example, a state variable *gps* of a mobile device may record in a boolean value whether the GPS is ON or OFF, another may record whether or not the present value of *Thermostat*, etc. Actions model the adaptations of the devices, e.g. turn OFF the GPS and reduce the temperature of autonomous heating. State variables not affected by an action keep their values.

Contexts are defined in the same way, but with the crucial difference that context variables cannot be changed by actions; the device environment changes them exogenously.

Definition 8 (Contexts). *Given a set of Context Variables $CVars = \{w_1, \ldots, w_m\}$, and a set of corresponding domain values $\{W_1, \ldots, W_m\}$, a Context c_x is an assignment $c_x : w_i \mapsto d \in W_i$ that for each $i = 1, \ldots, m$ maps each context variable w_i to its current value $c(w_i) \in W_i$.*

Definition 9 (Conditions). *We call $\mathcal{C}$ the language containing all possible conditions. For every action a, the condition C (part of ECA rule) is a formula $C_a \in \mathcal{C}$ which is a Boolean combination of*

- *comparisons of state variables (v_i op d), where $v_i \in SVars$, $d \in D_i$, and op $\in \{=, \neq, <, >, \geq, \leq\}$ is a comparison operator;*
- *comparisons of context variables (c_i op d), where $c_i \in CVars$, $d \in W_i$, and op is as above.*

Given a condition $C \in \mathcal{C}$, represented as a Boolean combination of *state* and *Context* variables comparison we now define how to evaluate its truth value.

Definition 10 (Interpretation). *An **interpretation** $\mathcal{I}$ for $\mathcal{C}$ is a function $\cdot^{\mathcal{I}}$ that maps each comparison of state variables (v_i op d) occurring in P_a to a truth value $(v_i$ op $d)^{\mathcal{I}} = f(d)$ and, analogously, each comparison of context variables (c_{xi} op d) to a truth value $(c_{xi}$ op $d)^{\mathcal{I}} = f(d)$ with f being a fuzzy membership function. Given $C_a, C'_a \in \mathcal{C}$ we recursively define the interpretation of a formula as:*

- $(\neg C_a)^{\mathcal{I}} = 1 - C_a^{\mathcal{I}}$
- $(C_a \wedge C'_a)^{\mathcal{I}} = min(C_a^{\mathcal{I}}, C_a'^{\mathcal{I}})$
- $(C_a \vee C'_a)^{\mathcal{I}} = max(C_a^{\mathcal{I}}, C_a'^{\mathcal{I}})$

With reference to the above definition, given a set of conditions $\hat{\mathcal{C}} \subseteq \mathcal{C}$ we can compute a total order among its elements by means of the interpretation functions. Indeed, given $C_a, C_b \in \hat{\mathcal{C}}$ we can always evaluate whether $C_a^{\mathcal{I}} \geq C_b^{\mathcal{I}}$ or $C_b^{\mathcal{I}} \geq C_a^{\mathcal{I}}$. Actually, an order among conditions can be easily reverted to a ranking among the corresponding actions. In other words, if $C_a^{\mathcal{I}} \geq C_b^{\mathcal{I}}$ we assume a is more likely to be executed than b.

Definition 11 (Executable Rule). *Let $ECARR = \{\langle a, C_a \rangle, \langle b, C_b \rangle, \ldots\}$ be an ECA Rules Repository, and $t \in (0, 1)$ be a threshold value. We say a is an **executable rule** iff both there is no rule b such that $C_b^{\mathcal{I}} > C_a^{\mathcal{I}}$ and $C_a^{\mathcal{I}} \geq t$.*

We may have more than one executable rule $a, a', a'', \ldots$. Indeed, it may occur that $C_a^{\mathcal{I}} = C_{a'}^{\mathcal{I}} = C_{a''}^{\mathcal{I}} = \ldots$. We see that as we do not have any order among $a, a', a'', \ldots$ we may execute any of them randomly. The reason why we introduce the threshold t is to avoid situations where the executed action has a low truth value (which corresponds to a high untruth value). Given a state-context $\tilde{C}$, in case there is no executable action, the CEP engine does nothing until the next change in $\tilde{C}$.

With respect to the metamodel presented in this section, we can encode preferences within the fuzzy membership functions. In fact, looking at Fig. 3, we see they are defined in terms of a set of parameters x, y, z, t. By changing these values, we modify the shape of the functions. Let us go back to our example ($time = 13 : 30$) and suppose we define the *fuzzy set* associated to time by means of a triangular function with $y = 13 : 30$. We may distinguish between an "always on time" user and a "more relaxed" one by setting, for instance, in the former case $x = 12 : 25$ and $z = 13 : 35$ while in the latter case $x = 13 : 00$ and $z = 14 : 00$. Hence, the truth value associated to C_a may change and then the possible selection of a as executable action. It is noteworthy that x, y, z, t can be either be set manually or be automatically learned by collecting information about the user's behavior.

The history of the user's behavior is stored in an ontological model through the values of the context and state variables describing the actions generally performed by the user and the related preferences. A triangular function elicits the variables values to describe the user's behavior: for example, the history of the places she usually visits (in this case, the state variable is *position*), or the times he usually returns at home or he's going to another place. The CEP engine will choose among the pool of rules identified in the *ECA Rules Repository* the rule that verifies the constraint with the threshold t with respect to the triangular function of variable in the condition. In case of multiple properties in the condition expressed with a fuzzy variables the minimum or maximum operator as specified in the corresponding fuzzy interpretation.

To make the formulas fuzzy, we can express the conditions using intervals, that is, the condition is not true for only one value of the formula, but for the values in these ranges. For example, the choice of points to be displayed on a map will not be shown only for an exact value of the radius of the area, but depending on user habits, this value can be included in a interval. For example, y is the current position, while the interval $[x, z]$ defines the length of the circumference of the diameter to be displayed (centered at y).

4   Prototype Instantiation of the Metamodel

4.1   Smart Home

The metamodel proposed in Sect. 3 was instantiated in the domain of smart home. Living in a smart home brings many benefits, especially at the level of comfort, safety, energy saving and so on. Systems integration, with its endless customization possibilities, significantly improves the domestic liveability. In smart home scenario it is in fact possible to control each device with the touch of a button or in a completely automated way, and have full control of our home. The practicality of an automated system is also expressed in the possibility to program specific functions at predetermined times or store scenarios, namely a series of commands that are activated simultaneously, designed to meet the needs of a particular condition based on state and context variables.

Nowadays, also the proximity environment domain is being considered as an added value of most applications, especially in social environments. This phenomenon is widely observed spreading in the social sphere, thanks to the enormous spread of smartphones with GPS. Using the GPS connection, we can model as context variable the *social network user position*. For example, depending on the context (location, time) points and user's habits, when one user is returning home or is wakes up in the morning, devices such as autonomous heating or rolling shutter, can interact with the user activating the change of device state, turn ON the autonomous heating system and pull up the rolling shutters, respectively.

4.2   Context-Aware SIoT Metamodel Instantiation

The instantiated metamodel exploits the *goals*, the objective that the user expects. Table 1 summarizes, in this exemplifying version, how the elements in the tuple $CaSIoTNM$ are instantiated. Table 2 presents an example of the instantiated (fuzzy) ECA rules. State and context variables are sensors in the external environments, context variables available on the user mobile device, events extracted from the sensors. In this instantiation we constructed an OWL 2 ontology[1] to represent all the described knowledge related to the defined

Table 1. Instantiation of the elements in the tuple $CaSIoTNM$ for Smart Home scenario.

Element	Instantiation
S_c	Entities that create the information flows entering the CEP engine: GPS device, smart home objects, human agent post and so on
CEP	Tool that operates according to a set of *processing rules*
$SIoTNOntology$	A formal naming and definition of the types, properties, and interrelationships of the entities that really exist according to Definition 2
S_k	Recipient of output(s): Human agents, devices and actuators
$Actions$	Performed actions based on the combination of continuous query primitives with context operators on received events, checking for correlations among these events
C_x	Sensors in the external environments
U_m	User habits (time lunch, sleep), the places already visited, how many times they were visited, preferences about smart devices states, type of medium supply, etc.

Table 2. Example of (Fuzzy) ECA rule for Smart Home Scenario.

EVENT: Fire-alarm
CONDITION: ($temperatureValue > thresholdofHeat$) and ($duration > thresholdofDuration$)
ACTION: Send Fire-alarm Post on social Network

EVENT: Recommend most used app at home
CONDITION: ($gps = true$) and ($gps.precision < x_1$) and ($location = y_2$) and ($time \sim 19:00$)
ACTION: Displays facebook, youtube, netflix, meteo apps

EVENT: Automatic ignition autonomous heating system
CONDITION: ($gps = true$) and ($season = winter$) and ($radius > x_2$) and ($radius < z_2 - x_2$) and ($time = 18:50$)
ACTION: Turn ON rolling shutter actuator

---

[1] https://www.w3.org/TR/owl2-overview/.

metamodel in Sect. 3 by using *Protégé Version 5.1.0²* editor. Figure 4 shows the class hierarchy graph of the instantiated ontology. CEP engine is responsible for observation, filtering, and pattern matching from data sources, based on the defined *ECA* rules, combining such notifications to sinks.

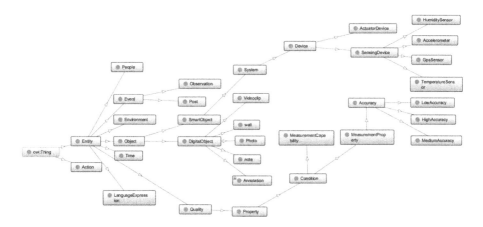

Fig. 4. Class hierarchy graph of the instantiated *SIoTNOntology*.

The proposed solution allows the communication between humans and smart devices to autonomously establish social relationships, providing automatic functionalities related to the home living, status change of smart home devices, include recommendations and so on.

5 Conclusion and Future Work

In the Big Data era, the huge amount of data flowing though IoT networks poses a big issue related to the discovery of objects that are able to provide data by executing specific services. The evolution of existing technologies and emerging standards is increasingly oriented to optimizing the use of mobile devices. The idea to use social networking concepts in the IoT solutions to allow objects to autonomously establish social relationships is gaining popularity in the last years. When Social Networks meet the Internet of Things, the resulting paradigm is called *Social Internet of Things(SIoT)*. In this paper we propose a formal Semantic CEP-driven SIoT network model to communicate and interact with smart things that humans use in daily life taking into account relevant aspects adaptation: context, users habits and profiles, information detached from external sources and sensors.

The proposed approach allows modelling and reasoning on complex adaptive architecture according to changed behavioural properties or context variables.

---

² http://protege.stanford.edu/.

We are currently implementing the prototype version by detecting all possible *ECA* rule in Smart Home Scenario. We see the presented model as a research vehicle to analyze the implications of socio-technical networks in the context of IoT, especially concerning the perception of these system in the eyes of human users. We guess that IoT, as it becomes part of our social lives, can help non-technical relations we continuously establish in a more technical advanced society and make our dependencies on systems more intuitive. We plan to additionally include wearable sensing system to monitor personal health data.

References

1. Atzori, L., Iera, A., Morabito, G., Nitti, M.: The social internet of things (siot)-when social networks meet the internet of things: concept, architecture and network characterization. Comput. Netw. **56**(16), 3594–3608 (2012)
2. Cugola, G., Margara, A.: Processing flows of information: from data stream to complex event processing. ACM Comput. Surv. (CSUR) **44**(3), 15 (2012)
3. Di Noia, T., Di Sciascio, E., Donini, F.M., Mongiello, M., Nocera, F.: Formal model for user-centred adaptive mobile devices. IET Software, Jan 2017
4. Ding, L., Shi, P., Liu, B.: The clustering of internet, internet of things and social network. In: 2010 3rd International Symposium on Knowledge Acquisition and Modeling (KAM), pp. 417–420. IEEE (2010)
5. Guinard, D., Fischer, M., Trifa, V.: Sharing using social networks in a composable web of things. In: 2010 8th IEEE International Conference on Pervasive Computing and Communications Workshops (PERCOM Workshops), pp. 702–707. IEEE (2010)
6. Holmquist, L.E., Mattern, F., Schiele, B., Alahuhta, P., Beigl, M., Gellersen, H.-W.: Smart-its friends: a technique for users to easily establish connections between smart artefacts. In: Abowd, G.D., Brumitt, B., Shafer, S. (eds.) UbiComp 2001. LNCS, vol. 2201, pp. 116–122. Springer, Heidelberg (2001). https://doi.org/10.1007/3-540-45427-6_10
7. Kim, J.E., Maron, A., Mosse, D.: Socialite: a flexible framework for social internet of things. In: 2015 16th IEEE International Conference on Mobile Data Management (MDM), vol. 1, pp. 94–103. IEEE (2015)
8. Kranz, M., Roalter, L., Michahelles, F.: Things that twitter: social networks and the internet of things. In: What can the Internet of Things do for the Citizen (CIoT) Workshop at The Eighth International Conference on Pervasive Computing (Pervasive 2010), pp. 1–10 (2010)
9. Luckham, D.: The Power of Events, vol. 204. Addison-Wesley, Reading (2002)
10. Mendes, P.: Social-driven internet of connected objects. In: Proceedings of the Interconn, Smart Objects with the Internet Workshop (2011)
11. Mongiello, M., Di Noia, T., Nocera, F., Di Sciascio, E.: Case-based reasoning and knowledge-graph based metamodel for runtime adaptive architectural modeling. In: Proceedings of the 31st Annual ACM Symposium on Applied Computing, SAC 2016, pp. 1323–1328. ACM, New York (2016)
12. Zadeh, L.A.: Fuzzy sets. Inf. Control **8**(3), 338–353 (1965)

Semantic Discovery in the Web of Things

Fernando Serena[(⊠)], María Poveda-Villalón , and Raúl García-Castro

Ontology Engineering Group, Universidad Politécnica de Madrid, Madrid, Spain
{fserena,mpoveda,rgarcia}@fi.upm.es

Abstract. While the number of things present in the Web grows, the ability of discovering such things in order to successfully interact with them becomes a challenge, mainly due to heterogeneity. The contribution of this paper is two-fold. First, an ontology-based approach to leverage web things discovery that is transparent to the syntax, protocols and formats used in things interfaces is described. Second, a semantic model for describing web things and how to extract and understand the relevant information for discovery is proposed.

Keywords: Discovery · Interoperability · Web of Things · Ontologies

1 Introduction

The Internet of Things is characterized by its inherent heterogeneity [1], which is evident when thinking about the diversity of things that can be accessed through the Internet. Such diversity does not apply only to the type of things, e.g., thermostat, traffic light; but also to many other aspects like their communication protocols, data formats and even the IoT standards [2] they implement. Furthermore, the range of possibilities for the aforementioned aspects are not expected to stop growing, so one can say that heterogeneity can only evolve.

The number of various things that are being made available through the Internet is growing steadily[1]. Therefore, IoT consumers cannot be asked to be aware of every possible aspect, platforms and individual things out there, so that it is necessary to rely on mechanisms and services that enable them to search for and discover what they want to consume. In other words, discovery is meant to cope and take advantage of the heterogeneity and large population of things in the IoT. For example, discovery is one of the Common Service Functions of the architecture proposed by the oneM2M standarization organization[2].

A detailed description of the open issues in discovery for the so-called Web of Things (WoT) is provided in Sect. 2, including a characterization of web

---

This research is partially supported by the European project VICINITY: Open virtual neighbourhood network to connect intelligent buildings and smart objects (H2020-688467) http://vicinity2020.eu/vicinity/.

[1] http://www.businessinsider.com/there-will-be-34-billion-iot-devices-installed-on-earth-by-2020-2016-5.

[2] http://www.onem2m.org/technical/published-documents.

I. Garrigós and M. Wimmer (Eds.): ICWE 2017, LNCS 10544, pp. 19–31, 2018.
https://doi.org/10.1007/978-3-319-74433-9_2

things based on the current discussion of the corresponding W3C Working Group (WG)[3], and outlining a desirable common data model for thing descriptions.

A particular approach for semantic discovery of web things, their interaction patterns and attributes regardless of specific communication protocols, syntax and data formats used in their web interfaces is provided as first contribution of this paper and it is described in Sect. 3. A use case that implements the proposed approach is also provided.

Since such approach is ontology-based, an overview of the developed ontologies for supporting the proposed solution is presented in Sect. 4. This description framework for the Web of Things in the form of an ontology which answers to what a thing is, where in the Web are its interfaces and how to extract and understand the discovery-relevant information from it represents the second contribution of the present work.

Existing approaches for WoT discoverability and related semantic models are outlined in Sect. 5 before concluding and discussing future work in Sect. 6.

2   Discovery in the Web of Things

Discovery in the IoT can be thought of as search on web pages: consumers issue some search criteria that can result in the discovery of a set of resources relevant to the consumer and possibly yet unknown. Although, inevitably, in order to yield useful results, it is necessary to have the means to characterize or describe resources so that potential matches with the provided search criteria can be detected. As it is well known, search engines work with documents and count on standards like HTML. Nevertheless, discovery services in the IoT are still orphaned in common formats and syntax for that purpose in a global scope.

Therefore, a common data model for describing things, their features and capabilities is required. In this sense, the W3C Web of Things WG is already working on defining and standardizing a Thing Description (TD) data model.

2.1   Web Things

The Web of Things (WoT) aims to make everything that belongs to an IoT ecosystem (e.g., devices, systems, or data) part of the Web, leveraging it as a platform. Thus, all individual things accessible through a web interface may belong to the WoT. Still, along with the description of the features and capabilities of these web things, their web interfaces have to be described as well.

At discovery time, web things intertwine what has traditionally been separated: resource and service discovery [3]. Discovery clients are not only interested in what web things are but also in where and how to reach them out on the Web. Regarding the "where", descriptions must inform about the corresponding dereferenceable links for accessing the thing; regarding the "how", descriptions should include relevant metadata that report on aspects to be taken into account when

---

[3] https://www.w3.org/WoT/WG/.

invoking each link, e.g., communication protocol, data formats and security constraints. In this way, descriptions of discovered things may provide complete "views" that can lead consumers to implement informed interactions, even automatically, and bringing a minimum support to IoT interoperability.

2.2   Description Scope

Not all thing attributes that are relevant for discovery can be expressed in a static and shareable description; mainly because they are dynamic, protected or both. For instance, the geo-location of certain physical things can be considered as sensitive and only be obtained under specific security and privacy constraints, through its endpoints. Besides, its value may dynamically vary as the physical thing changes its position. Therefore, if this casuistry is not taken into account, the location-based discovery of such kind of things will not be possible.

A solution to this would involve describing as well how data provided by secured endpoints map to specific thing attributes. By following this approach, descriptions might inform on how to automatically and securely retrieve and map their own missing attribute values, by means of what we call *access mappings*.

2.3   Access Mappings

The adoption of *access mappings* in the data model for web things leads to a wider scope solution: to gather values for any kind of thing attributes from its own web interfaces, significantly extending the support to interoperability in the IoT ecosystem. In order to achieve this, data models for web things should also support describing the exchanged data with mentioned links or endpoints, i.e., they should not just describe its format but also its content. Thus, rather than expecting to receive data from endpoints in a specific syntax, descriptions would inform consumers on how to process responses and extract useful information.

For instance, the description of a temperature sensor may tell that the data received after invoking an endpoint contains the latest measured value in Celsius and where to find such value in the response. Thanks to this, discovery clients might be able to issue search criteria for things measuring temperature in Celsius and get, extract and interpret values from the discovered things' endpoints.

3   Ontology-Based Approach for Discovery

Having a common data model turns out to be the cornerstone of interoperability in the Web of Things. Besides, the richer the model, the more interoperable things will be. Still, increasing the richness does not necessarily mean that the model has to be more complex, but rather better represent the ecosystem. Even having the richest model imaginable shared by all actors of the ecosystem is not sufficient to facilitate discovery. It is also desirable that approaches for discovery in WoT meet the following requirements:

– Depending on the context and use case, at least one of the following interaction patterns[4] for discovery should be supported: (a) finding things around spatial coordinates, (b) finding things on a network, (c) searching in directories, and (d) accessing thing metadata.
– Communication technologies used by things should not condition the process of discovery. They just have to be properly described in case there are endpoints that implement them.
– Requests should be expressed as queries based on the common data model.
– The model for describing things must be agnostic of whatever discovery interaction patterns are required in the use case; web things are what they are regardless of the mechanisms implemented to discover them.

In any case, all approaches for discovery in the WoT would mainly build on the ability of involved actors to generate, publish, understand and query thing descriptions. Not all actors of the WoT need to have all these abilities; it shall depend on the role each one plays in the ecosystem, e.g., consumers are not required to have the same abilities as publishers. In what follows, descriptions of the aforementioned abilities as well as their impact on the different approaches for discovery are provided.

Generate. Descriptions of things provided by web interfaces need to be generated so as to become part of the WoT and, in turn, to be interoperable in the ecosystem. Such generation may be performed manually, e.g., by the owner of the web thing; or automatically, by a hypothetical system capable of characterizing web things. Such a task of automatically describing the type of a certain thing plus some of its attributes and features might seem to be not too complicated if sufficient metadata about it can be obtained automatically as well, e.g., HATEOAS, CoRE Link Format. However, it is not the case of automatic description of their web interfaces, even if they were built using standards like OData[5], OpenAPI[6] or RAML[7].

Publish. Once a thing description is generated it has to be made available in a machine-readable format so that others can eventually consume it. Intuitively, there are at least two ways of publishing these descriptions: (a) the actual thing directly exposes its own description through an endpoint, (b) a third-party entity is given thing descriptions so as to be the directory of the ecosystem. Choosing one or the other may significantly affect the architectural approach to address the discovery problem, e.g., the former may be crucial in peer-to-peer solutions.

Understand. In order for actors to interact with a discovered thing, they must be able to read, parse and understand its description. Thus, it is required to have a well-defined set of predefined serialization formats and common syntax shared by all actors. The usage of the common data model in descriptions is what shall enable actors to understand such descriptions and to parse them correctly.

---

[4] https://www.w3.org/WoT/IG/wiki/Discovery_Categories_and_Tech_Landscape.
[5] http://www.hydra-cg.com/spec/latest/core/.
[6] https://openapis.org/.
[7] http://raml.org/.

Query. Search criteria can be considered as the queries that trigger the discovery process which is expected to end up providing a ranked set of matching thing descriptions to the issuer. In case a query language, e.g., SPARQL[8] is used for expressing semantic search criteria, all involved actors should at least know about its protocol, i.e., communications established between an issuer and a directory must implement the corresponding query language protocol. A high level of expressiveness of the query language used will likely broaden the possibilities for discovery requests, e.g., features for filtering and aggregating. However, its counterpart is that involved actors might need to be much more intelligent.

3.1   Semantic Discovery

Although all the aforementioned requirements and considerations are met and covered in a hypothetical Web of Things, there is still room for improvement in discovery and, in turn, in interoperability in general. In addition to the described abilities, actors can infer implicit information from thing descriptions by leveraging the semantics of the ecosystem by means of reasoning.

Those ecosystems that promote reasoning will allow actors of the discovery process to query about things whose specific type may be not known to the issuer, but its abstract type is. Further, some discovery queries may express interest in things that measure humidity in general, no matter if it is relative or absolute. In both cases, it is the explicit definition of semantics into the common data model what supports the ability to reason within the whole ecosystem. In this paper, we propose an approach for discovery that takes advantage of domain semantics and implements its common data model in the form of an ontology.

In Computer Science, the term ontology is used to refer to a "formal, explicit specification of a shared conceptualisation" [4]. First of all, "share" reflects the notion that an ontology captures consensual knowledge, that is, it is not private of some individual, but accepted by a group. In our case, the shared conceptualization to be represented in this ontology is the domain of WoT being discussed in the W3C WoT WG. For doing so, it is needed to describe the concepts, properties and constraints that apply to the given domain. All those entities need to be described explicitly, so that we cover as much as possible of the world phenomenon that we are trying to represent. Next, being formal refers to the need of implementing the ontology following a machine-readable ontology language that can be easily processed. For doing so, the proposed ontologies are formalized following Description Logics and being implemented in the W3C Web Ontology Language standard OWL.[9]

3.2   Use Case: VICINITY

VICINITY is an H2020 European project that aims to be an open virtual neighbourhood to connect IoT infrastructures. In VICINITY, a peer-to-peer

---

[8] https://www.w3.org/TR/sparql11-query/.
[9] https://www.w3.org/TR/owl-ref/.

network is created, which is composed of IoT infrastructures and value-added services that are integrated so as to become semantically interoperable, while IoT providers can keep control over their data. All nodes in the network share a common data model, namely the VICINITY ontology network[10].

The VICINITY architecture implements the present ontology-based approach for discovery in the WoT as follows:

– Any node of the network can issue discovery requests in the form of SPARQL queries expressed with the VICINITY ontology.
– Queries are issued to a cloud-based central directory that holds descriptions of all things in the VICINITY ecosystem.
– Nodes wanting to integrate their assets into VICINITY are responsible for sending their corresponding descriptions to the central directory.
– For each SPARQL query that the central repository receives, it returns a set of query-relevant thing descriptions to the issuer.
– As nodes receive thing descriptions as query results, they still have to figure out whether such descriptions contain all query-relevant data that allows them to make an informed evaluation of its own discovery query. As we mentioned in Sect. 2.2, there might be cases for which some additional information has to be collected at discovery time, e.g., geo-location.
– In case some extra information is needed for discovery, issuer nodes (securely) invoke the query-relevant remote endpoints, taking advantage of provided access mappings in descriptions so as to correctly understand responses.
– Nodes evaluate the SPARQL query and yield the found things.

As just described, the discovery process in VICINITY is distributed. Nodes rely on the central directory to provide them with as much query-relevant information as it knows, but both extension of description scope and SPARQL query evaluation take place at client side.

4   Semantics for Understanding Thing Descriptions

As presented above, the proposed approach for discovery in the WoT is based on the semantic description of web things and of the way of accessing them. In order to fill in the gap for this goal some ontologies are being developed. The following sections will briefly present such ontologies, namely the WoT ontology (describing "what", "where" and "how" they are accessed) and a Mapping ontology (describing the how the information should be understood).

For the sake of readability, prefixes will be used for representing ontology namespaces along the section, including text and figures. The list of prefixes used and their corresponding ontologies and namespaces are listed in Table 1.

---

[10] http://vicinity.iot.linkeddata.es/vicinity/.

Table 1. Prefix listing of references ontologies

Prefix	Name	URI
wot	WoT ontology	http://iot.linkeddata.es/def/wot
map	Mapping ontology	http://iot.linkeddata.es/def/wot-mappings
core	VICINITY core ontology	http://iot.linkeddata.es/def/core
om	Ontology of units of Measure (OM) 1.8	http://www.wurvoc.org/vocabularies/om-1.8/
rdf	RDF model	http://www.w3.org/1999/02/22-rdf-syntax-ns
rdfs	rdf(s)	http://www.w3.org/2000/01/rdf-schema
owl	OWL ontology	http://www.w3.org/2002/07/owl

4.1 WoT Ontology

This section provides an overview of the WoT ontology as well as a brief description of the development process and resources available.

The WoT ontology has been developed to define "what", "where" and "how" (see Sect. 2) things can be discovered or accessed in the Web of Things. In this sense, the shared conceptualization to be represented in this ontology is the domain of the Web of Things, that is, it will describe the virtual counterpart of physical objects according to the Web Thing Model discussed in the W3C.

As most engineering projects, the ontology development life cycle usually starts with the Ontology Requirements Specification activity. In order to extract requirements for the WoT ontology, the documentation provided by the WoT Interest Group (IG) of the W3C,[11] was analysed. While the complete list of requirements initially defined for the WoT ontology are available online[12], in the following an excerpt of the main requirements is provided in the form of competency questions [5] or natural language sentences:

1. What is a thing in the web thing context? The abstract concept of a physical entity that can either be a real-world artefact, such as a device, or a virtual entity that represents physicality, such as a room or group of devices.
2. What is a property? A property provides readable and/or writeable data that can be static (e.g., supported mode, rated output voltage, etc.) or dynamic (e.g., current fill level of water, minimum recorded temperature, etc.).
3. What is an action? The Action interaction pattern targets changes or processes on a Thing that take a certain time to complete.
4. What is an event? The Event interaction pattern enables a mechanism to be notified by a Thing on a certain condition.
5. A thing interaction can be available over different or multiple protocols.
6. Each thing has at least an interaction pattern.
7. An interaction pattern can have different endpoints.
8. Each interaction pattern has an endpoint.

---

[11] http://w3c.github.io/wot/current-practices/wot-practices.

[12] http://vicinity.iot.linkeddata.es/vicinity/requirements/wot/report.html.

9. Each endpoint has minimum two attributes: URI and media-type.
10. An endpoint can be associated with a thing without determine the interaction patterns.

After defining the first set of requirements, though modification and addition of requirements is allowed during the development, the ontology implementation phase has been carried out through a number of sprints in which some requirements are selected in order to be incorporated in the current model. The current conceptual model defined by the WoT ontology is depicted in Fig. 1. This ontology introduces some new concepts closely related to the WoT domain, namely:

– *Thing*: this concept represents anything (both physical and non-physical) which has a distinct and independent existence and can have one or more web representations.
– *Interaction pattern*: this concept represents, in the context of WoT, an exchange of data between a web client and a Thing. This data can be either given as input by the client, returned as output by the Thing or both.
– *Data format*: this concept represents the input data or output data of a given interaction pattern which includes information such as the data type used and which unit of measurement is the data represented in, if needed.
– *Endpoint*: this concept indicates the web location where a service can be accessed by a client application.

The main concepts defined in the ontology, as shown in Fig. 1, are `wot:Thing`, `wot:InteractionPattern`, `wot:DataFormat` and `wot:Endpoint` according to the above definitions. It is worth noting that the class `wot:Thing` defines things in the context of the Web of Things and does not intend to be the top class of all

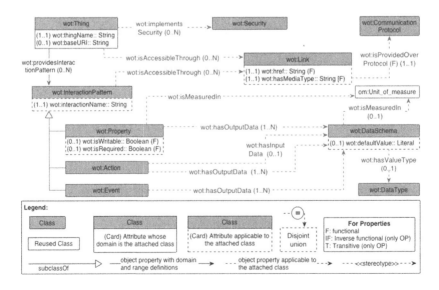

Fig. 1. General overview of the WoT ontology

possible concepts as `owl:Thing` does. According to the model, a particular thing is linked to the interaction patterns it provides by means of the object property `wot:providesInteractionPattern`. An interaction pattern can be either a *property*, an *action* or an *event*, represented by the concepts `wot:Property`, `wot:Action` and `wot:Event`, respectively.

As shown in Fig. 1, a thing or an interaction pattern can be associated to one or more endpoints either directly or through its interaction patterns by means of the object property `wot:isAccessibleThrough`. The main information provided by the endpoint class is about the web location in which the service is provided which is indicated by the attribute `wot:href`. Every endpoint should have a value and only one value for such attribute. Attached to such endpoint the information about the expected media type can be specified by means of the property `wot:isProvidedOverProtocol` which links instances of endpoints to the individual that represents the possible web protocols.

Finally, some interaction might have input or output data associated, or both, for example for writable properties. In order to model that, the relationships `wot:hasInputData` and `wot:hasOutputData` were created. These properties allow the connection from a given interaction pattern to an instance that will be linked to a certain data type and a certain unit of measure by means of the properties `wot:isMeasuredIn` and `wot:hasValuetype`, respectively. This modelling decision responds to the use of the ontology design pattern for representing n-ary relationships as it is needed to relate the given interaction patterns with both the unit of measure and the expected data type.

It should be mentioned that the presented ontology is under development and new concepts might be included or extended. Some ongoing lines of work on the ontology include the modelling of more complex datatypes, to detail security aspects, and to further describe the actions and events as they are defined in the W3C working group.

4.2 Mapping Ontology

Additionally to the WoT ontology, another model for describing how thing values should be understood (see Sect. 2) has been developed. The conceptualization to be represented in this ontology is the mechanism for accessing the values provided by web things. In this sense what is needed is to represent the mappings between the values provided under a given endpoint for example in JSON format to common semantic vocabularies.

The current conceptual model defined by the Mapping ontology is depicted in Fig. 2. In order to model this information, it should be first established what does a mapping mean in this context:

– *Mapping*: A mapping indicates the relation between a given key (provided as structure data in an on-line resource) and the RDF property to which the values should be mapped and the target type of object.

Taking this definition as starting point and together with sample data, the ontology shown in Fig. 2 was designed. The main concepts defined in such ontology are `map:Mapping` and `map:AccessMapping`. The former correspond to the mapping concept above-defined allowing the connection between a key provided within structure data in an on-line resource, represented by the datatype property `map:key`, to the RDF property to which it should be mapped, represented by the object property `map:predicate`.

The instances of the class `map:Mapping` can be further classified into one of its two subclasses, `map:ObjectPropertyMapping` and `map:DatatypeProperty Mapping`, depending on whether the predicate attached to them is an `owl: ObjectProperty` or an `owl:DatatypeProperty`, respectively. As it can be observed, `map:Mapping` is defined as the disjoint union of both subclasses, as an instance of `map:Mapping` can belong to any of the subclasses but only can belong to one of them.

As it can be observed in the figure, another difference between the subclasses of `map:Mapping` is the target element expected for the values transformed, for the case of the `map:ObjectPropertyMapping` the expected target should be an instance of `owl:Class` while for the case of `map:DatatypePropertyMapping` it should map values to instances of the class `rdfs:Datatype`. The mappings are linked to these target elements by means of the properties `map:targetClass` and `map:targetDatatype`, respectively.

The class `map:AccessMapping` is included in the model in order to link one or more mappings that are executed with a given endpoint. This allows the definition of the mappings independently of the endpoint in which they can be executed since the link to the endpoint is established from the access mapping. A thing description, represented by the class `core:ThingDescription`, may have zero or more access mappings attached by means of the object property `map:hasAccessMapping`. The object property `map:isExecutedAfter` indicates dependency on the order of execution between access mappings.

Finally, the object property `map:valuesTransformedBy`, which can only be applied to `map:ObjectPropertyMapping` instances, is used to estate that the obtained values from a resource when applying a mapping should be transformed according to the referenced `core:ThingDescription`. This predicate is oriented to support the WoT discovery feature proposed at the W3C IG, taken literally *"The relationship between things provides a further basis for discovery. The relationships are defined through the models for things, where a thing has properties whose values are other things."*[13]

5   Related Work

The IoT ecosystem has been very prolific in producing different mechanisms for resource and service discovery. Datta et al. [2] analyse the most representative technologies and architectures used for discovery and propose a set of categories, namely distributed and P2P discovery, centralized architecture, semantic based, among others. Regarding the semantic based category, it is DiscoWoT [6] the

---

[13] See for further information https://www.w3.org/WoT/IG/wiki/Discovery_TF.

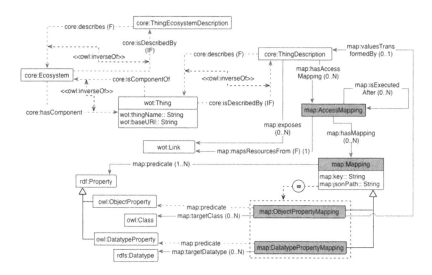

Fig. 2. General overview of the WoT mapping ontology

only one that is based on the Web of Things. Even if the proposed solution is very flexible to different "Discovery Strategies", it neither considers extending descriptions by means of accessing the discovered devices, nor supports describing endpoint security constraints.

The W3C WoT IG made a great effort on evaluating[14] the technology landscape relevant to the standardization initiative. It is clear from such report that there has been a great deal of development and evolution with regards to discovery in the IoT. However, semantic web technologies seem to have a minor representation in the landscape: just a SPARQL endpoint that centralizes all thing descriptions. In addition, we can claim that while the IoT domain has gathered a lot of attention and numerous ontologies[15] have been defined to cover it in many ways [7], the WoT field has not been object of much attention.

One of the ontologies for modelling WoT is SWOT-O which was developed in the context of the SWoT4CPS framework [8]. This ontology represents the main WoT elements as entities, properties, actions and events. However, the actions and events represented in this ontology seem to have a narrower scope than the actions and events defined in the W3C WoT working group. For the documentation given, the actions and events in SWoT-O are related to actuators while our intention is to attach them to a more general concept including all flavours of web things. In addition, this model does not include where and how to access the values provided by the web things interaction patterns.

Alam and Noll [9] have developed an ontology for representing Web of Things concepts. The main issue with this work is that no pointer to the OWL ontology implementation is provided which restrains its reuse. Additionally, as for the

---

documentation provided in the paper, this ontology does not consider interaction patterns modelling and actions.

Finally, the WoT ontology described by Charpenay et al. [10] proposes and extension of the Identifier-Resource-Entity pattern to include WoT resources. This ontology does not provide mechanisms to indicate where and how the resource values can be accessed and interpreted. Event though it is a good practice to extend upper level ontologies, the fact of importing DUL by means of the `owl:imports` predicate, makes this ontology too heavy for the given use case. More precisely, the WoT WG intention is to provide a neat lightweight core vocabulary, which of course could serve as the basis for further extensions.

6   Conclusions

Along this paper the problem of discovery in the Web of Things has been characterised, highlighting that even if a common data model for describing things is a requirement for bringing interoperability to the IoT ecosystem, it is also very convenient to make use of it when implementing any discovery solution. Besides, an ontology-based approach for discovery has been proposed, which builds on the benefits of explicitly describing the semantics of the WoT ecosystem. In addition, the core ontologies involved in such solution have been described.

Regarding the ontology development, we plan to reuse existing ontologies that could fit in the models presented in this paper, for example reusing the ontology described by Charpenay and colleagues [10] as it is also being developed in the context of the W3C WoT WG. In addition, we also plan to further describe the security concept in the ontology and provide examples of how to use the presented models including also connections with existing ontologies or datasets.

Finally, it is expected to evolve the proposed approach from the experience gained with the VICINITY project. Further, some experiments in other use cases will be performed with the intention of refining and generalizing the approach.

References

1. Zaslavsky, A., Jayaraman, P.P.: Discovery in the internet of things: the internet of things (ubiquity symposium). Ubiquity **2015**, 2:1–2:10 (2015)
2. Datta, S.K., Ferreira da Costa, R.P., Bonnet, C.: Resource discovery in Internet of Things: current trends and future standardization aspects. In: WF-IOT 2015, IEEE 2nd World Forum on Internet of Things, Milan, Italy, December 2015
3. Cirani, S., Davoli, L., Ferrari, G., Léone, R., Medagliani, P., Picone, M., Veltri, L.: A scalable and self-configuring architecture for service discovery in the internet of things. IEEE Internet Things J. **1**(5), 508–521 (2014)
4. Studer, R., Benjamins, V.R., Fensel, D.: Knowledge engineering: principles and methods. Data Knowl. Eng. **25**(1–2), 161–197 (1998)
5. Grüninger, M., Fox, M.S.: Methodology for the design and evaluation of ontologies. In: IJCAI 1995, Workshop on Basic Ontological Issues in Knowledge Sharing (1995)
6. Mayer, S., Guinard, D.: An extensible discovery service for smart things. In: Proceedings of the Second International Workshop on Web of Things, WoT 2011, pp. 7:1–7:6. ACM, New York (2011)

7. Gyrard, A., Bonnet, C., Boudaoud, K., Serrano, M.: Lov4iot: a second life for ontology-based domain knowledge to build semantic web of things applications. In: Future Internet of Things and Cloud (FiCloud), pp. 254–261. IEEE (2016)
8. Wu, Z., Xu, Y., Yang, Y., Zhang, C., Zhu, X., Ji, Y.: Towards a semantic web of things: a hybrid semantic annotation, extraction, and reasoning framework for cyber-physical system. Sensors **17**(2), 403 (2017)
9. Alam, S., Noll, J.: A semantic enhanced service proxy framework for internet of things. In: Proceedings of the 2010 IEEE/ACM International Conference on Green Computing and Communications and International Conference on Cyber, Physical and Social Computing, pp. 488–495. IEEE Computer Society (2010)
10. Charpenay, V., Käbisch, S., Kosch, H.: Introducing thing descriptions and interactions: an ontology for the web of things. In: Proceedings of the 1st Workshop on SemanticWeb Technologies for the Internet of Things (SWIT) at ISWC (2016)

Challenges When Moving from Monolith to Microservice Architecture

Miika Kalske[✉], Niko Mäkitalo, and Tommi Mikkonen

Department of Computer Science, University of Helsinki, Helsinki, Finland
{miika.kalske,niko.makitalo,tommi.mikkonen}@helsinki.fi

Abstract. One of the more recent avenues towards more flexible installations and execution is the transition from monolithic architecture to microservice architecture. In such architecture, where microservices can be more liberally updated, relocated, and replaced, building liquid software also becomes simpler, as adaptation and deployment of code is easier than when using a monolithic architecture where almost everything is connected. In this paper, we study this type of transition. The objective is to identify the reasons why the companies decide to make such transition, and identify the challenges that companies may face during this transition. Our method is a survey based on different publications and case studies conducted about these architectural transitions from monolithic architecture to microservices. Our findings reveal that typical reasons moving towards microservice architecture are complexity, scalability and code ownership. The challenges, on the other hand, can be separated to architectural challenges and organizational challenges. The conclusion is that when a software company grows big enough in size and starts facing problems regarding the size of the codebase, that is when microservices can be a good way to handle the complexity and size. Even though the transition provides its own challenges, these challenges can be easier to solve than the challenges that monolithic architecture presents to company.

1   Introduction

One of the more recent avenues towards more flexible installations and execution is the transition from monolithic architecture to microservice architecture. The motivation for this transition comes from the fact that constantly maintaining a monolithic architecture has resulted in difficulties in keeping up in pace with new development approaches such as DevOps, calling for deployment several times a day. In contrast, microservices offer a more flexible option, where individual services comply with the single responsibility principle (SRP) [1], and they can therefore be scaled and deployed independently [2]. Although partially overlooked in a recent paper addressing liquid software design space [3], such architecture clearly supports building liquid software, as more liberally updated, relocated, and replaced than their traditional, usually monolithic counterparts. In this paper, we study the reasons why the companies decide to make the transition from monolithic architectures to microservices, and identify the challenges

© Springer International Publishing AG, part of Springer Nature 2018
I. Garrigós and M. Wimmer (Eds.): ICWE 2017, LNCS 10544, pp. 32–47, 2018.
https://doi.org/10.1007/978-3-319-74433-9_3

that companies may face during this transition. The study is based on different publications and case studies conducted about these architectural transitions from monolithic architecture to microservices.

The rest of the paper is structured as follows. Section 2 discusses the background of the paper. Section 3 compares monolithic and microservice based architectures from several different viewpoints. Section 4 introduces challenges encountered in the transition from a monolithic architecture to microservices. Towards the end of the paper, Sect. 5 draws some final conclusions.

2 Background and Motivation

Microservices are small services that comply with the single responsibility principle (SRP) [1]. Each service is focused only on one functionality. This kind of approach makes it clear where the boundaries between different services are and where code changes should go. Consequently, microservices are by nature loosely coupled [4]. Loose coupling gives developers a chance to make independent changes to services without affecting the rest of the codebase. Because microservices are not tied to each other, they can be scaled and deployed independently [2]. Such architecture is also a key enabler for building liquid software, as more liberally updated, relocated, and replaced than their traditional, usually monolithic counterparts.

All these qualities make microservices desirable option for existing monolithic applications. Scaling of monolithic application is always harder than scaling microservices because one has to scale the whole application and deploy the whole codebase instead of scaling the part of the application that demands more resources [6]. The current development of cloud services make automatic scaling of resources very easy and cost-efficient. Microservices make most out of this automatic scaling. When developing and deploying a big monolithic applications companies cannot take the full advantage of these functionalities.

As applications grow in size during the many years of development, it becomes harder to maintain and make changes to them [5]. It is possible to maintain and develop the monolithic software but eventually it becomes obvious that changes to the architecture of the whole application has to be made. This kind of trend was first noticed in companies which have a lot of traffic, many developers and large codebase. Companies such as Amazon [7], Netflix [8], LinkedIn [9], SoundCloud [10] and many more have made the transition to microservice architecture because their existing monolithic application was too hard to maintain, develop and scale.

Monolithic applications have their downsides when the application codebase grows big and the changes have to be made rapidly. Fine-grained scaling is also impossible with monolith, because the whole application needs to be deployed every time. However, when teams start developing new a application, there are business requirements to develop new features fast in the beginning so the company can survive. Monolithic applications make it simple to develop, deploy, test and scale application when the size of the codebase is relatively small [11].

Most of the applications have monolithic architecture because of these reasons. Monolithic approach is enough in the beginning and it is possible that the size of the codebase and need for fine-grained scaling is never needed. Which means that it is better to stay with the monolith and avoid the technical and organizational challenges that microservice architecture comes with. There are also differing opinions. It can be argued that the refactoring of the existing monolith is too demanding task and instead the organization should spend more time at the start of the process to evaluate the architecture and functionalities that are required [12]. It is much easier to introduce accidental tight coupling in a monolithic than in microservices. Breaking up these tight couplings can be hard and require a lot of time and understanding of the application.

Whether the decision is to start with microservices or monolith that later will be refactored towards microservices, there are multiple technical challenges that needs to be solved in order to use microservices. Microservices add more distribution which adds more points of failure. This brings up many questions such as how to handle failures, how services communicate between each other, how transactions are handled and so on [1]. If monolithic application for some reason stops running in production, it is very fast to recognize that because nothing is working. With microservices, if one service stops responding other services still work and these kind of error situations needs to be handled properly. Communication between microservices is one of the big questions to get right. Getting the communication wrong can lead to a situation where microservices lose their autonomy and thus the main benefits of the whole approach can diminish [1]. On top of that, the communication between multiple microservices can introduce performance issues if the services are too fine-grained [34]. It seems to be an agreed consensus that the complexity should be within services instead of messaging pipes [2]. One challenge is also to handle the orchestration of the microservices in production. Luckily in the last few years many new tools for supporting this have been made such as Kubernetes [32] and Mesos [33] to name two.

In most of the cases, the need for architectural change from monolithic to microservices is realized when the codebase and the size of company has grown big. In these cases, there are new refactoring and organizational challenges on top of the existing ones that come with the microservice architecture. Refactoring of the existing software can be a daunting task. In order to successfully make the refactoring, a good test coverage is required. Otherwise, there is a chance that during the introduction of microservices new bugs might end up in the existing functionalities. It might also be hard to find and define which parts of the existing software should be split up to microservices and what are good candidates for microservices. One of the methods is to find seams from the existing software [1]. A seam is a part of the code that can be isolated and work alone in separation from the rest of the codebase [13]. Finding the seams requires good knowledge about the business use cases. However, this knowledge should already be in the organization. Either in the codebase, if the monolith has good modular architecture or even if the modules are not well defined then at least the use cases should be pretty clear.

On top of the technical challenges, adopting microservice architecture requires organizational changes [1]. The organization needs to adapt accordingly to the new architecture. Every team needs to take ownership of the services or service that they own. This means developing, testing, deploying and taking care of the service in production. DevOps culture needs to be adopted as teams now need to deploy, monitor and address issues also in production [14]. Teams have to set up their own continuous integration (CI) and continuous delivery (CD) pipelines. Microservices also require the composition of the teams to change. It is very typical that in organizations where monolithic applications are built, that the developers, quality assurance and operations work as separate teams. An organization which uses microservices, these horizontal borders needs to be broken and teams should be vertical in the sense that every team should consist of people from development, quality assurance and operations. Melvin Conway's paper *How Do Committees Invent* states the following: "Any organization that designs a system (defined more broadly here than just information systems) will inevitably produce a design whose structure is a copy of the organization's communication structure." [15]. In other words, organizations that build microservices also need to adapt their communication structure to this new style of architecture. Otherwise, the conflict between organization structure and the structure of architecture design will cause problems.

3 Comparison of Monolithic and Microservice Architecture

Monolithic architecture is the standard way to start application development because it is more straightforward. A monolith application is developed and deployed as a single unit containing all the needed parts. A typical monolith application consists of UI-layer, business logic layer and data access layer which communicates with the database as can be seen from the Fig. 1. Monolithic architecture is a good way to start development because it makes the initial development faster than with microservices [16].

However, as the codebase grows in size, the problems of monolithic architecture increase [11]. The new features and modifications of old features are harder to implement because the developer has to find the correct place to apply these changes. It takes a long time to get familiar with the big codebase. This means that it takes time for new developers to get up to speed as they feel lost and cannot find the correct place to apply changes. With big monolith codebase refactoring changes can reflect many parts of the software. This might lead to that developers fear to make big refactoring tasks, because their changes effect numerous places and testing that everything still works is a big task. This can even result in situations where refactoring is ignored because it is too risky. Which will lead to code that is not clean. Because developers are not familiar with the codebase, it is very likely that the code duplication level raises as it is almost impossible to find existing code which would already do the same thing.

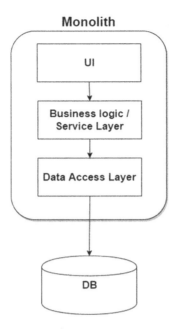

Fig. 1. Typical monolithic application consisting of three layers.

Also, it is very likely that the modularity of the codebase goes down as the codebase grows, as there are no hard module boundaries [11].

There are also other reasons to split up the monolith than just the size of the codebase. One of the reasons is team structure [1]. If the teams are located in different geographical areas and their communication is very slow, it makes sense that they take ownership of different parts of the code. This eases up the development as now the teams in different geographical areas do not have conflicts about modifying parts of the software. The team that has the ownership of a service can decide what happens inside that service and the other teams only have to care about the interface of the service. With this kind of approach the communication doesn't have to be as fast and as fine-grained as before. Also, if a team has ownership of a service it is more likely that the code stays cleaner and technical issues are solved faster as there is no one else to blame about the quality of the code. This division also means that if the team wants to publish a new version of the service to production it is a lot faster and easier, because the team doesn't have to communicate and coordinate the changes with other teams so much.

In general, it can be said that if the following requirements apply to the organization, then monolithic approach might be the correct choice: the number of the teams is low, the codebase is relatively small and it will stay that way for the coming years, the teams are close to each other geographically and their communication is easy. On top of these, the complexity of the domain plays a big factor and it is not easy to say when to use monolithic approach instead of microservices or vice versa. It is possible to have a monolithic that has good modularity and clean code but it requires more work to keep that modularity when working with monolith instead of microservices as microservices provide the modularity in their nature and make it harder to break the modularity [16].

A typical monolithic application can be seen in the Fig. 1. A layered architecture with three layers is very common especially in enterprise applications. As we can see, there is usually only one database which means that if some of the data would require better scaling, this kind of architecture does not support it. This limits the choices that the teams can make to support the business requirements and scaling requirements. For example, most of the data would fit fine in a relational database management system, but some parts of the application data require greater scalability and performance which for example Cassandra would provide. One database also means that schema changes have to be coordinated between multiple teams which slows the development.

In Fig. 2 we can see that with microservices it is possible to select the database engine per microservice. This kind of pattern is called database per service [17]. This gives teams more freedom to select their tools. Designing and scaling of the database are easier when the database consists of fewer tables and the microservice has full control of the data and the schema of the database. Some of the microservices can even be without database, if they for example write to disk. From Fig. 2 we can also see that microservices usually communicate with each other and the UI can request data from multiple services.

Table 1 contains comparison of these two architecture styles. As we can see, both of them have pros and cons. As a conclusion about the table we can notice

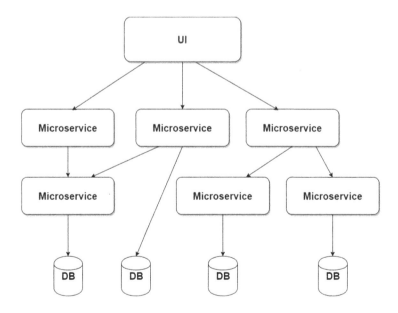

Fig. 2. Example of microservice architecture.

that microservice architecture style becomes attractive when we are working with big codebase. With smaller projects the technical challenges that microservices bring out might not have enough time to pay back. Also, if the DevOps skills of the team are lacking then it might be better to stick with monolith in the beginning.

Table 1. Comparing monolith and microservices

Category	Monolith	Microservices
Time to market	Fast in the beginning, slower later as codebase grows	Slower in the beginning because of the technical challenges that microservices have. Faster later
Refactoring	Hard to do, as changes can affect multiple places	Easier and safe because changes are contained inside the microservice
Deployment	The whole monolith has to be deployed always	Can be deployed in small parts, only one service at a time
Coding language	Hard to change. As codebase is large. Requires big rewriting	Language and tools can be selected per service. Services are small so changing is easy
Scaling	Scaling means deploying the whole monolith	Scaling can be done per service
DevOps skills	Doesn't require much as the number of technologies is limited	Multiple different technologies a lot of DevOps skills required
Understandability	Hard to understand as complexity is high. A lot of moving parts	Easy to understand as codebase is strictly modular and services use SRP
Performance	No communicational overhead. Technology stack might not support performance	Communication adds overhead. Possible performance gains because of technology choices

4   Challenges in Adopting Microservice Architecture

The challenges with adopting microservice architecture can be divided in two parts; the technical challenges and the organizational challenges [1]. Both of these are equally important to get right. The challenges are a bit different whether the application development will be started from scratch compared to converting a big existing codebase from monolith to microservices. In this paper, we focus on the challenges that are related to refactoring existing monolithic application towards microservice architecture. Most of these challenges needs to be addressed also when starting with microservices from the beginning. The biggest differences are that, there is no need for a big organizational change and refactoring is not needed, but the selection of services and their business requirements might be harder, if the teams decide to start with microservice architecture from beginning.

4.1 Technical Challenges

There are various technical challenges that needs to be solved before it is possible to utilize microservice architecture. When the starting point is a monolithic application, the organization is then most likely familiar with the domain already and have an idea where the seams of application can be found [1]. The biggest problem in these cases is to separate these services. It can take a lot of time and effort to refactor the services out from the monolithic architecture. This is why the refactoring towards microservices should be done in small parts. Also, when implementing new functionalities, they should not be appended to monolith even though it might be faster. Instead, organizations should expand their microservices offering and add new microservices to replace the old monolithic code [18]. By applying this mechanism organization is slowly moving most of the codebase towards microservices. It is extremely important to be careful when doing this refactoring, because there is the possibility of introducing new bugs in existing features. This is why good test coverage is needed before starting this process.

Testing can be seen as an enabler to the whole refactoring project. If most of the testing is done manually, then it might be good idea to first get the automatic test coverage up and postpone the refactoring towards microservices. Good automatic test coverage helps refactoring, and it also gives the option to get more out of the microservices. Microservices can be released frequently only if it is possible to validate that the software does what it needs to do [1]. There are multiple automatic testing strategies which developers can apply to their application depending on its needs. Continuous integration and continuous delivery both go hand in hand with microservices [19]. Without these two practices, it comes very hard to handle the multiple services, their deployments and validating the actions of the service.

After the automatic test coverage is in place it comes feasible to start thinking about the other challenges. The first thing to do is to define the microservices and their responsibility areas. It is important that the decomposition of services is correct [1]. This is important, because it is expensive to make a lot of changes across the services. Instead it is easy to change functionality inside one service, but when the changes effect multiple services and their interfaces, then the task becomes harder and more time consuming. This is where the earlier experience working with monolith and designing its components is helpful as developers should already have a good understanding about the business concepts of the application. It is probably best to start from the easiest and most obvious services and when the organization has more knowledge about microservice architecture then the services can become more fine-grained. Existing microservices can be split up to smaller services, when there is better understanding about the service composition.

When splitting up the services, attention should be paid to the fact that the services do not become too fine-grained. Microservices can introduce a performance overhead especially if the communication is done over network [1]. For example, if the communication is done using REST over HTTP each inter-service call adds overhead from the network latency and from marshalling and unmarshalling the data. If the services are too fine-grained there will be a lot of traffic between them and as each call adds overhead the outcome can be a system that does not perform well enough.

One of the biggest challenges is the integration between different microservices [2]. It is not recommended to tie the integration between services to some specific technology, because the teams might want to use different programming languages when implementing services. Instead using a technology which does not require a specific programming language is better choice. There are also multiple other challenges when thinking about the integration of microservices. The interface of microservice should be simple to use and it should have good backwards compatibility so when new functionalities are introduced, the clients using the service do not have to be necessarily updated. Like every good interface, it should also hide the implementation details inside.

Using microservices in production environment provides new challenges that needs to be handled. There can be hundreds of different services running in production and many services can have multiple instances running to comply with the scale that is needed from the application. This big amount of microservices organizations run in production means that there has to be tools to automatically to deploy, scale and manage these services. Manual deployment process is not an option when deployments to the production environment are made multiple times per day. Docker and similar technologies enable easier development and deployment of microservices [30]. Docker makes microservices easily portable and isolated [31]. There are no conflicts of dependencies or the need to configure each environment. With Docker developers can easily imitate the production environment in their local development environment. If the decision is to use Docker in production environment, then there are multiple tools to handle the scaling, deployment and management of these containers. These tools such as Kubernetes make it easier when solving these challenges [32]. Kubernetes provides multiple features like horizontal scaling, service discovery, load balancing and so on.

In addition to the infrastructure challenges, there are also challenges like logging and monitoring which need more attention with microservices than when working with a monolithic application [30]. In case of failures, there needs to be good logging in microservices. This logging has to be easily searchable and all services should aggregate logs to one place so problem finding becomes easier. When there is only one monolithic software running in production, it is a lot easier to monitor that. The monolithic application might be scaled to multiple nodes, but still there is less nodes or containers to monitor than when running microservices in production. This means that when there is more to monitor, there should also be good automated tools which notify the persons who need to act when a microservice fails. Because there are more moving parts it becomes more likely that a service will go down or have other problems such as high latency. Users might not notice that one microservice is down and it might seem that everything is working properly. When running monolith in production the users will immediately notice that the whole service is not working.

When the organization has more than a few microservices, then it should also take in to consideration the possibility that a service might not respond [20]. The design of microservices has to be fault-tolerant. With distributed system that has a lot of services it is inevitable that at some point a service might be under heavy load and cannot respond in timely manner or the service might down. This where circuit breaker pattern becomes useful. Circuit breaker pattern handles failures fast and can provide fallback which returns default data instead of waiting for the response from a dependency [20]. Circuit breaker monitors for failures and when there are enough failures the subsequent calls to the dependency won't be made and instead an error is returned [22]. This means that instead of adding more load to the dependency by making new calls to it, an error is returned immediately to the user which gives the dependency time to recover from the load. Also, a fallback method can be provided if it is possible. For example, when a product service fails to fetch personalized product recommendations, it could fallback to recommendations that are tied to that product as a default or instead just return nothing as recommendations and the UI could then handle this case. This kind of approach means that the user might not even notice that the microservice serving the recommendations is down. There are multiple ready solutions which can be used in microservices. The most famous one is probably Hystrix [21]. Hystrix is a library that provides latency and fault tolerance to distributed systems. Using Hystrix is simple and makes it easy for developers to make their calls to dependencies latency and fault tolerant.

Data management is an important part of every application. There are many important questions such as whether to use relational database or NoSQL, what database provider suits best for the use cases of the application and which kind of schema the database should have. Microservices provide the freedom to use multiple database engines. This pattern, which is called database per service, comes with its own challenges [17]. Multiple different databases means that managing them is harder and the organization might not have that much of knowledge about the database. Previously if the monolith application used traditional relational database then using ACID (Atomicity, Consistency, Isolation, Durability) transactions was easy. Now when there are multiple services which each have their own database the transactions are harder to handle and more time needs to be spent dealing with the transactions. Instead of transactions microservices can agree on eventual consistency of data [23]. This means that the changes done by other services might not be persisted immediately, but they will be eventually persisted, when the service has processed the message. If previously the user had to wait for the whole transaction to complete now the user might not be able to immediately explore the data that the dependency service will create. Figure 3 illustrates the one database per service approach. In this case, the service owns

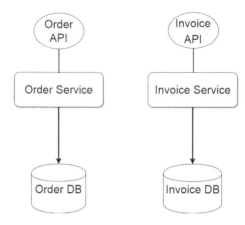

Fig. 3. A database per service.

the data and if for example the order service needs to know something about the invoices it has to go through invoice API. This leads to loose coupling of the services. If the team managing invoice service has to modify invoice database schema they can do it without changing any other service than invoice service as long as the API stays the same.

It is also possible to use one single database for all the services [24]. This approach is illustrated in Fig. 4. One database for all services is however problematic as now the database schema is tightly coupled [23]. One database also mean that services have access to data that should only be available through calls to other services. This can result in loss of modularity as it is very easy to rather query the data from different table directly instead of making a service call to proper service which should return this data. In Fig. 4 we can see that the order service has access

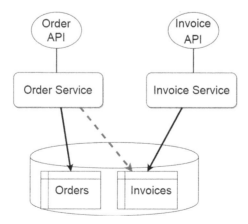

Fig. 4. One shared database for all services.

also to the schema of invoices. This makes it now easy for order service developers to get data from invoices without going through the invoice API. Which leads to tight coupling during development time, if team developing invoice service wants to change the schema they now have to coordinate this effort with multiple other teams [24]. Shared database diminishes many good sides of microservices and use of one shared database is not recommended [1]. Instead, when refactoring towards microservice architecture also the monolith database should be split up to multiple databases which can be accessed only by the service that handles that business context.

4.2   Organizational Challenges

Besides the technical challenges that microservices provide, there are organizational challenges that needs to be addressed when moving from monolithic architecture to microservice architecture. Even if the organization solves all the technical challenges, the structure and skills of organization should also support the new architecture [1].

One of the organizational challenges is the structure of the organization. In order to develop good application, the organization must align their structure with the structure of the application architecture [25]. If previously with monolithic application the organization had big teams which had clear roles like quality assurance, development and database administration then this kind of organization structure does not work with microservices. Conway's law states that the organization which designs the system will produce a system which structure is a copy of the organizations structure [15]. If the structure of the organization is monolithic then microservices approach does not work. The organization must split these big teams to smaller teams which can work autonomously. This way the structure of the architecture is in line with structure of the organization and they do not conflict with each other.

Figure 5 contains a monolithic organization which consists of teams which have very specialized focus areas. The teams are very good in their specialized areas but when delivering a business functionality, they need to collaborate with

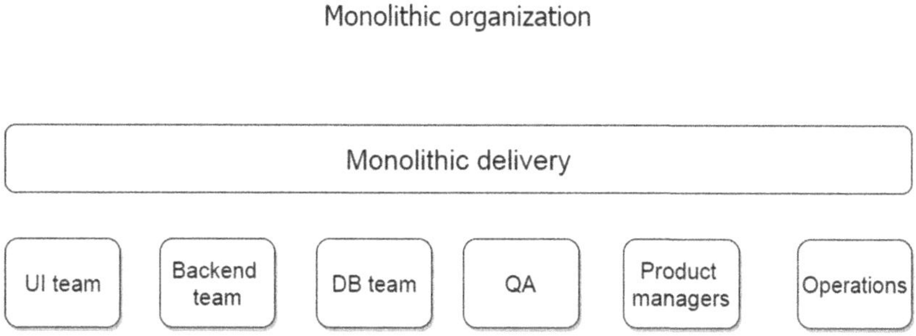

Monolithic organization

Fig. 5. Monolithic organization which delivers monolithic application.

each other and there is a hand-off process before a release can be made [26]. This kind of structure results in slower development cycles. Figure 6 shows an organization that is structured around microservices and products. When teams are organized like this they have more autonomy considering their releases. Now there is no hand-off process to a third party and teams do not have to wait for other teams to complete their changes. If there are new business requirements for invoicing then the team that is responsible for invoice service can deploy their changes to production when they are ready. This kind of structure reduces the need for fine-grained communication as teams can work separately. Teams have full control of their service and deployment timetable which introduces ownership of the product to the teams. They will also develop product specific skills on top of their technical skills which means that for example the accounting service team will have better business capabilities considering that area.

Microservices organization

Fig. 6. Organization structure that supports microservices.

When organization adopts microservice architecture style, the teams should have more freedom and responsibility but less process [26]. This means that the teams can deploy their service to the production when they need to instead of waiting for approval from someone else. Teams own their codebase and are responsible for the functionality of the service. They no longer can blame someone else about their failures and if there are problems in the production the team that is responsible for that service has to fix it. Ownership of code brings developers pride in appearance, improvement and commits developers to long-term involvement instead of always thinking that the problems in the codebase are someone else's problems and the next person will clean up the mess [27]. The ownership also gives teams freedom to develop the service as they want. It might still be sensible to have some constraints but there are far less constraints with microservices than with monolith. This kind of change is very dramatic. It might be scary to suddenly be fully responsible of the code, if before the architectural refactoring people had the chance to hide from responsibility. It takes time that teams adopt to this new responsibility and see the good sides of it. A good middle ground would be to have an operations team in the beginning which still has the main responsibility of production so teams have time to adopt that they own the codebase [1]. When teams are comfortable with owning the codebase then they can gradually also take over the production responsibility of their service.

When teams take full responsibility of their service, they might require new skills in order to deploy and fix problems in production. This means adopting DevOps mentality. DevOps can be described as "a set of practices intended to reduce the time between committing a change to a system and the change being placed into normal production, while ensuring high quality" [28]. Since fast change cycle is one of the main points of microservices, the deployments need to be fast and smooth. This kind of deployment process is called continuous delivery. It aims to shorten the release cycle of application by making developers and operations work together [29]. In a monolithic organization developers just committed code and then the deployments were responsibility of operations team. Now every team needs to be able to handle deployments. There might not be enough people with corresponding skills so team members need to learn new skills and enhance their deployment process. When operations and developers are working together in same team they have similar goals but the education and adaptation takes time and patience.

5   Conclusion

Based on the different challenges that organizations face when they move from monolith architecture to microservice architecture we can conclude that this transition is not easy and it will require a lot of time and effort from various parts of the organization. Making a system distributed introduces new challenges that needs to be addressed. Even though microservices can be considered novel software architecture, they are still somewhat mature in the sense that the tooling around microservices is pretty good and most of the challenges can be solved by applying open sourced tools made by companies which have already made the transition from monolith to microservices. These tools do not however solve the problem of refactoring and removing the tight coupling of codebase. Most of the focus will of course be on the technical side of the challenges, but organizations should not forget the Conway's law. The structure of the organization has to be similar as their architecture. So, the technical and organizational challenges have to be both solved in order to be successful with microservices.

Refactoring to microservices is a big process which can take a long time and this process requires buy-in from every part of the organization. This transition is still doable, as previous examples have showed us. Organization that is considering this transition should however evaluate the cost and the reward of the transition and think about their own problem base. Microservice architecture is not a silver bullet that works for every organization and in some cases the challenges outweigh the rewards. However, for some organizations it is the only way to continue the rapid development and deliver software fast to their customers.

Acknowledgements. The research was supported by the Academy of Finland (project 295913).

References

1. Newman, S.: Building Microservices, Designing Fine-Grained Systems, 1st edn. O'Reilly Media Inc., Sebastopol (2015)
2. Lewis, J., Fowler, M.: Microservices a Definition of this New Term, March 2014. https://martinfowler.com/articles/microservices.html
3. Gallidabino, A., Pautasso, C., Ilvonen, V., Mikkonen, T., Systä, K., Voutilainen, J.-P., Taivalsaari, A.: On the architecture of liquid software: technology alternatives and design space. In: Proceedings of the 2016 13th Working IEEE/IFIP Conference on Software Architecture, pp. 122–127. IEEE (2016)
4. Richardson, C.: Microservices—Pattern: Microservice Architecture, March 2014. http://microservices.io/patterns/microservices.html
5. Thones, J.: Microservices. IEEE Softw. **32**(1), 116 (2015)
6. Villamizar, M., Garcés, O., Castro, H., Verano, M., Salamanca, L., Casallas, R., Gil, S.: Evaluating the monolithic and the microservice architecture pattern to deploy Web applications in the cloud. In: Proceedings of CCC 2015, pp. 583–590 (2015)
7. Munns, C.: I Love APIs 2015: Microservices at Amazon, October 2015. https://www.slideshare.net/apigee/i-love-apis-2015-microservices-at-amazon-54487258
8. Mauro, T.: Nginx—Adopting Microservices at Neflix: Lessons for Architectural Design, February 2015. https://www.nginx.com/blog/microservices-at-netflix-architectural-best-practices/
9. Ihde, S.: InfoQ: From a Monotlith to Microservices + REST: the Evolution of LinkedIn's Service Architecture, March 2015. https://www.infoq.com/presentations/linkedin-microservices-urn
10. Calcado, P.: SoundCloud: Building Products at SoundCloud - Part 1: Dealing with the Monolith, June 2014. https://developers.soundcloud.com/blog/building-products-at-soundcloud-part-1-dealing-with-the-monolith
11. Richardson, C.: Microservices—Pattern: Monolithic Architecture, March 2017. http://microservices.io/patterns/monolithic.html
12. Tilkov, S.: Don't Start with a Monolith When Your Goal is a Microservice Architecture, June 2015. https://www.martinfowler.com/articles/dont-start-monolith.html
13. Feathers, M.: Working Effectively with Legacy Code. Prentice-Hall, Upper Saddle River (2004)
14. Balalaie, A., Heydarnoori, A., Jamshidi, P.: Microservices architecture enables DevOps: migration to a cloud-native architecture. IEEE Softw. **33**(3), 42–52 (2016)
15. Conway, M.E.: How do committees invent. Datamation **14**(4), 28–31 (1968)
16. Fowler, M.: Microservice Premium, May 2015. https://martinfowler.com/bliki/MicroservicePremium.html
17. Richardson, C.: Microservices—Pattern: Database per Service, March 2016. http://microservices.io/patterns/data/database-per-service.html
18. Clemm, J.: A Brief History of Scaling LinkedIn, July 2015. https://engineering.linkedin.com/architecture/brief-history-scaling-linkedin
19. Balalaie, A., Heydarnoori, A., Jamshidi, P.: Migrating to cloud-native architectures using microservices: an experience report. In: Celesti, A., Leitner, P. (eds.) ESOCC 2015. CCIS, vol. 567, pp. 201–215. Springer, Cham (2016). https://doi.org/10.1007/978-3-319-33313-7_15
20. Montesi, F., Weber, J.: Circuit breakers, discovery, and API gateways in microservices. arXiv preprint arXiv:1609.05830 (2016)

21. Netflix Inc.: https://github.com/Netflix/hystrix (2013)
22. Fowler, M.: https://martinfowler.com/bliki/CircuitBreaker.html, March 2014
23. Hasselbring, W.: Microservices for scalability: keynote talk abstract. In: Proceedings of the 7th ACM/SPEC on International Conference on Performance Engineering, pp. 133–134. ACM, March 2016
24. Richardson, C.: http://microservices.io/patterns/data/shared-database.html, November 2015
25. Newman, S.: https://www.thoughtworks.com/insights/blog/demystifying-conways-law, June 2014
26. Mauro, T.: https://www.nginx.com/blog/adopting-microservices-at-netflix-lessons-for-team-and-process-design/, March 2015
27. Nordberg, M.E.: Managing code ownership. IEEE Softw. **20**(2), 26–33 (2003)
28. Bass, L., Weber, I., Zhu, L.: DevOps: A Software Architect's Perspective. Addison-Wesley Professional, Boston (2015)
29. Wettinger, J., Andrikopoulos, V., Leymann, F.: Enabling DevOps collaboration and continuous delivery using diverse application environments. In: Debruyne, C., Panetto, H., Meersman, R., Dillon, T., Weichhart, G., An, Y., Ardagna, C.A. (eds.) OTM 2015. LNCS, vol. 9415, pp. 348–358. Springer, Cham (2015). https://doi.org/10.1007/978-3-319-26148-5_23
30. Stubbs, J., Moreira, W., Dooley, R.: Distributed systems of microservices using docker and serfnode. In: 2015 7th International Workshop on Science Gateways (IWSG), pp. 34–39. IEEE, June 2015
31. Merkel, D.: Docker: lightweight linux containers for consistent development and deployment. Linux J. **2014**(239) (2014). Article no. 2
32. Kubernetes: https://kubernetes.io/, March 2017
33. Mesos: http://mesos.apache.org/, May 2017
34. Richards, M.: Microservices Antipatterns and Pitfalls, 1st edn. O'Reilly Media Inc., Sebastopol (2016)

IoT Application Deployment
Using Request-Response Pattern
with MQTT

Antti Luoto[✉] and Kari Systä

Tampere University of Technology, Tampere, Finland
{antti.l.luoto,kari.systa}@tut.fi

Abstract. As IoT devices become more powerful they can also become full participants of Internet architectures. For example, they can consume and provide RESTful services. However, the typical network infrastructures do not support the architecture and middleware solutions used in the cloud-based Internet. We show how systems designed with RESTful architecture can be implemented by using an IoT-specific technology called MQTT. Our example case is an application development and deployment system that can be used for remote management of IoT devices.

Keywords: Internet-of-Things · IoT · REST · MQTT

1 Introduction

We assume that devices in the Internet of Things (IoT) get more powerful and capable for complex tasks. Thus, the execution is moving towards the edge devices. This means those devices become programmable and participate in rich set of interaction with other peers in the Internet.

When IoT systems should implement functionalities of Internet systems, the implementation architectures need to be adapted to the constraints of IoT systems. In this paper we use application management as an example of a service, but the discussion is valid for many other services too. The architectures used for the management operations can either be based on technologies and approaches used in traditional Internet-based information systems or on solutions that are optimized for hardware and networking constraints of IoT. This paper explores this dilemma by showing how designs based on Internet architectures can be re-implemented on top of Message Queuing Telemetry Transport (MQTT) based IoT architecture. The work is based on earlier work [1] that demonstrates how a web-based tool can be used both for development and remote deployment of applications to IoT devices. In this system all communication between different components is based on REST [9]. Depending on the task, any component of the system may assume either client or server role. In addition, the resources in all

© Springer International Publishing AG, part of Springer Nature 2018
I. Garrigós and M. Wimmer (Eds.): ICWE 2017, LNCS 10544, pp. 48–60, 2018.
https://doi.org/10.1007/978-3-319-74433-9_4

nodes are assumed to be directly addressable with a unique address. This leads to assumption of symmetric network architecture.

The network infrastructures of IoT systems are typically asymmetric: edge devices connect to the server but the servers cannot directly contact the edge devices. These constraints are enforced by various firewalls and Network Address Translation (NAT) systems. Thus, the REST-based system can properly work only if all devices are in the same local network.

MQTT is a lightweight protocol designed for device to device communication in IoT environments. MQTT uses a publish-subscribe (pub/sub) pattern for the communication and a centralized broker handles all subscriptions and message deliveries. Because of that, communication is limited to devices sending messages to broker and broker forwarding the messages to active subscriptions. This design is convenient if the system includes firewalls since only the broker needs to be accessible by all the components. A problem in REST-based original work [1] was that devices behind a firewall could not be accessed by other components.

Our research question is that how a REST-based system can be refactored to use MQTT in network where a firewall or NAT hides the IP address from other components. The core technical challenge is how to convert the request-response pattern assumed by REST to the pub/sub protocol of MQTT.

The rest of the paper is structured as follows. In Sect. 2 we introduce MQTT more in detail, present a comparison of MQTT and HTTP and suggest a solution to implement request-response in MQTT. In Sect. 3 our proof of concept is described and compared to the original HTTP work. In Sect. 4 we evaluate the work. After describing our work, we compare our work to the work made by others in Sect. 5. Finally, in Sect. 6 we provide some concluding remarks and thoughts for the future work.

2   Mapping of HTTP Concepts to MQTT

MQTT uses pub/sub communication pattern [20]. This means that senders do not send messages directly to recipients. Instead, the messages are just published for possible receivers. Similarly, the receivers express interest by subscribing to forthcoming messages. MQTT includes a special *broker* component which manages the subscriptions and publishing of the messages. To direct messages to intended recipients, the subscriptions and publishing in MQTT are directed to *topics* which may form hierarchical structures. Topics are constructed so that the different levels in the hierarchy are separated by a slash character. For example, if abc is a first-level topic then abc/123 is a second-level topic. The subscriber can use wild cards to subscribe to multiple topics in the hierarchy. A special character + is used as a single-level wild card and # character is used as a wild card for multiple levels. For example, a subscriber of topic abc/+ gets messages sent to topics abc/123, abc/xy, and to all other topics that start with abc/ and also have only one additional level. Since our aim is to refactor a REST-based architecture to work with MQTT, we present a brief comparison between the main features of both approaches. The comparison is constructed similarly to the

Table 1. The counterparts of HTTP (left) and MQTT (right).

Resource	MQTT client
URL	MQTT topic
HTTP request and response	MQTT message
Statelessness	With or without state
Client-Server	Publisher-subscriber

one made about REST and actor model in [17]. The comparison is summarized in Table 1.

Resource/MQTT client. Both HTTP resources and MQTT clients subscribing to messages can be seen as individual and isolated entities. In addition, they are both the fundamental parts of each approach which also define the used vocabulary for the service. For the most part, the information available in the system and the domain functionality is encapsulated in these concepts.

URL/MQTT topic. In REST all resources have a unique resource identifier (URL) that is accessed with the CRUD operations. In HTTP systems this means that an address is a combination of a host address and the path to the resource within the host. In MQTT the end-point addressing is replaced with topic hierarchies. MQTT allows, but does not enforce, designs where each resource has a dedicated topic (tough there is a danger that someone else has subscribed to that topic). Thus, the topic hierarchy in MQTT can be constructed by copying the URL structure of the corresponding REST-based architecture. Even the syntax – slash (/) used as a separator – is similar. So, as an example `http://example.com/abc/123` can be presented as a three-level-topic `example.com/abc/123` in MQTT.

HTTP request and response/MQTT message. HTTP communication is based on request-response paradigm where each request gets a response that contains at least a status (for example 200, 202, 404) and optionally also content as a payload of the response. In addition, the messages follow the uniform interface and apply standard operations on the resources – for example POST, GET, PUT and DELETE. In MQTT the messages are unidirectional and MQTT clients do not get any responses. Thus, if the application depends on a response, a separate response message has to be sent to the original sender. Furthermore, the messages in MQTT do not have standard types like HTTP.

Statelessness/With or without state. HTTP is a stateless protocol. There are some mechanisms in MQTT that retain information about the state of the client (for example *persistence* that keeps some information about the client on the broker in case of a lost connection) but using those is not mandatory. MQTT can be used as a stateless protocol when needed.

Client-Server/Publisher-subscriber. In HTTP the requests are always sent to a known server and resource. Although any entity can take either client or server role, each message is sent by a client to a dedicated server. MQTT has also an asymmetric communication pattern, but the client cannot address the message to a certain subscriber.

In using pub/sub architecture instead of HTTP-based REST, two fundamental issues need to be solved: design of an addressing mechanism that matches the URL-structure of the REST architecture, and implementation of the response mechanism that the application layer assumes. To answer these issues, the topics and contents of the messages have to be designed so that the response messages are directed to the original sender and matched to the original message. Fundamentally there are two places to encode the required information: message content and the topic hierarchy. Many combinations of those can be used to implement responses. We give two examples.

(1) Before sending any request, the caller subscribes to a unique topic for the response for the forthcoming request. In this case, the content of the response message consists of a status code and a payload assumed by the application. The topic hierarchies need to designed so that the topic for the reply message can be derived from the request automatically. Unsubscription from the response topic needs to be done so that the number registered topics in a long-living system stays limited.

(2) Each caller has a generic response topic that it subscribes to, and all responses to that caller are sent to that topic. The response message needs to include identification information about the original message and the client needs to match the response to the correct request. This option moves a part of the responsibility of directing a response to the correct request from the broker to the client. The broker is not assumed to interpret application-specific content of the response topic. If an application creates multiple requests - and they may be active simultaneously, then the matching of the response to correct topic becomes even more complicated. Compared to the previous option, a smaller number of topics is needed and they are not created and removed dynamically.

After analyzing the options, we selected the first option since it requires the least modifications to our application code, and since the amount of devices in IoT systems is expected to grow, a flexible topic structure is beneficial. The downside is the need for creating response topics dynamically and subsequently a need to remove them dynamically, too.

3 Proof of Concept

3.1 Original System

The original system consists of three active components: Integrated Development Environment (IDE), runtime environment and Resource Registry (RR). The IDE runs on web browser, and it is used for programming, deploying and managing the applications on devices. The runtime environment is pre-installed on the participating IoT devices and it essentially makes devices small application servers. The runtime environment, that is implemented with node.js [22], provides a REST API for installing, starting, stopping and removing applications.

The runtime environment can execute multiple installed applications simultane-ously. All devices and installed applications need to register themselves with the RR that maintains information about them. RR also provides an API for discov-ery of devices, device capabilities, installed applications and services provided by the applications. The architecture of the system is shown on the left in Fig. 1. The arrows depict communication between the components: IDE deploys and manages applications in devices, devices register themselves and applications to RR, and IDE queries devices and applications from RR. All the communication in the original system is implemented using HTTP. Further information about the original system can be found from [1,14].

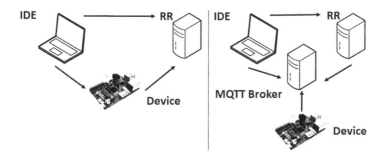

Fig. 1. Left: the original framework with HTTP. Right: HTTP replaced with MQTT.

3.2   Motivation: Network Limitations

The original system works well if all components are in the same network and there are no firewalls or NAT systems between the components. In reality the networks impose limitations. For example, the devices are often behind NAT and firewall for security or other reasons. We have experienced these problems in practice when demonstrating the system outside of our laboratory network. Our RR and many devices run in our research network, but we have wanted to bring the IDE and some example devices to remote locations where the connection is based on local wireless networks or portable 4G access points. Due to the limitations of those networks, some communication presented on the left in Fig. 1 was not possible because the devices were not addressable from the server-side components located in the university premises.

We wanted to see if MQTT can solve these problems. In addition, we have learned from IoT practitioners that MQTT is a rising technology in IoT domain and thus we wanted to test if our systems can be made MQTT compatible. Thus, we wanted to port our system to MQTT-based communication to ensure that our earlier research results can be applied under realistic network configurations, and to make demonstration of our system easier.

3.3   MQTT Implementation

We use MQTT.js [19] library and Mosquitto [18] MQTT broker. We implemented the communication from IDE to devices and from devices to RR seen in Fig. 1 with MQTT. Only communication that requires interaction between IDE to RR has been left using HTTP. We assume that RR as the central server is accessible from all components of our system. The resulting architecture is presented on the right in Fig. 1. We think that communication from IDE to devices and from devices to RR is enough for a proof of concept to show MQTT working in our use case. However, we do not foresee any problems in implementing communication from IDE to RR with MQTT as well.

From the different options to implement the request-response pattern with MQTT presented in Sect. 2, we selected the one where a unique topic is created for every request and response. The reason is that we want the broker to handle the directing of the messages so that the clients do not have to receive extra messages and decide what to do with them. It also requires less changes to our system. The topic hierarchies designed for our system are presented in Fig. 2. One notable detail in the hierarchies is the relation of replies to corresponding requests. In our solution each request is given a unique identification (rID) and a reply-topic for each rID is created before the request. Device identifications (dID) are used as unique identifiers for devices.

The left hierarchy in Fig. 2 consists of the following structure. The first level 'device' is a topic describing the problem domain - we are deploying applications to devices. Each device in the system has a separate branch which is identified with a unique dID. For example, a device with an identification XX has a topic starting with `device/XX`. The devices manage their own branches that direct the messages to them. Essentially this implements the addressing scheme discussed in Sect. 2: the beginning of the topic (`device/<dID>`) corresponds to IP address (domain name) and the rest corresponds to the path of URL. For details, see Table 2 where a mapping between some URLs of the system and MQTT topics is given. The level 'app' of each dID branch is for applications installed on the devices. The branches following from here are for requests and replies addressed to the applications. It would be easy to extend the hierarchy by adding a level

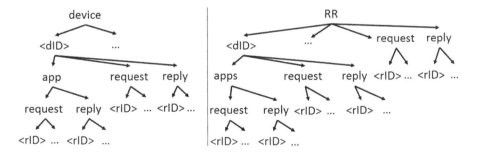

Fig. 2. Topic hierarchies for MQTT implementation. Left: device. Right: RR.

Table 2. Mapping of the URLs to MQTT topics when a device sends requests to RR.

URL	MQTT topic
RR-host-address	RR/request/< rID>
RR-host-address/< dID>/apps/< appID>	RR/< dID> /apps/request/< rID>

for application IDs. For example then it would be possible to address a certain application with a topic (`device/<id>/app/<appID>`).

The topics enabling communication with RR are seen on the right in Fig. 2. The first level indicates that the hierarchy is meant for RR. The topics `RR/request` and `RR/reply` are used for registering devices. Device identification is not used yet because unregistered device does not have a dID yet. On the second level each registered device has a separate branch identified by dID. 'Apps' branch is used for managing the applications running on the device or retrieving information about them. For example, it is used by a device to publish the current state of all its applications to RR using (`RR/<dID>/apps/request/<rID>`).

The sequence charts in Fig. 3 describe how a HTTP request-reply relates to MQTT request-reply. One can think that logically HTTP POST and HTTP response correspond to one pair of MQTT publications but in order to do the publishing, response subscriptions for both the parties need to be made. The sequence in the Fig. is about device registering itself to RR. For the RR to receive registrations, it needs to subscribe to a topic for RR related requests with a wild card (+). The device in turn, subscribes to a topic where it knows to expect the response. Then the device sends a registration request to a topic that contains a unique identifier for the request and is also subscribed by RR with the wild card. RR will then send a response to the response topic subscribed by the device. The status code in the reply tells whether the registration was successful or not. After the registration, the device can unsubscribe from the response topic.

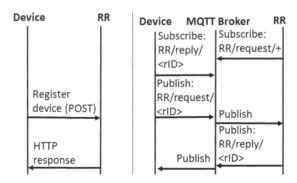

Fig. 3. Left: register a device with HTTP. Right: register a device with MQTT.

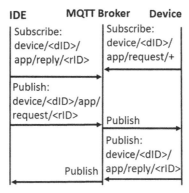

Fig. 4. An application is deployed to a device.

In Fig. 4, the situation is similar to the device registration case with the difference that the communication happens from the IDE to a device. In this case, a user deploys an application using the IDE. Initially the device (that has already been registered and thus has a dID) must have subscribed to a topic that is used for deploying applications to that device. Before sending the deployment message, the IDE subscribes to a topic dedicated for the response sent by the device. During the deployment, the IDE first creates a unique rID, subscribes to a reply topic of that rID and publishes a message to the topic that the receiving device has subscribed to. After completion of the deployment, the device publishes the response to the unique topic expected by the requesting IDE. The response contains information whether the deployment was successful or not. The IDE can unsubscribe from the reply topic finally.

4   Evaluation

The proof of concept works as expected and allows demonstrations outside of our lab. The original demo did not work if IoT devices were behind a firewall because IDE could not access the devices directly. The MQTT implementation has a centralized broker that is accessible from everywhere. As a result our demonstrations worked as expected. The required changes to the original system were limited and local. The adaptation to MQTT was done by replacing the source code that sends the HTTP requests with a source code that publishes an MQTT message and subscribes to the reply.

The next code example show how the original Javascript code snippet using HTTP is refactored for MQTT. The operation shown in the example is a device registering to RR The original code simply sends an HTTP POST to a URL hosted by RR and saves the returned dID for later use. The handling of the response in refactored code is a bit more complex because it needs to be converted to string and the response status and message body are not automatically parsed. While the snippet is an example from our case, the solution can be generalized so that for using MQTT in request-response style, dedicated request-reply topics with request IDs offer one flexible solution. The solution also provides the other benefits of MQTT such as lower resource consumption and ability to use normal pub/sub pattern when needed.

```
var options = {uri: RRInfo.url, method: 'POST', json: deviceInfo};
request(options, function(err, res, body) {
  if(!err && res.statusCode == 200) {
    //Read dID from HTTP response
    resourceRegistryInfo.idFromRR = body.toString();
    //Save dID to config file... (removed from this snippet)
  } else {//Error handling...}
});
//****The previous code refactored to use MQTT****
//Subscribe for response and register the device. Use unique request ID.
client.on('connect', function () {
  client.subscribe('RR/reply/' + rId);
  client.publish('RR/request/' + rId, JSON.stringify(deviceInfo));
});
//Listen for responses and parse the status code from the body.
client.on('message', function (topic, message) {
  if(topic == 'device/reply/' + rId) {
    if (message.toString().substr(0, 3) == '200') {
      //Read dID from MQTT response. It is after the status code.
      deviceInfo.idFromRR = message.toString().substr(5, message.length-1);
      //Save dID to config file... (removed from this snippet)
      client.unsubscribe('RR/reply/' + rId);
    } else {//Error handling...}
  }
});
```

We did not discover any performance issues while testing. The maximum size of an MQTT message is about 256 Megabytes and the size of the messages in our system has been under 10 kilobytes. Temporary topics are removed by the requester after receiving the response which increases the amount of traffic a bit but prevents the system from growing memory usage continuously. The method uses complex topics though simple and short topic structures could use less resources [13]. On the other hand, a flexible topic structure is important when adding new features. Still, since MQTT is IoT optimized, using it should help saving the resources when compared to HTTP. Our preliminary results with 1000 request-replies suggests that MQTT uses less CPU time and memory even with request-reply pattern but the detailed analysis is left for future work.

Robustness and reliability requires future work. In HTTP-based systems the clients either get a response or an error condition. In the current MQTT system conditions like network errors may lead to situations where client never gets any notice and the requesting subsystem has no way to discover what went wrong. The quality of service (QoS) of MQTT could provide partial solution but most probably some additional logic needs to be added. The QoS level used by us is MQTT level "zero" which means that there are no guarantees of delivery of the messages. However, we have not discovered any cases of undelivered messages in our test network.

If extra security is needed in REST, there are standard mechanisms for encryption, authentication and authorization. In the pub/sub systems basically anybody can subscribe and publish. This increases risks if all entities in the system are not trusted. MQTT also provides security features such as authentication and authorization but those are not used in this work.

5   Related Work

There is some research on making request-reply over pub/sub architecture [6,12,25] but they are on general level rather than solutions for specific network architecture problems in IoT. More recent studies and techniques take IoT into account. A draft document by Advancing Open Standards for Information Society [23] addresses the problem of using MQTT for request-response pattern by stating that request-response is needed when IoT device reads data from server/other device or vice versa, and when IoT device needs to set a value in server/other device or vice versa with a confirmation that the operation was successful.

Open Mobile Alliance Lightweight Machine-to-Machine (OMA LWM2M) is an IoT protocol that supports device and application management [24]. It has overhead for our purposes since it has an object and resource model that we do not need (we already have a resource model) and it uses CoAP that can not communicate to parties behind NAT as easily as MQTT. While tunneling, port forwarding or particular connection requests can be used with CoAP [15], we thought MQTT is more simple and enough for our needs. Several authors [3,10,27] mention the benefits of MQTT when communicating beyond NAT.

There is also some research about the relation of MQTT and REST. Collina et al. [5] studied a broker that bridges MQTT and REST by exposing MQTT topics as REST resources and vice versa, so that it is possible to use MQTT via REST but they do not try to use MQTT similarly to REST. Chan and Liu [4] implemented an MQTT proxy in their REST architecture comparing latency and performance between the protocols. They do not discuss how to implement functionality similar to REST with MQTT.

Some tool tutorials [11] (visual Java programming environment), [2] (example with Emitter.io broker), [7] (Java based IoT framework) [26] (complex messaging middleware) describe solutions which use request-reply over MQTT. However, we did not see enough benefits to utilize such tools with our approach of minimal refactoring. Other techniques to implement the functionality exist as well. HTTP long polling could work but we wanted to use MQTT because it should support IoT better. HTTP is not designed for pushing data and thus it is not as efficient [21]. Websockets could be another alternative often used in web browsers to create full-duplex communication. However, websockets are not designed for constrained devices and do not support IoT domain well [16].

Pulga [8] is an MQTT broker, targeted to be run on low-resource devices, that can deploy binary applications. In contrast, we use broker that is installed on a desktop server and deploy source code. However, there seems to be relatively few scientific publications about using MQTT in request-response (or REST) style.

6   Conclusions and Future Work

We presented a work where originally REST-based communication was substituted with MQTT by using it in request-response manner. The use case of the work was an IoT development and deployment framework presented in [1]. The initial motivation for the work came from the problems of using HTTP to access devices that are behind a firewall. Another reason is that MQTT is more suitable for IoT devices with limited resources, and MQTT is used in practical IoT implementations. The main technical challenges in our research were related to the implementation of request-response paradigm. Our solution is based on separate response message and design of topic hierarchy with specific request and reply topics. In addition, a status code needs to be added to the content of the response. Nevertheless, the similarities between the concepts of REST and MQTT helped us in the design work.

One way to extend the work would be to implement the whole system to support MQTT. Currently, only the communication that prevented us from demonstrating the system remotely have been implemented with MQTT. For example, the IDE still uses REST for communicating with the RR. The security aspects require further analysis and research since the current implementation assumes that all participating entities trust each other. By adding authentication and encryption technologies the security could be improved. In addition, the system should be evaluated with a larger scale set-up and amount of data. The number of messages, required processing and energy consumption should be measured to answer the questions raising from the growing IoT phenomenon.

References

1. Ahmadighohandizi, F., Systä, K.: Application development and deployment for IoT devices. In: CLIoT 2016: The 4th Workshop on CLoud for IoT (2016)
2. Atachiants, R.: Stock explorer: using pub/sub for request/response (2016). https://www.codeproject.com/Articles/1159256/Stock-Explorer-Using-Pub-Sub-for-Request-Response. Accessed 03 Feb 2017
3. Bellavista, P., Zanni, A.: Towards better scalability for IoT-cloud interactions via combined exploitation of MQTT and COAP. In: 2016 IEEE 2nd International Forum on Research and Technologies for Society and Industry Leveraging a Better Tomorrow (RTSI), pp. 1–6. IEEE (2016)
4. Chen, H.W., Lin, F.J.: Converging MQTT resources in ETSI standards based M2M platform. In: 2014 IEEE International Conference on Internet of Things (iThings), and Green Computing and Communications (GreenCom) and IEEE Cyber, Physical and Social Computing (CPSCom), pp. 292–295. IEEE (2014)

5. Collina, M., Corazza, G.E., Vanelli-Coralli, A.: Introducing the QEST broker: scaling the IoT by bridging MQTT and REST. In: 2012 IEEE 23rd International Symposium on Personal, Indoor and Mobile Radio Communications (PIMRC), pp. 36–41. IEEE (2012)
6. Cugola, G., Migliavacca, M., Monguzzi, A.: On adding replies to publish-subscribe. In: Proceedings of the 2007 Inaugural International Conference on Distributed Event-Based Systems, pp. 128–138. ACM (2007)
7. Documentation for Eclipse Kura: MQTT namespace guidelines. https://eclipse.github.io/kura/ref/mqtt-namespace.html#mqtt-request/response-conversations. Accessed 05 Oct 2016
8. Espinosa-Aranda, J.L., Vallez, N., Sanchez-Bueno, C., Aguado-Araujo, D., Bueno, G., Deniz, O.: Pulga, a tiny open-source MQTT broker for flexible and secure IoT deployments. In: 2015 IEEE Conference on Communications and Network Security (CNS), pp. 690–694. IEEE (2015)
9. Fielding, R.T.: Architectural styles and the design of network-based software architectures. Ph.D. thesis, University of California, Irvine (2000)
10. Fremantle, P.: A reference architecture for the internet of things. WSO2 White Paper (2014)
11. Gunawan, L.A.: Request/response pattern over MQTT (2014). http://www.bitreactive.com/mqtt-request-response/. Accessed 05 Oct 2016
12. Hill, J.C., Knight, J.C., Crickenberger, A.M., Honhart, R.: Publish and subscribe with reply. Technical rep, DTIC Document (2002)
13. HIVEMQ: MQTT essentials part 5: MQTT topics & best practices. http://www.hivemq.com/blog/mqtt-essentials-part-5-mqtt-topics-best-practices. Accessed 05 Oct 2016
14. Hylli, O., Ruokonen, A., Mäkitalo, N., Systä, K.: Orchestrating the Internet of Things dynamically. In: First International Workshop on Mashups of Things and APIs (MoTA) Co-located with MIDDLEWARE 2016 (2016, to appear)
15. Jaffey, T.: MQTT and CoAP, IoT protocols (2014). https://eclipse.org/community/eclipse_newsletter/2014/february/article2.php. Accessed 03 Feb 2017
16. Karagiannis, V., Chatzimisios, P., Vazquez-Gallego, F., Alonso-Zarate, J.: A survey on application layer protocols for the Internet of Things. Trans. IoT Cloud Comput. **3**(1), 11–17 (2015)
17. Kuuskeri, J., Turto, T.: On actors and the REST. In: Benatallah, B., Casati, F., Kappel, G., Rossi, G. (eds.) ICWE 2010. LNCS, vol. 6189, pp. 144–157. Springer, Heidelberg (2010). https://doi.org/10.1007/978-3-642-13911-6_10
18. Mosquitto: Mosquitto - an open source MQTT v3.1/v3.1.1 broker. https://mosquitto.org/. Accessed 05 Oct 2016
19. MQTT.js: The MQTT client for Node.js and the browser. https://www.npmjs.com/package/mqtt. Accessed 05 Oct 2016
20. MQTT.org: MQTT. http://mqtt.org/. Accessed 05 Oct 2016
21. Nicholas, S.: Power profiling: HTTPS long polling vs. MQTT with SSL, on Android (2012). http://stephendnicholas.com/archives/1217. Accessed 05 Oct 2016
22. Node.js: About node.js. https://nodejs.org/en/about. Accessed 08 Nov 2016
23. OASIS MQTT Technical Committee: Request/reply message exchange patterns and MQTT version 1.0 working draft 02 (2015). https://www.oasis-open.org/committees/download.php/56280/reqreply-v1%200-wd02.docx. Accessed 05 Oct 2016
24. Rao, S., Chendanda, D., Deshpande, C., Lakkundi, V.: Implementing LWM2M in constrained IoT devices. In: 2015 IEEE Conference on Wireless Sensors (ICWiSe), pp. 52–57. IEEE (2015)

25. Rodríguez-Domínguez, C., Benghazi, K., Noguera, M., Garrido, J.L., Rodríguez, M.L., Ruiz-López, T.: A communication model to integrate the request-response and the publish-subscribe paradigms into ubiquitous systems. Sensors **12**(6), 7648–7668 (2012)
26. Solace Systems: Request/reply (MQTT). http://dev.solacesystems.com/get-started/mqtt-tutorials/request-reply_mqtt/. Accessed 05 Oct 2016
27. Uehara, M.: A case study on developing cloud of things devices. In: 2015 Ninth International Conference on Complex, Intelligent, and Software Intensive Systems (CISIS), pp. 44–49. IEEE (2015)

Wireless Brain-Computer Interface for Wheelchair Control by Using Fast Machine Learning and Real-Time Hyper-Dimensional Classification

Valerio F. Annese[1], Giovanni Mezzina[2],
and Daniela De Venuto[2($\boxtimes$)] (iD)

[1] School of Engineering, University of Glasgow, Glasgow G12 8TA, UK
v.annese.1@research.gla.ac.uk
[2] Department of Electrical and Information Engineering,
Politecnico di Bari via Orabona 4, 70125 Bari, Italy
g.mezzina23@gmail.com, daniela.devenuto@poliba.it

Abstract. This paper presents a noninvasive brain-controlled P300-based wheelchair driven by EEG signals to be used by tetraplegic and paralytic users. The P300 - an Evoked Related Potential (ERP) - is induced for purpose by visual stimuli. The developed Brain-Computer Interface is made up by: (i) acquisition unit; (ii) processing unit and (iii) navigation unit. The acquisition unit is a wireless 32-channel EEG headset collecting data from 6 electrodes (parietal-cortex area). The processing unit is a dedicated µPC performing stimuli delivery, data gathering, Machine Learning (ML), real-time hyper-dimensional classification leading to the user intention interpretation. The ML stage is based on a custom algorithm (t-RIDE) which trains the following classification stage on the user-tuned P300 reference features. The real-time classification performs a functional approach for time-domain features extraction, which reduce the amount of data to be analyzed. The Raspberry-based navigation unit actuates the received commands and support the wheelchair motion using peripheral sensors (USB camera for video processing, ultrasound sensors). Differently from related works, the proposed protocol for stimulation is aware of the environment. The experimental results, based on a dataset of 5 subjects, demonstrate that: (i) the implemented ML algorithm allows a complete P300 spatio-temporal characterization in 1.95 s using only 22 target brain visual stimuli (88 s/direction); (ii) the complete classification chain (from features extraction to validation) takes in the worst case only 19.65 ms $\pm$ 10.1, allowing real-time control; (iii) the classification accuracy of the implemented BCI is 80.5 $\pm$ 4.1% on single-trial.

Keywords: BCI · Machine learning · Classification · EEG · ERP
P300

1 Introduction

Brain-Computer Interface (BCI) systems allow the user to control external devices, i.e. independent of peripheral nerves and muscles, with only brain signals. The first BCI system was implemented by W. Grey et al. in 1964 [1]. In [1], Grey et al. presented the

© Springer International Publishing AG, part of Springer Nature 2018
I. Garrigós and M. Wimmer (Eds.): ICWE 2017, LNCS 10544, pp. 61–74, 2018.
https://doi.org/10.1007/978-3-319-74433-9_5

development of a mind-controlled cursor. This work represents a milestone: the demonstration of the possibility of controlling devices with a specific brain signal belonging to the cognitive area fueled an exponential growth in the field of BCI.

Nowadays, BCI systems cover a wide range of applications [2–10] such as locomotion (wheelchair [2], car [3, 4] robot or neuro-prosthesis [5]), rehabilitation (the "Bionic Eye" [6]), communication (the P300 speller [7]), environmental control (the "Brain Gate" [8]) and entertaining (neuro-games [9]). Generally, they can be categorized basing on the particular Brain Activity Pattern (BAP) to be detected, i.e. sensorimotor rhythms (SMR), amplitude modulation of slow cortical potentials (SCP), visual cortex potentials (VEPs) or Event-Related Potentials (ERPs) [10]. Among the ERPs, the most commonly used potential for BCI applications is the P300. The P300 is a large positive deflection detectable in the EEGs when a rare stimulus ("target") is discriminated from multiple different frequent stimuli ("non-target"). This kind of stimuli delivery protocol is commonly known as "oddball paradigm" [11, 12]. The P300, reaching its peak around 300 ms after the target stimulus, reflects the stage of stimulus classification and, for this reason, can be also used for diagnostic purpose [13, 14]. Although individual differences in P300 latency and amplitude have also been reported in [13], P300 is detectable for every human being, with a high degree of repeatability. In the field of BCI for locomotion, strong interest was shown in the implementation of brain controlled wheelchairs [15], due to the inestimable impact that this technology can have on the quality of life of paralytic, tetraplegic and motor impaired subjects. Despite the extensive research [2–10, 15], the high computational times to perform both machine learning (ML) and classification make the system very challenging in a real-life scenario. In this context, this paper presents a P300-based BCI for the brain-control a wheelchair i.e. without need for any physical interaction. Differently from SMR and SCP based BCI, the developed BCI bases its operation on the P300, which does not require intensive user training (P300 component results from endogenous attention-based brain function). Furthermore, P300-based BCIs generally achieve a higher detection rate [15]. The complete architecture is made up by three sub-systems: (i) the acquisition unit; (ii) the processing unit and (iii) the navigation unit. The main improvement of the proposed BCI systems with respect to the state of the art are: (i) the use of a novel custom algorithm (t-RIDE) for fast ML and (ii) a fully spatio-temporal features-based approach for the real-time hyper-dimensional classification, addressing the need for computational speed. In particular, the adaption of t-RIDE [3, 4, 11–14], for ML stage allows a complete P300 spatio-temporal characterization using only 22 target brain visual stimuli (88 s for each addressable command). Additionally, the functional approach for the classification based on spatio-temporal features extraction (FE), allows fast interpretation of the user's intention (worst case: 19.65 ms $\pm$ 10.1 ms) keeping high success rate 89.54% $\pm$ 4.03 (tested on 5 subjects). Section 2 outlines the architecture of the BCI system, focusing on each sub-system composing the architecture. Section 3 presents the testing of the platform and the experimental results basing on a dataset from 5 healthy subjects. Section 4 concludes the paper.

2 The Architecture

The overall architecture can be divided into three sub-systems: (i) the acquisition unit, (ii) the processing unit and (iii) the navigation unit. The acquisition unit collects EEG data from the user and wirelessly (Bluetooth) sends them to the processing unit. The processing unit is the core of the systems, solving the main functions of the architecture i.e. (i) stimuli generation and delivery, (ii) data collection and synchronization, (iii) Machine Learning, (iv) real-time hyper-dimensional classification, (v) user intention interpretation. Once the processing unit interprets the user's intent, it wirelessly (TCP/IP) sends the relative command to the navigation unit. The navigation unit is responsible for the command actuation and it controls the navigation through its sensors i.e. ultrasonic proximity sensors (for obstacle avoidance) and USB camera (for video processing/streaming). Figure 1 shows a high-level schematic of the developed BCI architecture.

Fig. 1. Schematic overview of the developed BCI architecture.

2.1 The Acquisition Unit

The acquisition unit is a wireless (Bluetooth) 32-channels EEG headset. Conditioning integrated circuits are embedded in the electrodes performing "in loco" amplification, filtering and digitalization. Despite the employed acquisition unit is the one used in [16–23], the locations of the electrodes have been chosen according to previous P300 studies [24] and, in a later stage, reduced in number basing on the relevance in experimental conditions. EEG recordings are performed using six electrodes i.e. C_Z, CP_1, CP_2, P_3, P_z, P_4 (international 10–20 standard, see Fig. 2a). The recording scheme is monopolar. The reference electrode is AF_z while the right ear lobe (A_2) is used as ground. The filtering processing includes two stages: 2–30 Hz bandpass (Butterworth, 8th order) and 48–52 Hz notch (Butterworth, 4th order) filters. Both the filters are embedded into the acquisition front-end. The sampling rate is 500 Hz with 24-bit resolution while the input range is ± 187.5 mV. Using a multiplexer, EEG data are directed to the 2.4 GHz Bluetooth XVV-MEGA22M00 module for the transmission. Figure 2b present a schematic of the acquisition unit.

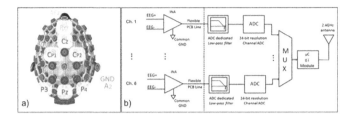

Fig. 2. (a) Location of the electrodes recorded in this work; (b) Schematic of the acquisition unit.

2.2   The Processing Unit

In our implementation, the processing unit is a PC (Intel i5, RAM 8 GB, 64 bit). The processing unit performs several functions in parallel and, for this reason, is the key part of the whole system.

Stimuli Generation and Delivery. The stimulation protocol is designed according to the oddball paradigm using visual stimuli. There are four delivered visual stimuli, individually and randomly flashing on a display (25% occurrence probability) with an inter-stimuli time of 1 s. The stimulus persists on the screen for 200 ms. Each stimulus is linked to a particular command to be sent to the navigation system i.e. start/go ahead, turn right, turn left, stop/go backwards. Neurophysiological studies [24] revealed that P300 latency and amplitude are related to the stimulus physiognomy (such as duration, contrast, color, etc.). For this reason, each command is linked to a different stimulus in terms of shape and color. Differently from a classic oddball paradigm, there is no pre-defined target stimulus. The user selects which stimulus is the target one, basing on his intention. Thus, only that particular stimulus, which is linked to the desired command, will evocate the P300. Figure 3 proposes a real example from our dataset (on C_Z electrode), showing the differences in the brain activity depending on the type of the stimulus. Only when a target stimulus is delivered, a clear positive peak rises approximately 300 ms after the stimulus onset.

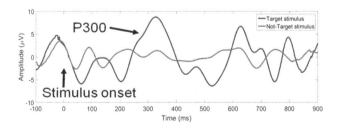

Fig. 3. The P300 can be detected only when a target stimulus is detected (Cz).

Data Collection and Synchronization. The processing unit receives six real-time EEG signals from the acquisition unit by Bluetooth protocol. Subsequently, each channel undergoes a further filtering stage, aiming to reduce both noise and artifacts (eyes and head movements). The channels are pre-processed in parallel. The implemented numerical filter is a 6th order low-pass Butterworth filter with $f_{3dB} = 15$ Hz. The next pre-processing stage is the channels synchronization with the delivered stimuli. For this aim, filtered EEG signals are firstly decomposed in 1 s segment (called – in this work – trial). The EEG trial starts as soon as the rising edge of the stimulation arrives. A 6th order fitting polynomial of the evaluated trial is subtracted to the signal in order to center and scale the trial, without losing the P300 information. Finally, all the trials are organized into a 3D matrix DATA $\in R^{S \times N \times M}$ where S is the number of samples into a single trial (500 in our implementation), N is the number of monitored channels (6 in our work) and M is the number of delivered stimuli (target and not-target).

Machine Learning. The P300 latency is heavily affected by inter-subject and trial-to-trial variability and it ranges from 290 ms to 447.5 ms [3, 4, 11–14, 24]. Additionally, its amplitude is affected by high variability: it can reach even 37.7 μV depending on the subject [3, 4, 11–14, 24].

Due to this inter-subject variability, the system needs to be tuned on the particular user. The subject-optimization is achieved by a stage of Machine Learning (ML) to be performed on the first use of the system. In this case, the neurophysiological protocol delivered to the user is slightly different form the one above-described. In fact, the user performs a supervised oddball test targeting N known stimulus (N $\geq$ 22 in our work, as demonstrated in Sect. 3.2). For the ML stage, the processing is performed offline.

P300 Extraction for ML. The ML stage implemented in this BCI is based on a novel algorithm, named tuned-Residue Iteration Decomposition (t-RIDE). The improvements achieved by t-RIDE with respect to the state of the art for P300 extraction has been presented in [12]. In [12], it was demonstrated on a dataset of 12 subjects that (i) t-RIDE is 1.6 times faster than ICA (i.e., t-RIDE: 1.95 s against ICA: 3.1 s); (ii) t-RIDE reaches 80% of accuracy after only 13 targets; (iii) t-RIDE can be performed even on a single channel (differently from ICA). t-RIDE is a custom tuned version of RIDE [12] for P300 extraction which include three additional steps to RIDE: pre-processing, window optimization and spatial characterization. t-RIDE iteratively estimates the computation window which optimize the P300 extraction. Only one signal derived from the average of P_Z and C_Z is considered – at first - for window optimization. A first default window is defined as $250 - 400$ ms after the stimulus. The procedure for window optimization is based on an iterative approach. After n_{IT} iterations, the algorithm selects the optimized window i.e., the one with the highest P300 amplitude. As soon as the optimized window is defined, the DATA matrix is processed by t-RIDE. Time-domain results from each channel are subsequently interpolated in order to extract the spatial characterization (P300 topography). In this stage, the system stores the vectors $L = (l_1, ..., l_N) \in R^N$ and $A = (a_1, ..., a_N) \in R^N$ containing respectively the expected P300 latencies and amplitude for each channel (N = 6).

Feature Extraction (FE) for ML. The P300 pulse extracted by t-RIDE undergoes a phase of FE to be used as 'golden reference'. Basing on specialized medical guidelines and literature investigation, five features have been selected. For the FE on the jth

channel, the trial x(i) is windowed by a rectangular 200 ms window (number of samples n_s = 100) centered on the expected latency l_j. The extracted features are:

1. The **Simmetry** quantifies the symmetry degree of the signal with respect to the expected latency:

$$f_1 = 1 - \left| \frac{2}{ns - 1} \sum_{i=1}^{ns} [x(i) - x(ns - i)] \right| \tag{1}$$

2. The **Convexity** identifies the convexity degree of the considered data points with respect to the expected latency:

$$f_2 = 1 \leftrightarrow \sum_{i=1}^{\left(\frac{ns}{2}\right)-1} \frac{\partial x(i)}{\partial i} \geq \sum_{i=\left(\frac{ns}{2}\right)+1}^{ns} \frac{\partial x(i)}{\partial i} ; otherwise \ f_2 = 0 \tag{2}$$

3. The **Triangle area (TA)** delivers the area of the triangle inscribed into the potentially P300 component deflection:

$$f_2 = 0.5 \cdot \begin{vmatrix} x1 & y1 & 1 \\ x2 & y2 & 1 \\ x3 & y3 & 1 \end{vmatrix} \tag{3}$$

where (x_1, y_1) is the minimum value in the 100 ms before the P300 learned latency as well as (x_2, y_2) is the minimum value of the 100 ms on its right side. (x_3, y_3) are the coordinates of maximum value of the extracted data points.

4. The **Peak to Max distance (PMD)** quantifies how close is the maximum point of the single trial with respect to the expected one:

$$f_4 = \left\{ \frac{(ns+1)}{2} - \left| \frac{(ns+1)}{2} - index(\max(x)) \right| \right\} \frac{2}{(ns+1)} \tag{4}$$

5. The **Direction changes index (DCI)** quantifies the number of considered waveform direction changes. It can be obtained by counting the slope sign changes, referring to signal derivative.

Thresholds/Weights Definition for ML. The features distributions are analyzed by a statistical method that extracts, for each feature and channel, the 25th and 75th percentiles and median value. A demonstrative picture for a generic feature is shown in Fig. 4a. Thresholds definition is based on the percentiles. The weights definition is based on the median values by evaluating the subtraction between the median value of the j-th feature vector referred to the target responses and the not-target ones (distance d in Fig. 4a). The learning step assigns their values in descending order starting from 0.3 for the best feature to 0.1 for the worst one. The remaining 3 features assume decreasing weights with 0.05 steps between 0.3 and 0.1. These values allow obtaining a sum that provides a maximum of 1.

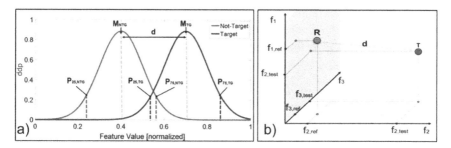

Fig. 4. (a) Demonstrative picture of the statistical analysis performed during the ML. (b) Visual interpretation of the classification approach (only 3 features for clarity).

Machine Learning Finalization. At the end of the ML and FE phase, the processing unit has learned the following subject-depending parameters:

(i) $\mathbf{UP} \in R^{5 \times 6}$ ($up_{i,j}$ = upper threshold for i-th feature referred to the j-channel);
(ii) $\mathbf{DN} \in R^{5 \times 6}$ ($dn_{i,j}$ = lower threshold for i-th feature referred to the j-channel);
(iii) $\mathbf{W} \in R^{5 \times 6}$ ($w_{i,j}$ = i-th weight referred to the j-channel);
(iv) $\mathbf{S} \in R^{6}$: (s_j = responsivity - detection rate of the j-th channels);
(v) $\mathbf{L} \in R^{6}$ (l_j = expected P300 latencies for the j-th channel);
(vi) $\mathbf{A} \in R^{6}$ (a_j = expected P300 amplitude for the j-th channel).

Hyper-Dimensional Real-Time Classification. For each subject, the "golden" learned P300 can be represented by a single point in a n-dimensional space where the features are the bases (n = number of features). Figure 4b proposes a visual interpretation of the situation, supposing n = 3. The real-time classifier performs a FE on incoming streaming EEG data and compares the results with the "golden" reference: the decision about the absence/presence of P300 is based on the n-dimensional distance between reference and incoming trial exploiting thresholds. In order to reduce the computational times, the classification is performed on a down-sampled (from 500 sps to 100 sps) and windowed (M samples centered on the expected latency, M = 20 – 200 ms) version of EEG trials. The classifier implements 5 rules to decide presence/absence of the P300 component.

When the classification is over, the processing unit sends to the navigation one a 2 bits code informing about the actuation through TCP/IP wireless communication.

1st rule: Data validation. Data are validated only if the they are similar in amplitude to the learned values in **A**:
Continue classification $\leftrightarrow$ max $(EEG_i) < ai + \varepsilon$ *otherwise* 'report error' and 'stop'.
2nd rule: Single Feature on single channel. As soon as a new stimulus occurs, the processing unit performs the FE on the single-trial for each channel basing on **L**. This leads to the computation of $\mathbf{f} \in R^{5 \times 6}$ where its generic element $f_{i,j}$ expresses the value of the i-th feature on the j-th channel. This procedure leads to the creation of the matrix $\mathbf{F} \in R^{5 \times 6}$ adopting the following decisional rule:

$$F_{i,j} = \begin{cases} 0 & \leftrightarrow & f_{i,j} < dn_{i,j} \\ 0.5 & \leftrightarrow & dn_{i,j} \leq f_{i,j} \leq up_{i,j} \\ 1 & \leftrightarrow & f_{i,j} > up_{i,j} \end{cases} \quad (5)$$

3rd rule: All features on single channels. A weighted sum of **F** defines the presence of the P300 on the j-th channel, through the calculation of the vector $\mathbf{R} \in R^6$, where the generic element is:

$$r_j = w_{1,j} \cdot F_{1,j} + \ldots + w_{5,j} \cdot F_{5,j} \text{ for } j = 1, 2, \ldots, 6 \quad (6)$$

4th rule: P300 presence/absence on single channel. Afterwards, the classifier adopts the a single threshold decision comparison to evaluate the presence/absence of P300 on the j-th channel:

$$y_j = \begin{cases} 0 & \leftrightarrow & r_j \leq y_t \\ 1 & \leftrightarrow & r_j > y_t \end{cases} \quad (7)$$

Where y_j is the generic element of $\mathbf{Y} \in R^6$ and y_t is a decision threshold set to 0.5. The rule yt = 0.5 means that on the j-th channel, at least 3 features have been detected.

5th rule: P300 presence/absence on all the channels. The classifier validate the P300 presence only if the P300 is simultaneous detected on 5 out of 6 channels detect w.r.t. channels, which deliver a high detection rate (vector **S**).

2.3   The Navigation Unit

The navigation unit is responsible for (i) actuating the commands sent by the processing unit and (ii) supporting the navigation. The core of the navigation unit is Raspberry Pi 2 (Model B+) equipped by a Wi-Fi antenna (for the communication with the processing unit), an USB camera and a SD. Using a DC-DC converter (XL-1509), a nominal supply voltage of 7.4 V voltage is stabilized to 5 V, delivering the power supply for the board. For actuating the commands sent by the processing unit, GPIO pins on Raspberry control the DC motor drivers. Particularly, two 12 V DC motors are used in this work to demonstrate running of wheelchair in forward, reverse, left and right direction. L293D motor driver is used to interface with Raspberry Pi, which is TTL compatible. Two H bridges of L293D can be connected in parallel to increase its current capacity to 2A. Then, GPIO pins can be enable, disable or modulate (by PWM) the pins of the L293D. Finally, a relay is used to quickly change the motor direction. The PWM modulates with adequate set of cross-velocity the motor providing rotation. The rotation is possible along predefined destinations, in term of (distance, angle) couple that are relative to the wheelchair's location, which corresponded to locations in the environment that the participants might select to reach. For instance, a rotation on the left side is traduced in a couple (distance, angle) of (2 m, −60°), while a right rotation reach the position (2 m, 60°) starting from the initial position of the wheelchair. The PWM preset allows a maximum translational and rotational velocities of

$\omega_{max} = 0.3$ m/s and an average velocity of 0.16 m/s. On the other hand, two servo-motors control the orientation of the USB camera, which streams a real-time video to the processing unit. The navigation unit supports the navigation by two different approaches: (i) obstacle avoidance and (ii) real-time modification of the neurophysiological protocol delivered to the user (w.r.t the protocol presented in Sect. 2.2.1). The obstacle detection and avoidance is based on three ultrasonic proximity sensors (HC-SR04) which point in three different directions (straight and sideways): when an obstacle is detected ahead with a distance lower than 1 m, the wheelchair stops. Differently, when the wheelchair detects a side obstacle that is not in its trajectory, Raspberry alerts the processing unit, which adapts the neurophysiological protocol preventing the choice of that specific direction. In this case, the processing unit does not deliver the visual stimuli linked to the command until further notice from the navigation unit. This procedure leads, de facto, to a modification of the oddball: the protocol is adaptive and is aware of the surroundings, proposing to the user only selections that are consistent with the environment. This approach, performing environment-related stimuli delivery, is a key-point of our platform and overcomes the static protocols presented in related works [2–10].

3   Experimental Results

The entire architecture has been tested on a dataset from 5 different subjects (age: 26 ± 3). The subjects performed at first the learning protocol and, subsequently, the real-time wheelchair control.

Machine Learning. In the testing stage, the neurophysiological paradigm for ML consist in a supervised oddball test (the target is known) presenting 30 target stimuli (i.e. 120 s). The supervised oddball test is reiterated for each addressable direction and data are processed offline. The P300 amplitude range was $3 - 8$ µV with a mean value of 4.7 µV $\pm$ 0.61 µV; the P300 latency was included in the range 300–403 ms, with a mean value of 349.25 ms $\pm$ 35.52 ms. Figure 5a summarizes the overall accuracy considering the channel-to-channel responsivity (array named S). The boxplots in Fig. 5a have been obtained by statistically treating the responsivity of each channel, on

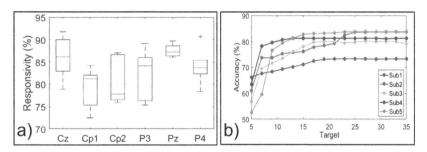

Fig. 5. (a) Boxplot representation of the responsivity vs. electrode position; (b) Accuracy (all the subjects) vs. n°. of target stimuli for training;

5 subjects. Considering the median values, the highest responsivity are reached by P_Z, C_Z, P_3, which obtain a value of 87.3%, 86.2%, 84.1%, respectively.

Real-time classification. The online validation approach included two different tests: (i) single direction repetitive selections and (ii) pattern recognition. In the first approach, the user is asked to select repeatedly a single target. The reached classification accuracies computed in these conditions are: sub_1: 73.68 ± 5.3%; sub_2: 83.71 ± 4.6%; sub_3: 80 ± 3.1%; sub_4: 81.30 ± 4.8%; sub_5: 83.84 ± 5.8% (best: 89%, worst: 68.38%).

Differently, the pattern recognition test consist in the selection of a known stream of directions (10 commands covering all the addressable directions). The performed accuracies computed in this test are: sub1: 67.9 ± 6.7%; sub2: 72.5 ± 7.1%; sub3: 67.5 ± 4.4%; sub4: 69.2 ± 8.5%; sub5: 70.6 ± 3.7% (best: 80% worst: 50%). Figure 5b outlines the accuracy of the system as a function of the number of targets used to train the BCI. The graph shows separately the subjects accuracy. It is worth noting that, 4 subjects on 5 reaches the accuracy steady state by using only 15 target stimuli. It corresponds to a ML stage of about 60 s for each direction. This lower limit is directly connected to the capability of the ML algorithm (t-RIDE) to reach the complete the P300 spatio-temporal characterization in the same number of targets (15 Targets → 90% of accuracy in P300 characterization) [12]. In the worst case, the system needs at least 22 targets (i.e. 88 s) to recognize the intentions with an accuracy of 83.7% (Sub.2). The best case (Sub.4) requests only 10 targets and thus a ML duration of 40 s/direction, obtaining an accuracy of 81.3%. From this analysis we can state that t-RIDE allows to drastically reduce the duration of the training, since it needs only 22 target stimuli for a worst-case complete characterization of P300 (88 s). The shortening of the training phase allows reducing the effect of the "habituation" that typically spoils the P300. t-RIDE computational time was only 1.95 s and it does not requires a minimum number of channels.

Timing. Since the application is in real-time, special attention should be devoted to timing in order to guarantee the correct functioning. The fixed communication latency from EEG headset and gateway is 14 ms. The classifier needs to buffer 1 s data after the stimulus in order to perform the computation. The worst-case computational time for each feature extraction on single channel and single trial was 0.653 ± 0.32 ms. The worst-case total time for the FE stage on 6 channels was 19.58 ± 9.7 ms. The successive definition of the matrix **F** was performed in 0.026 ± 0.011 ms on all the channels. The computational time (for 6 channels) for the spatial validation was 0.041 ± 0.008 ms. Given this computational details, the worst-case total time needed by the classifier to complete the classification for all the channels was 19.65 ± 10.1 ms. The FE stage is the most time consuming part of the process. The communication time between processing and navigation unit takes about 3.35 ns (only 2 bits to be sent by Wi-Fi). As soon as Raspberry Pi receives the command, the actuation is performed in 3 ms (worst-case). The overall architecture complete a single actuation (from EEG raw data acquisition triggered by stimulus delivery to PCS actuation) in 1.03 s (worst-case). Timing is not related to the subject but Fig. 6 highlights the variability of this parameter.

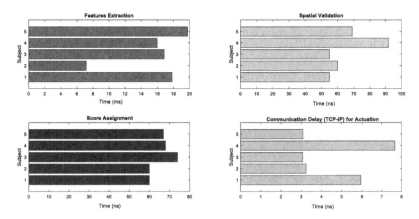

Fig. 6. Timing details for different tasks performed by the classifier.

4   Conclusion

The aim of the present work was the study, the design, implementation and test of a brain-computer interface based on P300. The implemented neural interface allows remote control of a wheelchair. The ML stage is based on the custom algorithm t-RIDE, which trains the following hyper-dimensional real-time classifier performing in real time the FE on raw data for the detection of presence/absence of P300. The system has been validated on a dataset of 5 subjects driving the wheelchair by their mind. The average classification accuracy on a single direction was $80.51 \pm 4.1\%$. The average classification accuracy in the detection of a 10-direction pattern was $69.6 \pm 1.9\%$. The classifier completes its process on all the channels in 19.65 ± 10.1 ms (worst-case). According to the achieved results, the oddball protocol used for training can be reduced to 88 s/direction (worst case). The computational time for ML is 1.95 s. Future perspectives include the use of biocompatible and flexible electronics in order to increase the wearability degree of the system [25, 26], the optimization of the wireless network [27–30] and the design and fabrication of an Application Specific Integrated Circuit (ASIC) [31–35].

References

1. Graimann, B., Allison, B., Pfurtscheller, G.: Brain–Computer Interfaces: A Gentle Introduction. Springer, Heidelberg (2009)
2. Grychtol, B., Lakany, H., Valsan, G., Conway, B.A.: Human behavior integration improves classification rates in real-time BCI. Neural Syst. Rehabil. Eng. **8**(4), 362–368 (2010). https://doi.org/10.1109/TNSRE.2010.2053218
3. De Venuto, D., Vincentelli, A.S.: Dr. Frankenstein's dream made possible: Implanted electronic devices. In: Proceedings of Design, Automation and Test in Europe, DATE, pp. 1531–1536 (2013). Art. no. 6513757

4. De Venuto, D., Annese, V.F., Mezzina, G.: An embedded system remotely driving mechanical devices by P300 brain activity. In: Proceedings of the 2017 Design, Automation and Test in Europe Conference and Exhibition, DATE (2017). ISBN 978-3-9815370-8-6

5. Ortner, R., et al.: An SSVEP BCI to control a hand orthosis for persons with tetraplegia. IEEE Trans. Neural Syst. Rehabil. Eng. **19**(1), 1–5 (2011)

6. Barnes, N.: Visual processing for the bionic eye: Research and development of visual processing for low vision devices and the bionic eye (2012)

7. Farwell, L.A., Donchin, E.: Talking off the top of your head: toward a mental prosthesis utilizing event-related brain potentials. Electroenceph Clin. Neurophysiol. **70**(6), 510–523 (1988)

8. Hochberg, L.R., et al.: Neuronal ensemble control of prosthetic devices by a human with tetraplegia. Nat. J. **442**, 164–171 (2006)

9. Nijholt, A.: BCI for games: a 'state of the art' survey. In: Stevens, Scott M., Saldamarco, Shirley J. (eds.) ICEC 2008. LNCS, vol. 5309, pp. 225–228. Springer, Heidelberg (2008). https://doi.org/10.1007/978-3-540-89222-9_29

10. Fernando, L., Alonso, N., Gomez-Gil, J.: Brain computer interfaces, a review. Sensors **12**(2), 1211–1264 (2012)

11. De Tommaso, M., Vecchio, E., Ricci, K., Montemurno, A., De Venuto, D., Annese, V.F.: Combined EEG/EMG evaluation during a novel dual task paradigm for gait analysis. In: Proceedings of the 2015 6th IEEE International Workshop on Advances in Sensors and Interfaces, IWASI 2015, pp. 181–186. (2015). art. no. 7184949. https://doi.org/10.1109/iwasi.2015.7184949

12. De Venuto, D., Annese, V.F., Mezzina, G.: Remote Neuro-Cognitive Impairment Sensing based on P300 Spatio-Temporal Monitoring. IEEE Sens. J. **16**(23), 8348–8356 (2016). PP (99), art. no. 7562544, https://doi.org/10.1109/jsen.2016.2606553

13. Annese, V.F., Mezzina, G., De Venuto, D.: Towards mobile health care: Neurocognitive impairment monitoring by BCI-based game. In: Proceedings of IEEE Sensors (2017). art. no. 7808745 2017. https://doi.org/10.1109/icsens.2016.7808745

14. De Venuto, D., Annese, V.F., Mezzina, G., Ruta, M., Sciascio, E.D.: Brain-computer interface using P300: A gaming approach for neurocognitive impairment diagnosis. In: 2016 IEEE International High Level Design Validation and Test Workshop, HLDVT 2016, pp. 93–99 (2016). art. no. 7748261. https://doi.org/10.1109/hldvt.2016.7748261

15. Fernández-Rodríguez, Á., Velasco-Álvarez, F., Ron-Angevin, R.: Review of real brain-controlled wheelchairs. J. Neural Eng. **13**(6), (2016). 061001

16. Annese, V.F., De Venuto, D.: Gait analysis for fall prediction using EMG triggered movement related potentials. In: Proceedings of 2015 10th IEEE International Conference on Design and Technology of Integrated Systems in Nanoscale Era, DTIS 2015 (2015). art. no. 7127386. https://doi.org/10.1109/dtis.2015.7127386

17. De Venuto, D., Annese, V.F., Ruta, M., Di Sciascio, E., Sangiovanni Vincentelli, A.L.: Designing a cyber-physical system for fall prevention by cortico-muscular coupling detection. IEEE Des. Test **33**(3), 66–76 (2016). art. no. 7273831. https://doi.org/10.1109/mdat.2015.2480707

18. Annese, V.F., De Venuto, D.: Fall-risk assessment by combined movement related potentials and co-contraction index monitoring. In: Proceedings of IEEE Biomedical Circuits and Systems Conference: Engineering for Healthy Minds and Able Bodies, BioCAS 2015 (2015). art. no. 7348366. https://doi.org/10.1109/biocas.2015.7348366

19. Annese, V.F., De Venuto, D.: FPGA based architecture for fall-risk assessment during gait monitoring by synchronous EEG/EMG. In: Proceedings of 2015 6th IEEE International Workshop on Advances in Sensors and Interfaces, IWASI 2015, pp. 116–121 (2015). art. no. 7184953. https://doi.org/10.1109/iwasi.2015.7184953

20. Annese, V.F., Crepaldi, M., Demarchi, D., De Venuto, D.: A digital processor architecture for combined EEG/EMG falling risk prediction. In: Proceedings of the 2016 Design, Automation and Test in Europe Conference and Exhibition, DATE 2016, pp. 714–719 (2016). art. no. 7459401

21. Annese, V.F., De Venuto, D.: The truth machine of involuntary movement: FPGA based cortico-muscular analysis for fall prevention. In: IEEE International Symposium on Signal Processing and Information Technology, ISSPIT 2015, pp. 553–558 (2015). art. no. 7394398. https://doi.org/10.1109/isspit.2015.7394398

22. De Venuto, D., Annese, V.F., Sangiovanni-Vincentelli, A.L.: The ultimate IoT application: a cyber-physical system for ambient assisted living. In: Proceedings of IEEE International Symposium on Circuits and Systems, pp. 2042–2045, July 2016. art. no. 7538979. https://doi.org/10.1109/iscas.2016.7538979

23. De Venuto, D., Annese, V.F., Defazio, G., Gallo, V.L., Mezzina, G.: Gait analysis and quantitative drug effect evaluation in parkinson disease by jointly EEG-EMG monitoring. In: Proceedings of 2017 12th IEEE International Conference on Design and Technology of Integrated Systems in Nanoscale Era, DTIS 2017 (2017)

24. Patel, S.H., Azzam, P.N.: Characterization of N200 and P300: Selected Studies of the Event-Related Potential. International Journal of Medical Sciences 2(4), 147–154 (2005)

25. Annese, V.F., De Venuto, D., Martin, C., Cumming, D.R.S.: Biodegradable pressure sensor for health-care. In: 2014 21st IEEE International Conference on Electronics, Circuits and Systems, ICECS 2014, pp. 598–601 (2014). art. no. 7050056. https://doi.org/10.1109/icecs.2014.7050056

26. Annese, V.F., Martin, C., Cumming, D.R.S., De Venuto, D.: Wireless capsule technology: Remotely powered improved high-sensitive barometric endoradiosonde. In: Proceedings of IEEE International Symposium on Circuits and Systems, pp. 1370–1373. July 2016. art. no. 7527504. https://doi.org/10.1109/iscas.2016.7527504

27. Annese, V.F., De Venuto, D.: On-line shelf-life prediction in perishable goods chain through the integration of WSN technology with a 1st order kinetic model. In: 2015 IEEE 15th International Conference on Environment and Electrical Engineering, EEEIC 2015, pp. 605–610 (2015). art. no. 7165232. https://doi.org/10.1109/eeeic.2015.7165232

28. Annese, V.F., Biccario, G.E., Cipriani, S., De Venuto, D.: Organoleptic properties remote sensing and life-time prediction along the perishables goods supply-chain. In: Proceedings of the International Conference on Sensing Technology, ICST, pp. 130–135. Jan 2014

29. De Venuto, D., Annese, V.F., de Tommaso, M., Vecchio, E., Vincentelli, A.S.: Combining EEG and EMG signals in a wireless system for preventing fall in neurodegenerative diseases. Ambient Assisted Living, pp. 317–327. Springer, Cham (2015)

30. Biccario, G.E., Annese, V.F., Cipriani, S., De Venuto, D.: WSN-based near real-time environmental monitoring for shelf life prediction through data processing to improve food safety and certification. In: Proceedings of the 11th International Conference on Informatics in Control, Automation and Robotics, ICINCO 2014, vol. 1, pp. 777–782 (2014)

31. De Venuto, D., Carrara, S., Ricco, B.: Design of an integrated low-noise read-out system for DNA capacitive sensors. Microelectron. J. 40(9), 1358–1365 (2009). https://doi.org/10.1016/j.mejo.2008.07.071

32. De Venuto, D., Castro, D.T., Ponomarev, Y., Stikvoort, E.: Low power 12-bit SAR ADC for autonomous wireless sensors network interface. In: 3rd International Workshop on Advances in Sensors and Interfaces, IWASI 2009, pp. 115–120 (2009). art. no. 5184780. https://doi.org/10.1109/iwasi.2009.5184780

33. De Venuto, D., Ohletz, M.J., Ricco, B.: Automatic repositioning technique for digital cell based window comparators and implementation within mixed-signal DfT schemes. In: Proceedings of International Symposium on Quality Electronic Design, ISQED, pp. 431–437. Jan 2003. art. no. 1194771. https://doi.org/10.1109/isqed.2003.1194771

34. De Venuto, D., Ohletz, M.J., Ricco, B.: Digital window comparator DfT scheme for mixed-signal ICs. J. Electron. Test. Theory Appl. (JETTA) **18**(2), 121–128 (2002). https://doi.org/10.1023/A:1014937424827

35. De Venuto, D., Ohletz, M.J., Ricco, B.: Testing of analogue circuits via (standard) digital gates. In: Proceedings of International Symposium on Quality Electronic Design, ISQED, pp. 112–119. Jan 2002. art. no. 996709. https://doi.org/10.1109/isqed.2002.996709

Case Study: Building a Serverless Messenger Chatbot

Jyri Lehvä[(✉)] ⓘ, Niko Mäkitalo ⓘ, and Tommi Mikkonen ⓘ

Department of Computer Science, University of Helsinki, Helsinki, Finland
{jyri.lehva,niko.makitalo,tommi.mikkonen}@helsinki.fi

Abstract. Major chat platforms, such as Facebook Messenger, have recently added support for chatbots, thus making chatbots more accessible for the end users. This paper presents a case study on building and designing a Messenger chatbot for a media company. The chatbot uses a Serverless Microservice architecture which was implemented using Amazon Web Services (AWS) including API Gateway, Lambda, DynamoDB, SNS and CloudWatch. The paper presents the architecture and reports the findings regarding the design and the final implementation. These findings are also compared to other recent studies around the same emerging topic.

Keywords: Chatbot · Internet Bot · Serverless computing
Microservices · AWS · AWS Lambda · Facebook Messenger

1 Introduction

Companies such as Facebook, Google, Apple and Amazon have recently started promoting conversational UIs such as chatbots and bots that can be commanded with voice and text [18]. That has resulted in growing interest interest regarding how such technology could be used to improve business in many domains.

In this paper we report a two-month case study where a chatbot was built for a media company in early 2017. The goal of the project was to design a scalable, modern architecture for a chatbot that follows liquid software principles [14]. Hence in the paper we present such an architecture and explain the design behind our solution. We also report the findings and experiences gained from building the given solution. The chatbot has been beta tested with 150 real users but is still not launched to production by the time of writing this paper.

The chatbot was built for Facebook Messenger platform [7], which lets developers to build chatbots that are directly available in the widely used Facebook Messenger applications. The architecture followed the Serverless Microservices approach and was built using Amazon Web Services [9,11,12,15]. Serverless platforms are said to have many benefits compared to server-based approaches; The infrastructure used for running the serverless platforms are managed by the cloud provider which removes the need to worry about server management, which is

© Springer International Publishing AG, part of Springer Nature 2018
I. Garrigós and M. Wimmer (Eds.): ICWE 2017, LNCS 10544, pp. 75–86, 2018.
https://doi.org/10.1007/978-3-319-74433-9_6

an inexpensive solution, and which can scale up rapidly [10, 13, 16]. While these are great benefits, some studies say that serverless services can be hard to debug [13, 17]. Thus, in addition to designing the architecture and building a chatbot, this case study also tries to find out if these benefits apply to the project, and if the implemented serverless service is hard to debug.

The rest of the paper is structured as follows. In Sect. 2 we describe the case study. In Sects. 3 and 4 we introduce the used technologies. In Sect. 5 we describe the designed architecture. In Sect. 6 we report the results of the case study, and in Sect. 7 we discuss about the results. Finally, in Sect. 8, we outline some future work and draw some final conclusions.

2   Case Study: Chatbot for a Media Company

The media company's vision of the chatbot was to build an assistant that could help the users to follow up the latest news of their interests easier. Together with the company, we analyzed and defined the chatbot to have a set of features.

Major features of the chatbot included the following:

- Customizable dialogues
- Read latest news
- User interface for reading latest news
- Order customizable news packages
- Select delivery time for the news packages
- Receive breaking news as they happen
- Subscribe for a weekend news package with a hardcoded delivery time

Other requirements included a possibility for adding natural language processing (NLP) features later on, as these were left out from the project's first phase. The idea of these NLP features is to try finding users' intents from free text input and then trying to react with a proper reply. The architecture also had to have a support to add other chat platforms such as Slack or Telegram later if so wished.

Technical requirements were found out when more carefully analyzing the major features that were requested by the media company. The main requirements are:

- The chatbot had to have a data structure or format for the dialogue. For that the team decided to use JSON notation where the dialogue is written as so called states. Each state had an id, message sent to the user and info about the next state to follow.
- There had to be a way to persist the state of the user between messages. The chatbot could not simply be 100% stateless. The reason for that was that there's a bunch of so called chat flows where the first step leads to a second

step and so on. The chatbot just had to know from which step the user is coming and sometimes even what the user had selected in the flow a couple of steps backwards.

- The future state paths could also contain conditional logic that depends on the past selections. For the conditional logic, the JSON had a list of function names per state which should be called when the user enters the state.

3   Facebook Messenger Platform

Facebook Messenger is a service for instant messaging with Facebook friends. It is available as an application for all major mobile platforms such as iOS, Android and Windows. In 2016 Facebook Messenger platform was extended so that it enables building chatbots that can have conversations with people on Facebook [7].

The conversations with chatbots can be started by searching for the chatbot by the name of the Facebook page they are linked to on the Messenger. The chatbots can also be discovered through direct links that can be advertised on Facebook or with Facebooks QR-code-like system called Messenger Codes which can be scanned using the Messenger application [7].

Facebook doesn't offer any solution to build the chatbot backend. Instead, the backend needs to be built and hosted somewhere else and Facebook leaves that up to the developer to decide where and how. The platform offers callbacks which call a webhook (configured by the developer) when a user sends a message to the chatbot. That way the message gets delivered to the backend. The chatbot can answer to the message by sending it to Facebook Send API which then delivers it to the user as a reply to the initial message.

The UI of the Messenger, which is shown in the Fig. 1, is completely in hands of Facebook. There is a variety of different kind of templates for the messages which can be used by the chatbots. These templates include swipeable carousels, lists, receipts, images, text, buttons, quick replies plus some other options.

4   Amazon Web Services (AWS)

AWS [5] is a cloud service platform built by Amazon company, offering a wide range of services for developing software. The services are hosted by Amazon in their cloud environment and the main idea is that the developer doesn't have to worry about traits such as availability, scalability or reliability as Amazon promises to handle them automatically depending on the needs of the developer and the application(s). The cloud service platform consists of tens of services and solutions for topics such as AI, messaging, storage, computing, game development, databases and analytics. Next, we shortly introduce some of the services that were used to build the chatbot. The exact tools we used for designing the serverless system are the following.

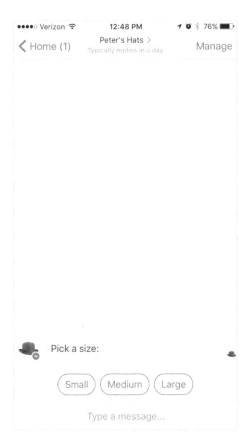

Fig. 1. Facebook Messenger UI with three quick reply buttons [7].

Lambda is the Serverless environment offered by AWS [6]. The code uploaded to Lambda can be triggered with events from Mobile apps, HTTP endpoints and other AWS services such as API Gateway, Simple Notification Service (SNS) or CloudWatch.

Simple Notification Service (SNS) is a web service that can be used to send notifications from the cloud [4]. The notifications can be send as push notifications to different kinds of clients such as mobile devices, as SMS messages, emails or HTTP/HTTPS requests. The SNS follows the publish-subscribe messaging paradigm where messages are being sent to the subscribers every time there is a new message which removes the need of subscribers from constantly polling for new messages. Benefits of SNS include option to configure retry policies if the message delivery fails for some reason, easy to set up from the web-based AWS Management Console and pricing depends directly on the number of messages being delivered through the SNS. First 1 million messages each month are free [4].

CloudWatch is a monitoring system for AWS cloud resources [2]. It provides easy way to read logs, set up alarms, monitor system performance and resource utilization and set up web dashboards to make visualizations of all those together. CloudWatch also supports making scheduled events to invoke other AWS resources such as the SNS or Lambda.

API Gateway can be used as a gateway for incoming requests for other AWS resources, such as Lambda [1]. When the requests come through API Gateway and continues to Lambda, they always take advantage of the Amazons worldwide edge locations to provide the requests the lowest latency as possible. API Gateway lets the developer also to set up caching logic to prevent some requests from hitting the backend systems at all. Other benefits include easy setup of RESTful endpoints for existing services, security controls and throttling of incoming requests during traffic spikes.

DynamoDB is a NoSQL database that supports both document and key-value store models [3]. It promises a bunch of features such as seamless scaling, high availability, secondary indexes, free-text search, strong consistency and cross-region replication. It's easy to set up and Amazon provides web interface to browse the tables in the database.

5   Towards Serverless Chatbot Architecture

The main motivation for serverless computing approach is that the developer doesn't need to manage servers. Instead, the developer can simply just upload the code (e.g. a function) to the serverless environment where the code gets executed when it's triggered by some event. Thus the developer is free from worrying about security updates or any other work related to keeping the environment up and running as all that work is outsourced to the service provider [5,9,10,13].

The serverless environment will do scaling automatically depending on the workload, and at times, when there's zero workload, it won't use any resources at all [10]. That can make serverless computing very cost efficient as the customer only pays when the code is being executed. Furthermore, this can be a good motivation to optimize the code in general. As an example, reducing the duration of the code execution from 1 s down to 200 ms would directly translate to 80% savings without making any infrastructural changes [10,16]. Due to not requiring system administration work, the serverless approach can also lead to cost savings in operational management [13].

Architecture of the Chatbot has been depicted in Fig. 2. The user sends a message using the Messenger application. The message goes to Facebook and triggers a callback to a webhook that contains URL pointing to the API Gateway. The API Gateway passes the event to "facebookWebhook Lambda function" that saves the user id to DynamoDB and formats the message to the internal format

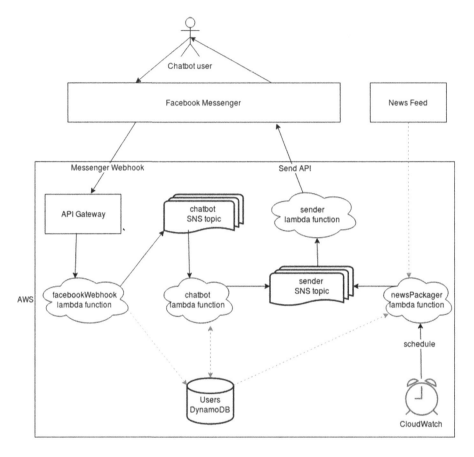

Fig. 2. Architecture of the chatbot.

used in the chatbot and passes it to "chatbot SNS topic" that forwards the event
to "chatbot Lambda function".

The chatbot Lambda function contains all the business logic of the chatbot.
The whole dialogue is located there as a JSON-file and the chatbot works almost
as a state machine following the states found from the dialogue. The user's state
is kept in DynamoDB, and if the user makes selections (e.g. selects which themes
to add to the news package) those are put to DynamoDB as well.

After the "chatbot Lambda function" finishes it passes the result to "sender
SNS topic" that forwards the event to the third Lambda function called "sender".
The senders job is to format the reply to a proper format that is accepted by
Facebook and then send it to the Facebook Send API that handles the delivery
of the message to the end users Messenger Application.

The architecture also contains a component called "newsPackager Lambda
function". The purpose of the function is to read news from a third-party API.
This process gets invoked once every minute by the CloudWatch scheduler. If
there's users who have subscribed to news packages, they get the news delivered

to their Messenger apps, or if there's new breaking news, then those gets delivered to users who have subscribed. Same logic also applies to sending the weekend news package for those who have subscribed.

6 Results and Experiences

Overall the designed architecture worked as expected. It also offers easy way to extend the system by adding other chat platforms without messing up the existing service since each task is separated as their own Lambda function. The service can be extended with other platforms simply by adding a new API Gateway, writing a new webhook and a sender using a new Lambda function for each new platform. The new API Gateway acts as a webhook for the incoming messages from the new platform and forwards them to a proper Lambda function that knows how to translate them to the format accepted by the chatbot Lambda function. Finally, the new sender would translate the replies from chatbot Lambda function to a format accepted by the new platform and send them there back to the users.

Even though the architecture consists of many different components calling each other, the latencies stayed low. One of our fears was that if each component added n milliseconds to the request time, then it could add up and make the chatbot respond too slow to the users. Luckily, that wasn't the case.

The scaling of the architecture was tested with 150 beta testers and a load test. During the beta testing there were no signs of errors about loads going too high or the Lambda invocations taking too long. The beta testing consisted of normal day to day usage and two scheduled notifications which were sent to all users at the same time trying to wake them up to use the chatbot to read news. This resulted to spikes in traffic. Lambda platform did what was promised and scaled up as needed without the developers needing to do any extra effort to achieve it.

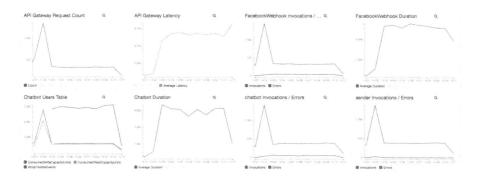

Fig. 3. CloudWatch Dashboard with throttled DynamoDB writes.

Bottlenecks of the architecture were revealed by using load testing. This was performed by using Apache Bench to call the chatbot with different amounts of concurrent connections, totaling thousands of requests during the whole testing session. To monitor what happens within the application a CloudWatch Dashboard with multiple widgets to visualize latencies, durations, throttling and invocations of the components in the architecture was set up.

It quickly became obvious that when moving to higher amounts of load compared to the loads caused by the tests with 150 real users, the DynamoDB became a bottleneck as it started to throttle the write requests, as can be seen in Fig. 3. The throttling happened due to hitting the limits of the provisioned capacity units. That caused a chain reaction to the Lambda functions which started to hit the timeout limits and failed as they were pending the throttled DynamoDB calls. Also the API Gateway latencies increased considerably when the throttling happened.

After increasing the amount of capacity units for the DynamoDB and running load tests, with even higher amount of concurrent connections and requests, there were no signs of errors and the whole application was handling the requests well. This further proved that the DynamoDB and the capacity units were the bottleneck. This scenario is shown in Fig. 4.

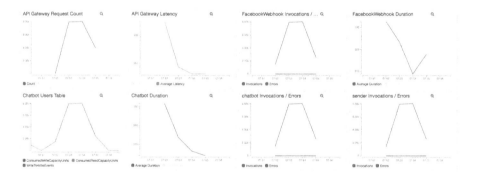

Fig. 4. CloudWatch Dashboard with increased DynamoDB capacity units.

Optimizations were made to the amount of DynamoDB calls after the tests since there was a couple of unnecessary calls being made. Many of them were replaced by adding more data to the payload sent between the Lambda functions. This removed the need of first writing something to DynamoDB and then querying it back in the second function. The tests also raised the team's attention to think how to configure the capacity units. The strategy was to increase the amount of the provisioned units for the production launch of the chatbot and then scale the amount to match the usage after monitoring the consumed capacity units over time with real users and real production usage scenarios manually after some time has passed.

The total costs of using the platform has been low. When the development time spent was about two months, there had been 2 different environments being used on the same AWS account, and the past 2 weeks had been a beta testing period with 150 beta testers, the whole cost for all that was less than one euro. A little surprise was that each invocation of a Lambda function costs 100 ms – even if the invocation runs the code less than 100 ms meaning that 5ms invocation counts as 100 ms, and 101 ms invocation counts as 200 ms invocation. That might leave some room for cost optimization in the future if there's many Lambda invocations that are fast and just invoke other Lambda functions. Luckily the time spent running each Lambda function and the memory it used gets logged automatically every time the function is invoked, which makes it easy to find out if there is room for improvements of Lambda functions.

The developers' experiences about the chosen approach were fairly positive. The chatbot seemed to be a good match for the serverless computing platform as the code can be mostly stateless, and the calls to database were simple, resulting to rather fast queries. The developer team had very positive feelings about the serverless environment in general after the project and will not hesitate to use it again if there's a project where it's a good fit.

There were some problems debugging Lambda functions at first, but after paying attention to logging and learning how to run Lambda function locally using the Serverless Framework [8] debugging and development got a lot easier. The first approach to read logs was to deploy the Lambda function to AWS and then trigger it from the Messenger chat and wait for the logs to appear on the CloudWatch web UI. That turned out to slow down the development as the developer would spend a lot of time deploying and triggering the Lambda functions and then wait for the logs to update. The more efficient way was to invoke the Lambda functions with the Serverless framework on developer's local machine. That way the function can be executed on terminal in an instant and the logs are shown right away so there was no need to wait for the deployment and the CloudWatch to update the logs which lead to way more faster development cycles.

Setting up new environments was easy and fast after setting up AWS account and creating a configuration file for Serverless Framework. The configuration file describes to the Serverless Framework which AWS-components are needed and how they are linked together and then creates the environment with a single command on terminal. After that the new environment is ready to use. That was a very efficient way of setting up own environments for each developer in the team and it also worked for setting up the final production environment.

7   Discussion

Other researches and articles [10,13,16,17] pointed out that serverless microservices can be very inexpensive, require close to zero effort to manage them as there's no need to manage servers and they are highly scalable. The findings from this case study were similar. The case study also had signs of the debugging problems but they were mostly solved by using the existing tools more efficiently. The reason why that has been an issue for the other research [17] could be explained by different platform as the research didn't use AWS. Other explanation could simply be that the tools have improved during the time after the research was released as the serverless platforms are all improving very rapidly. Though it's clear that the debugging and logging options are mostly limited to what the service providers are offering.

The beta test with 150 users gave insight on how the chatbot is used by real users. This information could be used to roughly estimate the loads and resource usage of the chatbot with different amounts of users. That combined with the results of the load tests showing the bottlenecks of the current setup was enough to point out where the focus should be when it comes down to scalability of the chatbot. While the current architecture is scalable, the limiting factor seems to be the DynamoDB and the provisioned capacity units.

As the results showed, there's no need to manage servers or make extra effort for the scaling, it could be that in the future that kind of tasks will be more and more a problem just for the platform providers than they are for the developers and architects, and that there could be less demand for that kind of expertise. These cloud platforms look more and more like a pile of different kind of puzzle pieces that require expertise to put together efficiently to form services for businesses. This lets the project teams to focus more on the business problems and the implementation of the code since there is less to worry about the hosting of the services. The flip-side of the coin is that the developers need to be aware of the pricing of the different services since this has effects on the architecture or business logic of the software.

8   Conclusions and Future Work

This case study presented an architecture for Messenger chatbot built on top of Amazon Web Services. The experiences gained from designing and building the chatbot were compared to other researches about same kind of topics. The designed chatbot architecture turned out to be extensible and scalable, requiring close to zero management and even to be cost efficient.

The future work for the chatbot application includes addition of Natural Language Processing and AI to add better support for free text input from the users. For those features, a bunch of web services will be benchmarked to find out if they can handle the needs of the chatbot. One of the biggest fear with NLP is the support for finnish language which might be quite lacking compared to more common languages like English, for instance.

Future work could also include cost optimization as the pricing model charges the Lambda invocations per 100ms of code execution time. It might sometimes make sense to run two fast scripts within one invocation instead of two invocations. Though, that should not become a problem unless the number of users increases dramatically.

Finally, trying out alternative databases and comparing them to DynamoDB from the point of view of automatic scaling should also be interesting. It might also be possible to automatically provision more capacity units for the DynamoDB by triggering events from CloudWatch as the amount of consumed capacity units changes and then programmatically increase or decrease the amount. Though there could be some latencies preventing this kind of solution from being able to address sudden spikes in the traffic.

Acknowledgements. The research was supported by the Academy of Finland (project 295913).

References

1. Amazon API Gateway. https://aws.amazon.com/api-gateway/. Accessed 9 April 2017
2. Amazon Cloudwatch. https://aws.amazon.com/cloudwatch/. Accessed 9 April 2017
3. Amazon DynamoDB. https://aws.amazon.com/dynamodb/. Accessed 9 April 2017
4. Amazon Simple Notification Service (SNS). https://aws.amazon.com/sns/. Accessed 10 April 2017
5. Amazon Web Services. https://aws.amazon.com/. Accessed 5 April 2017
6. AWS lambda. https://aws.amazon.com/lambda/. Accessed 10 April 2017
7. Facebook Messenger Platform. https://messengerplatform.fb.com/. Accessed 5 April 2017
8. The Serverless Application Framework. https://serverless.com/. Accessed 5 April 2017
9. Eivy, A.: Be wary of the economics of "serverless" cloud computing. IEEE Cloud Comput. **4**(2), 6–12 (2017)
10. Hendrickson, S., Sturdevant, S., Harter, T., Venkataramani, V., Arpaci-Dusseau, A.C., Arpaci-Dusseau, R.H.: Serverless computation with openLambda. In: Proceedings of the 8th USENIX Conference on Hot Topics in Cloud Computing, HotCloud 2016, pp. 33–39, Berkeley. USENIX Association (2016)
11. Pautasso, C., Zimmermann, O., Amundsen, M., Lewis, J., Josuttis, N.: Microservices in practice, part 1: reality check and service design. IEEE Softw. **34**(1), 91–98 (2017)
12. Pautasso, C., Zimmermann, O., Amundsen, M., Lewis, J., Josuttis, N.: Microservices in practice, part 2: service integration and sustainability. IEEE Softw. **34**(2), 97–104 (2017)
13. Roberts, M.: Serverless Architectures. https://martinfowler.com/articles/serverless.html. Accessed 9 April 2017
14. Taivalsaari, A., Mikkonen, T., Systä, K.: Liquid software manifesto: The era of multiple device ownership and its implications for software architecture. In: 2014 IEEE 38th Annual Computer Software and Applications Conference, pp. 338–343, July 2014
15. Thönes, J.: Microservices. IEEE Softw. **32**(1), 116–116 (2015)
16. Villamizar, M., Garces, O., Ochoa, L., Castro, H.E., Salamanca, L., Verano, M., Casallas, R., Gil, S., Valencia, C., Zambrano, A., Lang, M.: Infrastructure cost comparison of running web applications in the cloud using AWS Lambda and monolithic and microservice architectures. In: 2016 16th IEEE/ACM International Symposium on Cluster, Cloud and Grid Computing (CCGrid) (2016)

17. Yan, M., Castro, P., Cheng, P., Ishakian, V.: Building a chatbot with server-less computing. In: Proceedings of the 1st International Workshop on Mashups of Things and APIs, p. 5. ACM (2016)
18. Yao, M.: Does conversation hurt or help the Chatbot Ux? Smashing Magazine, Nov 2016

Four Key Factors to Design a Web of Things Architecture

Francesco Bruni[1], Claudio Pomo[2(✉)], and Gaetano Murgolo[3]

[1] Planetek Italia SRL, Bari, Italy
bruni@planetek.it
[2] Polytechnic University of Bari, Bari, Italy
c.pomo@studenti.poliba.it
[3] Engineering Consulting SRL, Bitonto, Italy
info@ecmg.it

Abstract. The spreading of Internet accesses and latest developments of Web technologies simplified the process of building architectures capable of collecting and sharing data. On the other side, a massive use of smart devices helped increasing the overall quality of the monitored process. This report illustrates how sensed raw data collected over an electrical plant by a smart device have been turned into a market valuable knowledge. Implementing and extending the Back-end Data Sharing Pattern, the proposed architecture underlines some key factors to be appointed when designing this kind of infrastructures and how they have been implemented in a real world use case.

Keywords: Internet of Things · Software architecture IoT
Web of Things · Back-end data sharing pattern

1 Scenario

The current *web of data era* made extremely easy collecting raw and semi-structured data and developing data processing pipelines capable of extracting metrics and insights. Indeed turning a raw information into a market valuable knowledge is the actual challenge and represents the goal of this work.

In order to monitor consumptions and prevent unforeseen events, the current work details an infrastructure capable of sensing and reporting collected data in a photo-voltaic plant. Exploiting a *smart device*, an extensive set of electrical parameters is collected and made available to other services designed to clean, normalize, aggregate and finally expose them over the Web.

Data collection contains a lot of measures about voltage, current, power consumption e so one. It's quite evident that the massive data collecting trend is highly correlated with the spread of *smart objects*. Being capable of sensing the world and communicating gathered results outside, they make raw sensed data available to other more sophisticated actors.

© Springer International Publishing AG, part of Springer Nature 2018
I. Garrigós and M. Wimmer (Eds.): ICWE 2017, LNCS 10544, pp. 87–91, 2018.
https://doi.org/10.1007/978-3-319-74433-9_7

On the other side, the proliferation of Web technologies made developing web applications easier than ever. Thanks to the increasing number of frameworks and programming languages, the effort spent deploying an up and running web application decreased over the last years up to minutes.

This report details a **Back-End Data Sharing** [1] based architecture suitable for exposing smart devices (processed) sensed data to end users. This work focuses only on the overall infrastructure and does not cover internal processing algorithms details.

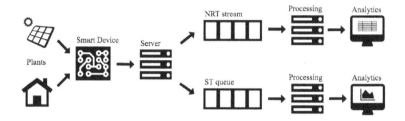

Fig. 1. Scenario overview

The proposed WoT [4] architecture overview is depicted in Fig. 1. The smart device splits up the gathered data into multiple JSON[1] encoded chunks. Uniquely identified by a *timestamp*, each chunk is then sent over an HTTP[2] request to the *Server* counterpart:

```
{
    "timestamp": 1491250500,
    "data":{
    "FVARL": {
        "FVARL-MIN": 92897,
        "FVARL-MAX": 120115,
        "FVARL-MEAN": 106675
        }
    ...
}
```

Listing 1.1. JSON encoded raw data

After a basic validation, the Server publishes received data over multiple queues and hands over control to the *Processing* module to run a well defined data processing pipeline. The *Analytics* module exposes the extracted knowledge (electrical parameters expressed as a time series) to end users. Furthermore, it allows administrator users the ability to assert the truthfulness and correctness of measurements.

---

[1] http://www.json.org.
[2] https://tools.ietf.org/html/rfc2616.

2   Architecture

In order to enforce the software reuse and modularity, each server side deployed component has been wrapped in a container. This approach turns a monolithic structure into a set of independent pieces capable of communicating each other and simplifies the scaling process.

Given the scenario and the overall complexity of the problem, the proposed architecture addresses four different aspects detailed in the next sections.

2.1   A Scalable and Fault Tolerant System

To afford long time running computations, multiple queue-based data structures have been deployed. Processing incoming data or start producing user customized reports should not impact the overall system capabilities with blocking calls and spinning loops. Nowadays, being asynchronous can be very effective if an immediate feedback could be delayed and handled later. As turning raw data into kwnoledge requires time, this process has been designed to be asynchronous. Specifically, data is sent to the Server component which, after a domain specific validation, replies with a well-defined response. Incoming server side data are then pushed over two different queues, as detailed below: an *Apache Kafka*[3] based *Near real time* (NRT) stream for admin oriented analytics and a *Redis*[4] based *Standard* queue (ST) for end users.

The involved queues have been spawned over multiple nodes and orchestrated by a designated component to be scalable and robust to unforeseen accidents since no single point of failure is present.

The underlined queue-based architecture recalls and partially implements the *Actor model* (AM) [3]: incoming messages are routed to specific actors (the request consumers) whose task is fixed and well designed. They can spawn other actors, edit received messages before retransmitting them, and make local decisions. As highlighted in the mathematical theory, AM decouples senders and communications and make concurrency easier to be implemented. No specific order of messages is required and no fixed size pool of actors needs to be allocated.

2.2   Per-User Customized Knowledge

Build on top of the *Angular.js* framework, two different web clients have been included in this architecture. Basically, they consume *RESTful* services exposed by the Server component.

To guarantee secure communications, client requests need to be authenticated. The JWT [2] protocol enforces this control and solves typical cross domain problems due to cookies. Besides, JWT encodes user information in the HTTP

---

[3] https://kafka.apache.org/.
[4] https://redis.io/.

request *Authorization* header. This approach allows server side application to infer user identity and acting consequently.

As implied by Fig. 1, incoming data have been initially processed by the server component and then sent over two different queues. Indeed different kind of users should have access to a different knowledge. This means that admin oriented analytics have been extracted in *real time* fashion and not shared with end users which have been granted access to a different set of informations. Thus superuser and user refer to different players and should be threated as different consumers.

2.3   React and Adapt

Sensing the physical world and pushing gathered perceptions to a server would be useless if the involved device was not able to adapt its behaviour to an external change.

Changing sensing rate or the Server component IP address should be reflected on the device. The provided architecture allows end user to reconfigure an operative smart device using a web client as well as monitoring this operation.

This feature masks the overall complexity and gives end user the power and the illusion to drive the entire system. Actually, the request is enqueued, validated by the Server component and, if still valid, notified to the smart device.

In this ecosystem we assume to use a smart device to sense the physical world and push this perception of reality to a server. We can use adjective smart to focus some feature about this device: capability to send significant and correct measure, able to act and react to an external change in the faster way as possible. Our device is able to adapt same parameter, based on user interaction with mobile or web application, in order to set up a specific configuration for a single user.

This feature masked complexity of underlying architecture and in the other hand give to users power, and illusion, to drive entire system. However user inputs passes through the server before reaching out the device, because data are pushed to the server based on publish/subscribe paradigm.

2.4   Handling Connectivity Issues and Notifiyng Anomalies

Detecting anomalies on sensed data can be challenging, since different types of anomalies require multiple acting approaches. Specifically, the architecture focuses on *connection issues*.

Missing data due to connectivity issues can be restored later if *fallback storage solutions* are implemented on the device side. Due to constrained storage capabilities, this approach could not easily implemented on typically *IoT* devices, but it is worth to consider it whenever such limit can be overcome. Storing data when Internet connection is not available implies focusing on two different aspects.

First of all, a correct evict data policy should be designed to avoid saturating the available capacity. Second, a retransmission logic needs to be implemented to assure stored data is sent when connectivity returns available.

From a user perspective, a delay will be experienced but no data will be lost in this scenario.

3   Conclusion and Future Work

In this work we presented a model for exposing electrical based measurements data over the Web to monitor consumptions, breakdown and preventing unforeseen events. We then discussed four aspects that characterized it. Actually, they all deal with the importance of *data* and it could make sense to explore three aspects. First of all, a set of *machine learning based algorithms* to detect anomalies; second, *harvesting multiple data sources* to publish an even more complete knowledge to end user; third, a *websocket based connection* between Server and Device as a more reactive way of keeping components chained each other.

By the designed infrastructure perspective, it could be useful to reorganize services into smaller components to match the *microservices architecture* [5] and thus deploying each service in a container.

References

1. Architectural Considerations in Smart Object Networking (2015). https://tools.ietf. org/html/rfc7452
2. JSON Web Token (JWT) (2015). https://tools.ietf.org/html/rfc7519
3. Agha, G.A.: Actors: A Model of Concurrent Computation in Distributed Systems (1985)
4. Guinard, D., Trifa, V., Wilde, E.: A resource oriented architecture for the Web of Things (2010)
5. Lewis, J., Fowler, M.: Microservices (2014). https://martinfowler.com/articles/ microservices.html

Liquid Transfer of User Identity

Sivamani Thangavel$^{(\boxtimes)}$ and Kari Systä

Tampere University of Technology, Tampere, Finland
{sivamani.thangavel,kari.systa}@tut.fi

Abstract. Most consumers own more than one device for accessing content from the Web. In this world Liquid Software allows users to switch the device and effortlessly continue tasks in the new device. This paper addresses on the needs and methods for transferring a user session and user information from one device to another. The identity should follow the moving application seamlessly instead of requiring repeated entering of credentials in each device. Such solution would make services that require authentication to work in a liquid fashion. The paper describes our on-going work on investigating how liquid transfer of user identity can be added to various ways of handing the user authentication.

Keywords: User identification · Liquid software · User sessions
Web session migration

1 Introduction

In most parts of the world an average consumer has at least two computing devices, a laptop and a smart phone. Owning a tablet and/or an e-reader which is becoming increasingly common, further increases the count of personal computing devices. The services and content accessed with these devices are the same, and the user should have a unified user experience through all of her devices. In a realization of this vision the applications and their state should move between the devices with minimum explicit actions by the user. The mechanism should also be as simple as possible for the application developers. In a completely liquid environment all applications installed by the user should move seamlessly between devices. This Liquid experience [13] could be achieved at the operating system level, in which the complete device state is transferred from one device to another, or at application level where the individual applications can move between devices.

Some of the software ecosystems, for example iOS and Mac by Apple and Android by Google offer some of that liquid experience, but those solutions are limited to the vendor-specific ecosystems. An alternative approach is to build a vendor-neutral ecosystem around Web technologies. In this paper we concentrate on Liquid Experience of Web applications. This means that all client devices are assumed to have a browser that hosts the applications.

© Springer International Publishing AG, part of Springer Nature 2018
I. Garrigós and M. Wimmer (Eds.): ICWE 2017, LNCS 10544, pp. 92–107, 2018.
https://doi.org/10.1007/978-3-319-74433-9_8

Our earlier research, for example [16,18], has mainly concentrated in client-side applications and largely ignored the fact that many web applications are tied to a server component. In this research we focus on a more server-centric application - a media service. In such services the user identity and authentication are important elements for both the service provider and consumer. From the user's point of view this could mean that the user can start reading the news (or watching the media) in a smart phone and continue the activity in a laptop. Internet services often include authentication of users, since then the service can be personalized to individual users. For example, if a media service has collected information about the user's interests it can provide personalized content. If multiple devices are used to consume the service the user typically needs to authenticate each device separately. The liquid user identity proposed in this paper frees the user from manual login in each device.

Another example, but not discussed in this paper is a web shop that allows liquid change from device to another keeping the content of carts and wish-lists along with user identity to make the shopping experience more pleasant.

In this paper we describe our on-going work on transferring the user identity from a device to another as a part of the Liquid Experience. We explore the technological alternatives, their benefits and challenges in implementing liquidity of the user identity.

1.1   Liquid Software

The term Liquid Software was first mentioned in [15]. The Liquid Manifesto [13] provides a more recent definition of Liquid Software: "an approach in which applications and data can flow from one device or screen to another seamlessly, allowing the users to roam freely from one device to another, no longer worrying about device management, not having their favorite applications or data, or having to remember complex steps."

From the users' point of view Liquid Software can be divided in three use cases: [6]:

1. Sequential screening - the user switches from one device to another to continue the activity
2. Simultaneous screening - the user uses multiple devices to perform a single activity (screen sharing of video, a slide show etc.)
3. Collaboration - Multiple users work together on an activity

Examples of existing and widely used liquid software include Google Docs and Apple Handoff. Google Docs provides liquid functionality by using a cloud service to synchronize the state of the content in the browsers. Synchronization is done between multiple users if they are accessing the same document and between devices if the content is being accessed by same user account. Apple Handoff supports the liquid functionality and provides application developers with APIs to make the applications liquid. This functionality is limited to Apple devices and applications and it also requires that the same iCloud user account is used in all the devices.

The earlier research, for example [16], discusses several elements of liquidity:

- Topology – is the system centered around some central point or completely de-centralized? In this research we assume rather centralized structure around the media service.
- Layering – how thin or thick is the client application? Client-code is responsible for rendering the content and user actions are typically send to server. Thus, our case can be considered rather thin.
- Client Deployment – are applications pre-installed or downloaded on demand? In this research we assume on-demand loading, although in the case of current commercial services the active users often prefer pre-installed applications for mobile use.
- Granularity – is the transfered item a component of an application, a complete application or some container including both application and some platform components? In this research we assume that the client application moves as a whole.
- State Identification – is the transferred application state recognized automatically or explicitly marked by the application developer? In this case, the state is primarily in the session and current applications store the state in the server. However, for some interactions client state could be transferred and any mechanism of earlier research could be used.
- Device Usage – whether the devices are used in parallel or sequentially. The default usage in our case is sequential, but simultaneous usage could be supported, too.
- UI Adaptation – how the application adapts to I/O characteristics of the devices? The research presented in this paper is agnostic regarding this.
- Primitives – is liquidity based on copying or moving? The research presented in this paper is agnostic regarding this.
- Discovery – how the applications and devices find each other? The research presented in this paper is agnostic regarding this.

These elements are further discussed in [17], but there is no prior research in handling of the user identity in the context of Liquid Software.

1.2 The Need for User Identity

The need for identifying a person/user/consumer could be based on economical, legal or logical reasons. For example, the service providers need the user identity to separate paying customers from non-paying, for targeted advertisement, and to handle situations where the user behaves against the agreements or law. In many cases user identification is an essential part of the business, but not much addressed in the research on Liquid Software.

User accounts also let the service to provide personalized services that are based on the preferences and interests of the user. This could be based on explicit configuration done by the user or by tracking which stories user has been interested in the past.

1.3 The Liquid Transfer

Most users save website credentials in the devices, so there is no need to login manually every time they access the website. This allows them to switch devices with no additional work, other than opening the website. This also provides latest content on all devices. Any item added to a cart in one device is also shown in the next device, when the website is opened.

OAuth protocol implementations store tokens/identifiers corresponding to the user in the devices he/she logged in. When a user has logged in to a website using an OAuth service once, the authentication can be kept valid for a long time using refresh tokens[1] [21]. This also allows the users to login once into the website in their devices and then freely switch between devices without having to reenter their credentials.

While the above mentioned techniques reduce the need to enter the credentials in private personal devices, they do not work well when a user wants to use a public device and they do not transfer the information about the current state. The following are the use cases which benefit from this research:

– When user changes password, it is easier to move the new identity by transferring the identity, rather than entering the credentials manually to all their personal devices.
– User shares his account to a public or borrowed device temporarily. Implementation should allow users to see and invalidate the active sessions under their account. He/She can later remove the device's session from the list of valid sessions, in case they didn't manually log out of their session in the device.
– The approach in this research allows the user to continue with an activity more smoothly, as it transfers information about the page and content, the user accessed before transfer.

In this research, we need to implement the transfer of the application and its local state to another device similarly to earlier research like in [18]. In the earlier research the focus has been transfer of the code and state, and the discovery in the centralized topology can be based, for example, on a QR-code. In this approach the server prepares a QR-code including a URL and a code similar to a session identifier. This identifier is rendered on the screen of the source device and the destination device scans the code with built-in camera and directs the browser to the URL encoded in the QR code. The included code allows the receiving client to get the session and local state of the origin. Other techniques like short-range radio connectivity could also be used instead of QR-code to implement liquid transfer, too.

If the user identity and authentication should be included in transfer the information should be in the QR-code or temporarily stored in the server for the

---

[1] https://developers.google.com/identity/protocols/OAuth2WebServer,
https://developers.facebook.com/docs/facebook-login/access-tokens/and-expiration-extension.

transfer. The different approaches to implement liquid transfer of session with user identity in the context of different authentication mechanisms is the focus of this paper.

1.4 Structure of the Paper

The rest of the paper is organized as follows. Section 2 describes the background of the work, the nature of the target services and the techniques for authentication and requirements for the liquid transfer. Section 3 describes the technical options and Sect. 4 gives information about our evaluating case that implements some of the technical options. Some related work is described in Sect. 5 and final conclusion are given in Sect. 6.

2 Background

2.1 Modern Media Service

Most of the media services are available in digitized form and the content can be consumed with multiple devices. At the same time the services are moving towards providing personalized content. When a media company delivers the content through the web, it is possible to personalize the content if the users are authenticated.

When the number of devices a subscriber uses increases, it becomes tedious for the subscriber to login, every time he/she is switching to a different device and navigate to the content, that was being read/watched/listened to, in the previous device.

The view point of this research is of a service provider, especially of a media company that provide news and other content to users. The focus is on registered users who also may be required to pay a subscription fee. However, a limited set of content is available without registration. The service is assumed to contain a discussion and commenting forum for registered users, too.

2.2 Techniques for Authentication

In the physical world the identification is done through ID cards (usually the ones with a photograph and personal details of the user), tickets, PINs (Personal Identification Numbers) that are widely used with bank cards, certificates, access cards, keys etc. In the virtual world of Internet the authentication is usually done through a combination of a unique id (user name or email address) and a secret key (password) that the user types in to the service [14]. The user id is often created by a user in a self-service fashion. Other possibilities include biometric data which is being supported by increasing number of consumer devices. The research presented in this paper does not analyze the different approaches, and the experimentations are based on simple user name and password.

The user id is used to identify the user and the password is used to validate the claim that id belongs to the user. This process is termed as Authentication.

Different user accounts may have different privileges in a system. A user of a media service could be allowed to post comments and not allowed to change any news content. A journalist working for the content can be allowed to post new content and also comments. The process of allowing or preventing a user from performing a certain action is referred to as Authorization. Every request that performs a restricted action will need to check if the request comes from authorized users.

Technically speaking the traffic between clients is implemented with HTTP(S) which is a stateless protocol. Thus, each request should have some form of authentication. This allows the server to make sure that it is only serving authorized users. Because it is impractical to send credentials in each request, the web standards and implementations include mechanisms to include authentication information to requests without exposing the original credentials. In this paper the focus is on how to integrate liquid behavior with the techniques to implement authentication of the requests.

2.3   Requirements for the Liquid Transfer of Authentication

The solution should be both secure and convenient to use. The security measures should protect the service provider against unauthorized access. For example, if the service or parts of it are for paying customers only, the solution for liquid experience should not make unauthorized use easier than in non-liquid case. From the users' point of view identity theft should be prevented as well as possible.

The solution used for liquidity do not aim at making the service more secure than it is without the liquid transfer, so this research does not address the total security. Instead we consider security risks that the liquidity can add and the possible mitigations. The high-level requirement include:

- Unintentional initiation of the transfer should not be possible. The interaction mechanism used to initiate the transfer should be controlled by an authenticated user.
- Stealing of the transferred information for unauthorized use should be prevented. This means that the information needs to stored securely and the traffic should use secure channels only.
- The liquidity mechanism should not enable unauthorized access to the service. Thus, the service should have mechanisms to control the transfer.

To support these high-level requirements we have already recognized a set of technical requirements. The current list includes:

- For sensitive operations such as changing the password or making new purchases, the service should mandate the user to re-enter the current password, especially when it is a transferred session.
- When a user changes password for the account, transferred sessions should be invalidated.

– Service should notify the user about transfers to devices never used before. In case of a suspected misuse it should be possible for the user to invalidate all existing sessions (all active sessions created with direct authentication and through session transfers).
– Server should have means to conclude the physical distance between the IP addresses between the source and destination devices. If the destination IP is in a network in the other side of the world, then the service should alert the user about possible misuse. Implementing accurate distance measurement is complex in practice. There are libraries[2] and services[3] which can be used to get the geographic location of an IP. The accuracy of the result is usually the nearest city. The solutions to improve the accuracy usually involve using landmarks (servers/devices with known locations) and measuring Round Trip Times [20]. HTML 5 geolocation API is a better option to use with Web applications. When GPS is available, it can be used to get higher accuracy. If user has connected one of the devices to VPN (Virtual Private Network), IP geolocation gives misleading information [19].

3   Considered Options

In this section we present some alternative mechanisms to transfer user identity when the application and usage session migrates from a device to another. The default scenario is *sequential use* but we assume these techniques can used in case of *simultaneous use*, too. *Collaborative use* is not in the scope of this research. In the following discussion we use term *session* for information that is related to client-server session – the local state can be transfered with any mechanisms described in [16].

3.1   Transferring Session Data

In the research we explored four different ways to transfer the user identity. The approaches are classified under two categories, based on how the information about authorized user and the specific session is handled. The service provider manages the user identity and authentication (login). This Subsect. 3.1 discusses the transfer of session identifier and session data used to keep the authentication persistent. Transfer of other application state data is discussed at the end of the Subsect. 3.2.

Server Side Session: This represents the approach in which only the session identifier is provided to the client side and the association between a session and its user identity is stored in the server side. Any session related data is stored on the server side. When the server receives a request with a session identifier, it looks up in the database to verify if the session ID is valid. If there are user

---

[2] http://www.ip2location.com/.
[3] `freegeoip.net`.

groups (readers, journalists, editors etc. in a media website), the server checks the session ID's corresponding user account to determine if the user is authorized to perform the action, corresponding to the request. This database lookup can create a bottleneck in the system, when the amount of requests received is high. It is also hard to scale as adding more servers means that the database has to be shared with all the servers.

1. The built-in mechanisms, *cookies*, of the browser is used to the manage the session. This mechanism does not require special measures from the client code of application. When a user logs in, the authentication is kept persistent by using a *session identifier cookie*. To improve security, the cookie can have 'httpOnly' attribute set to true to prevent client side JavaScript from reading it. If the 'secure' attribute has been set to true, it is attached to requests only when the connection is secure.

2. As a contrast to the fist option the client code is responsible for persisting session identifier. When a user logs in, the server provides an access token in plain text that needs to be attached to each subsequent requests to server. In this case the client stores the access token in a global variable or in a local storage or in a cookie. This token is attached to the header of all requests needing authorization. This method is vulnerable to session hijacking, as a hacker can read the client side script to find the storage mechanism and copy the access token.

When the session – including the identity – is transfered to a new device, the server creates a new session identifier for the new device and asso-ciates all data from old session to the new session. The transfer of the session is initiated at the source device and as a result the server pro-vides a short lived transfer token. In our experiments the current page's URL and the transfer token, is communicated to the destination with a QR-code: the source device gets and displays the QR-code. The destination device then reads the QR-code and makes a request to the URL. The server then provides the destination device with a new session identifier. A more detailed description of the evaluation experiment is given in Sect. 4.

Client Side Session: This represents approaches where the session identifier and the association between the session identifier and user is stored in the client side. The server encrypts or signs this information to prevent the client side from modifying the data. Any session related data is also stored in client side, as server has no persistence of the session. When a user logs in, server creates the session information and encrypts or signs it before sending it to the client. The contents of the session information depends on the implementation. In general, it has to include at least the user name and also user group information to check the privileges of a user. When an authorized client sends a request, it sends the session information along with the request. The server can decrypt or verify the signature to ensure that the client side has not tampered the information. It can verify if a user is authorized to perform an action by checking the contents of session information. This provides a flexible way to scale, as there is no database lookup needed to validate a session. This approach is particularly suitable for cases with multiple web servers to provide high availability, there is no need to synchronize session data between the web servers. The implementation of client side session can have several flavors, for example:

1. The session identifier and data are stored in a *secure cookie*. There are libraries like 'client-sessions' which implement client side session storage with tamper-free cookies [3]. A secure client side cookie protocol is discussed here [10].
2. The client sessions may be based on signed tokens. JWT(JSON Web Token) is a standard way of providing a signed and secure authorization claim token [9]. Server provides the token once authentication succeeds and client attaches the token to the Authorization header for subsequent requests. The content of a JWT is a base64 encoded string comprising of 3 parts separated by the dot character.
   (a) The header, which has the encryption algorithm and the type, which is always 'JWT'.
   (b) The payload, which has the data a website wants to associate with the authorization claim. The standard defines a few reserved claims like iss(issuer), exp(expiration time), sub(subject), aud(audience). It also allows the users to define custom claims.
   (c) The final part is the signature, which is created by combining the header and payload and signing it with a secret key. This helps the server to verify that this token was created by it.

Similarly to server-side session, when a transfer is initiated, the client side creates a QR code of the current page's URL and the session information. When the user scans QR code and opens the link in the browser in the destination device, the session continues in the destination device. Server does not need to differentiate the sessions with the source and destination device. It simply accepts any request with valid session information as authorized. The QR code in this case has longer data compared to server side session approaches. The length is usually within the QR code's maximum capacity of 3391 alphanumeric characters with the recommended *medium* error correction mode.(QR code can store a maximum of 4296 alphanumeric characters, when the error correction mode is set to low[4]). But longer data takes noticeably longer to scan using the mobile devices.

The following are the disadvantages of using client side sessions. The session information is considerably longer to transmit over the network for each access. The server cannot destroy a session once it is created. Although setting expiry time for the session information helps, it does not work for situations where active sessions of a user have to be destroyed (for example, when a user changes password). Whether the session data can be read by a hacker, depends on the strength of the key used for encryption. If a constant key is used for encryption, a hacker could try to get as many sessions as possible and do a cryptanalysis to figure out the secret key. It is also possible to do session replay attacks, if a hacker gets hold of a user's session information.

---

[4] http://www.qrcode.com/en/about/version.html.

3.2   Handling the Application State

There can be less sensitive data related to the session(for example, contents of the shopping cart), which is stored by client side script in a cookie or local storage. If this data is included to the QR code, the data is too long and there is noticeable delay in scanning. To reduce the delay, it is convenient to use an approach under server side sessions Sect. 3.1. When user requests transfer code, server stores all the cookies in that request to some database (except for the session cookie). If the application uses local storage, client can pass it as a parameter to the call to get transfer code. Server can store this data to database temporarily. When it gets the call from destination device with transfer code, it attaches all the stored cookies in the response and adds the persisted data of the transfer code request, to the response.

3.3   Use of Third Party Authentication

An external service can also be used for authentication, for example, many services allow users to authenticate themselves with the Facebook ID. From the user's point of view this is convenient since many users already have a Facebook id. Facebook also provides documentation and a JavaScript-library for the login procedure [2]. In this approach Facebook provides *access token* that needs to be used for subsequent requests to Facebook APIs to access the user account/profile. To provide liquid functionality, service provider manages the session with its own identifier and persists the *Facebook access token* in server side database. When a session is transferred, server associates the facebook ID with the new session in another device.

4   Evaluation with a Proof of Concept

This paper describes on-going research and we are currently implementing the various scenarios described in Sect. 3. Our plan is to create a lightweight implementation of all scenarios and then evaluate them against the requirements given in Subsect. 2.3.

The proof of concept is a simple service that provides weather news. Headlines and a short content are available publicly in the home page (See Fig. 1) but detailed content and the option to comment are available only to authorized users (See Fig. 2).

The proof of concept provides alternative authentication mechanisms by using service-specific credentials (created by signing up to the website) or with Facebook accounts. The prototype does not interact with user's Facebook profile and uses them purely to authenticate the user. When user transfers the session to a new device, it does not transfer the Facebook cookies tokens and hence does not enable automatic Facebook authentication in other websites - unless the user has saved authentication already. Once the user is authenticated (with local account or by Facebook authentication), the server creates a session identifier and stores it along with the user information to the database. The server

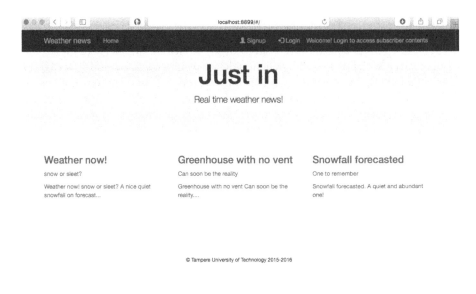

Fig. 1. Home page

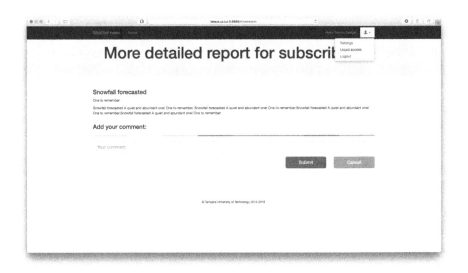

Fig. 2. Liquid access option

provides the session token to the client in the response to the authentication request. Client side persists this token and sends it with all subsequent requests. When a user opens a news item, the title is stored to a cookie by client side script.

JWT and secure client side sessions were considered for maintaining the sessions. They provide the advantage that all the session data is maintained in

Fig. 3. QR code to scan

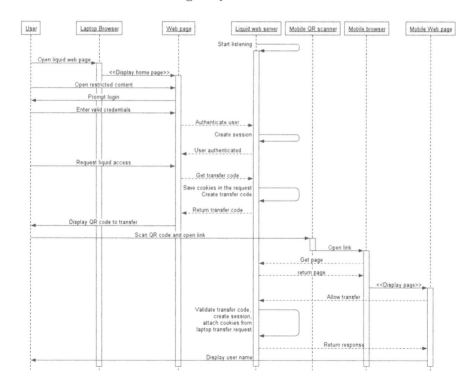

Fig. 4. Liquid transfer sequence

client-side and there is no need for a database lookup, to validate the session for every call to the server. But, this flexibility is outweighed by the issue that they cannot be invalidated by the server when needed (Examples scenarios where this is necessary are to log a user out of all sessions in case the user changes the password, if the server has to be patched up with a security fix and all sessions need to be recreated etc.). The advantage of not having to lookup the session in the database is also offset by the need to use cryptographic functions to validate the sessions/token and the cost of transferring a much longer data compared to a session identifier for every interaction between the client and the server.

When a user wants to switch to a new device, he/she uses the 'liquid access' command in the UI of the source device (see Fig. 2). The sequence of actions and interactions, from when a user logs in and switches the session to a different device is shown in Fig. 4. Liquid access request is sent to the server that provides a short lived code. The server stores all the cookies related to the session temporarily to a database. The code is added to the URL of the current page as a parameter and the resulting URL is shown as QR code in the UI. The user can scan this code with his/her mobile device. An example code along with the URL embedded in it is shown in Fig. 3 (The URL in plain text will be removed from the UI when the prototype is finalized). By scanning and opening the URL in the browser, the user account gets authorized and a new session is created. The server sends all the cookies from the source device session to the destination device along with the new session ID. The transfer is in practice, a copy/clone of the session and does not invalidate the authorization in the source device. By transferring the cookie that has the last accessed news item, the prototype is able to transfer both the user identity and the application state.

5   Related Work

There are browser technologies implementations by browsers to transfer a browsing session from one device to another. These approaches are based on user identity provided by the browser or platform vendor. These solutions store and retrieve the user's session in a server. Google Sync and Mozilla Weave were precursors of this concept. Currently, Mozilla FireFox Sync and Google Chrome Sync support users to move bookmarks, history, saved passwords and other settings between devices [5,12]. There is also prototype implementation as a browser extension, with a server component acting as the storage for the sessions [7]. The purpose of these systems are different since they aim liquidity on platform level instead of applications. (See discussion about granularity in Subsect. 1.1 [16]).

The first one needs the user to create an account for each of the browsers he/she uses and it does not provide option to synchronization of a session from one browser to another. The second one needs the user to install an application for each of the browsers that he/she wants to synchronize and also to create an account. It is challenging to support transfers between different kind of browsers, as some of them store cookies in files and some in database. The format is also not standardized. Some store the session information as plain text and some as binary. They also use different encryption mechanisms to save passwords for different sites (if the user chooses the option to save password, when the browser prompts them to do so).

These solutions are good if the user wants to transfer entire browsing history and context but they are not designed for transfer of user identity and state of individual applications. If a service provider wants the application to be easily transferable from one device to another, it is not reasonable to expect the users of the service to go through the trouble of creating a user account or install browser extensions. These browser synchronizing concepts also raise concerns of privacy as their browsing habits can now be tracked easily. A more sensible approach is for the service to provide a transferable authorization mechanism which allows users to authenticate themselves in one device and move the authorized session to a different device.

There is also existing research on using a proxy between server and client to support switching the device. The proxy collects and stores information about the sessions. When a user switches the device used for browsing, the information about source device's open sessions are retrieved from the proxy and handed over to the destination device [4,11]. There are also solutions that take a snapshot of the browser's state and stores it to a repository. A destination device loads the source device's snapshot from the repository to get the session transferred. This involves changes to the browsers which is complex [8]. Solutions involving proxy and repository introduces privacy and security issues, as access to them will give an attacker access to the details of user's browsing habits and may be even to sensitive information that is exchanged with web servers.

The solution proposed by Alapetite [1] focuses on use case where the user does not have a personal account with the website. This is useful for cases, where user makes a one time transaction and would not like to register for a user account. The approach transfers session by copying the session identifier to the new device. The website provider is responsible for implementing the liquid functionality and it saves all form data in the server side. This requires that any changes made by the user in the UI should be immediately communicated to the server. It uses QR code of a URL and session identifier, that the user meed to scan when she or he wants to switch to a mobile device. Once the user scans the QR code using a mobile device, the user is redirected to the page he/she was accessing in the source device. This research also includes a study that shows that it takes longer to manually type the URL to transfer the session, compared to scanning of the QR code. And an example the authors used a travel service, where users can book flights and can switch to a different device during the process. Once the user initiates transfer, the service provides a QR code, user scans the QR code in destination device and can continue the activity of booking flights. This solution uses server side sessions and QR codes, which are used by our solution too. The core use case is however different from ours, as we address the transfer of the identity and session of a logged in user while in Alapetite's work the users were anonymous.

6   Conclusions

The work is still ongoing and these conclusions present our intermediate results. However, it appears that there are several ways to add transfer of the application-specific user identity within the liquid transfer.

This research is done from the point of view of a provider of a media service who needs to control and manage the access per individual user. Thus, the liquid transfer needs a secure way to transfer the liquid identity too. Furthermore, the service owner needs a way to controls the transfer.

The mechanisms should not introduce any additional privacy threats, as the user is provided an explicit control over transferring a session to a different device. The user identity is not put at risk, as only the session is transferred and the service can avoid storing any sensitive user information to the sessions on the client side.

It should be noted that if the set of devices is fixed, the devices can store standard cookies for all commonly used services. Then the liquid transfer could be implemented without the mechanisms described in this paper. The benefits of the solutions realize when the number of services is large, if client-side sessions are preferred for scalability reasons, and if shared devices – like tablets – are used.

Standardizing a solution by having all the web content providers expose endpoints to initiate session transfer from one device to another and modifying the browsers to provide session transfer options by communicating with these endpoints, would make it easier to transfer complete browsing sessions securely and without compromising privacy.

References

1. Alapetite, A.: Dynamic 2D-barcodes for multi-device web session migration including mobile phones. Pers. Ubiquit. Comput. **14**(1), 4–52 (2010). http://link.springer.com.libproxy.tut.fi/article/10.1007%2Fs00779-009-0228-5
2. Facebook Login for the Web with the JavaScript SDK. https://developers.facebook.com/docs/facebook-login/web. Accessed 30 Mar 2017
3. Marier, F., Nyman, R.: Using secure client-side sessions to build simple and scalable Node.JS applications. https://hacks.mozilla.org/2012/12/using-secure-client-side-sessions-to-build-simple-and-scalable-node-applications-a-node-js-holiday-season-part-3. Accessed 5 Apr 2017
4. Canfora, G., Di Santo, G. Venturi, G., Zimeo, E., Zito, M.V.: Proxy-based hand-off of web sessions for user mobility. In: Proceedings of the Second Annual International Conference on Mobile and Ubiquitous Systems: Networking and Services (MobiQuitous -05) (2005). https://www.researchgate.net/publication/4193595
5. Google chrome support. https://support.google.com/chrome/answer/165139. Accessed 31 Mar 2017
6. Google Research team. http://services.google.com/fh/files/misc/multiscreenworld_final.pdf. Accessed 24 Mar 2017
7. Song, H., Chu, H.-H., Kurakake, S.: Browser session preservation and migration. In: International World Wide Web Conference (2002). http://wwwconference.org/proceedings/www2002/poster/80.pdf

8. Song, H., Chu, H., Islam, N., Kurakake, S., Katagiri, M.: Browser state repository service. In: Mattern, F., Naghshineh, M. (eds.) Pervasive 2002. LNCS, vol. 2414, pp. 253–266. Springer, Heidelberg (2002). https://doi.org/10.1007/3-540-45866-2_20

9. Jones, M., Bradley J., Sakimura, N.: Internet Engineering Task Force (IETF), May 2015. https://tools.ietf.org/html/rfc7519

10. Liu, A.X., Kovacs, J.M., Huang, C., Gouda, M.: A Secure cookie protocol. In: Proceedings of 14th International Conference on Computer Communications and Networks (2005). http://www.cse.msu.edu/~alexliu/publications/Cookie/cookie.pdf

11. Hsieha, M.-D., Wangb, T.-P., Tsaia, C.-S., Tsenga, C.-C.: Stateful session handoff for mobile WWW. Inf. Sci. **176**(9), 1241–1265 (2006). https://doi.org/10.1016/j.ins.2005.02.009

12. Mozilla official website. https://www.mozilla.org/en-US/firefox/sync. Accessed 31 Mar 2017

13. Taivalsaari, A., Mikkonen, T., Systä, K.: Liquid software manifesto: the era of multiple device ownership and its implications for software architecture. In: IEEE 38th Annual Computer Software and Applications Conference, COMPSAC, Västerås, pp. 338–343. IEEE, Sweden (2014)

14. Todorov, D.: Mechanics of User Identification and Authentication: Fundamentals of Identity Management, pp. 1–45. Auerbach Publications, London (2007)

15. Weiser, M.: The computer for the 21st century. Sci. Am. **265**(3), 94–104 (1991)

16. Gallidabino, A., Pautasso, C., Ilvonen, V., Mikkonen, T., Systä, K., Voutilainen, J.-P., Taivalsaari, A.: On the architecture of liquid software: technology alternatives and design space. In: The Proceedings of WICSA (2016)

17. Gallidabino, A., Pautasso, C., Mikkonen, T., Systä, K., Voutilainen, J.-P., Taivalsaari, A.: Architecting Liquid Software. J. Web Eng. (2017, to appear)

18. Voutilainen, J.-P., Mikkonen, T., Systä, K.: Synchronizing application state using virtual DOM trees. In: Casteleyn, S., Dolog, P., Pautasso, C. (eds.) ICWE 2016. LNCS, vol. 9881, pp. 142–154. Springer, Cham (2016). https://doi.org/10.1007/978-3-319-46963-8_12

19. Casario, M., Elst, P., Brown, C., Wormser, N., Hanquez, C.: HTML5 geolocation API. In: Book HTML5 Solutions, Essential Techniques for HTML5 Developers, pp. 263–280. Apress publishers (2011)

20. Eriksson, B., Barford, P., Maggs, B., Nowak, R.: Posit: a lightweight approach for IP geolocation. In: Journal ACM SIGMETRICS Performance Evaluation Review, pp. 2–11 (2012)

21. Hardt, D. (ed.): The OAuth 2.0 Authorization Framework, Internet Engineering Task Force (IETF), pp. 10–12, October 2012. https://tools.ietf.org/html/rfc6749

Engineering Task-Automation Systems for Domain Specificity

Carmelo Ardito[1], Giuseppe Desolda[1(✉)], and Maristella Matera[2]

[1] Dipartimento di Informatica, Università degli Studi di Bari Aldo Moro,
Via Orabona 4, 70125 Bari, Italy
{carmelo.ardito,giuseppe.desolda}@uniba.it
[2] Dipartimento di Elettronica, Informazione e Bioingegneria, Politecnico di Milano,
Piazza Leonardo da Vinci 32, 20134 Milan, Italy
maristella.matera@polimi.it

Abstract. Domain specificity is largely recognized as a means to foster the adoption of systems by specific communities of non-technical users. This paper presents an architecture for the development of Task-Automation Systems that can be customized in specific domains. It is one of the results of a human-centred design process we performed to support non-technical people to program the behaviour of smart objects by defining event-condition-action (ECA) rules. We illustrate the main modules of the proposed architecture, also describing how it supports the creation of ECA rules constrained by means of temporal and spatial conditions. Finally, we report on the development of a Task-Automation System customized by developing and comparing three different composition paradigms.

Keywords: Task-Automation Systems · Internet of Thing
End-User Development · Domain specificity

1 Introduction

In the last years, the spreading of low-cost technologies that integrate sensors and actuators has facilitated building the so-called *smart objects*. A smart object is an electronic device connected to the Internet, which embeds sensors to feel the environment and/or actuators to communicate with the environment [5]. The proliferation of such devices led to the Internet of Things (IoT), a novel paradigm where the Internet is connected to the physical world via ubiquitous sensors[1]. The IoT is breeding grounds for different research areas since several challenges need to be addressed, such as those related to energy consumption, communication protocols, programming languages and end-user development (EUD) [12, 23]. Many efforts are being devoted to improve technological features. Little attention has been instead dedicated to social and practical aspects: therefore, despite all the advances in the IoT field, end users still encounter difficulties when they try to make sense of such technology. The research community agrees on the fact that the opportunities offered by IoT can be amplified if high-level abstractions and

---

[1] http://www.rfidjournal.com/articles/view?4986.

© Springer International Publishing AG, part of Springer Nature 2018
I. Garrigós and M. Wimmer (Eds.): ICWE 2017, LNCS 10544, pp. 108–119, 2018.
https://doi.org/10.1007/978-3-319-74433-9_9

adequate interaction paradigms are devised to enable also non-programmers to customize and synchronize the behaviour of smart objects [31].

In line with this claim, Task-Automation Systems (TASs) have recently become a popular solution to support non-technical users, i.e., people without skills in computer programming, to synchronize smart objects by exploiting visual mechanisms [25]. Despite a wide availability of TASs, the adopted graphical notations often do not match the mental model of most users [32]. In addition, TASs are typically conceived as general purpose systems, but their generality often implies a scarce adoption by specific communities of end users [10].

This paper proposes an architecture that fosters the development of TASs that are customizable with respect to varying users and usage domains. The customization mainly consists in developing a specific User Interface (UI) that "speaks the language of the user", i.e., that proposes terminology, concepts, rules, and conventions the target users are comfortable with. In addition, the architecture addresses the smart objects synchronization by means of event-condition-action (ECA) rules. Such rules are based on a model, called *5 W*, which defines some specification constructs (*Which, What, When, Where, Why*) to build rules coupling multiple events and conditions exposed by smart objects, and for defining temporal and spatial constraints on rule activation and action execution. This model meets the mental model of the users, who can easily describe the ingredients of the ECA rules following the 5 W simple questions. Starting from the proposed architecture, this paper briefly illustrates the development of a TAS called EFESTO and its customization through the development of three different UIs.

The paper is organized as follows. Section 2 illustrates the architecture that drives the development of Task-Automation Systems, which can be customized by developing proper UIs that satisfy varying users and usage domains. Section 3 describes the implementation of the EFESTO platform and its customization with three UIs implementing different composition paradigms. Section 4 reports related works. Finally, Sect. 5 concludes the paper also outlining our future work.

2   Domain Specificity in Task-Automation Systems: A Platform Architecture

In this section, we illustrate an architecture that facilitates the development of Task-Automation Systems that are customizable with respect to varying users and usage domains. The architecture design was driven by the need to develop a general TAS to be easily customized by adapting in the interaction layer [2], thus facilitating its adoption in different domains where users are comfortable with specific terminology, concepts, rules, and conventions. The proposed architecture thus features a decoupling of the interaction layer from the other platform modules. Software design patterns, first of all the MVC (Model-View-Controller), already addressed this separation of concerns. In our work, however, the emphasis is not on programming practices to facilitate the development and maintenance of an interactive system; rather we want to stress the possibility to adapt easily the composition paradigm offered by a TAS, to comply with domain-specific requirements. It is indeed important to develop a general TAS that can be, however, easily customized as far as the provided composition metaphor is concerned [2].

The resulting TASs would allow people to exploit different composition paradigms to program the behaviour of smart objects by defining ECA rules whose events and actions are defined in term of: *Which* is the object, *What* event triggers the rule (What action has to be activated), and *When* and *Where* the event/action has to happen [15]. This characterization of rule events and actions is inspired by the 5 W model typically adopted in journalism to describe a fact.

2.1 Platform Organization

The architecture inherits some modules for service invocation and management already developed in the EFESTO mashup framework [14]. The focus of the new architecture

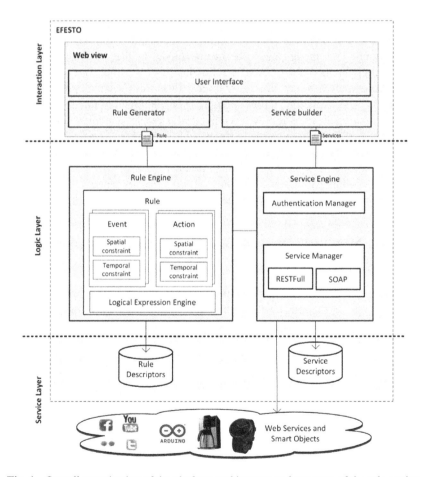

Fig. 1. Overall organization of the platform architecture and structure of the rule engine.

is however on the *Rule Engine*. As reported in Fig. 1, the architecture is organized in three layers, each one managing a separate aspect.

The *Interaction Layer* refers to the system client that manages the UI through which the users can create ECA rules. In addition, it implements two modules, the *Service Builder* and the *Rule Generator*. The first one is in charge of materializing in the UI the list of attributes of registered services, as resulting from the *Service Descriptor* reposi- tory. Thus, it is invoked each time users need to add an event or an action to the rule. The UI layer is in principle agnostic to the registered services; to build the visualization of available services, the Service Builder requests to the *Service Engine* the JSON file containing the list of available services, each of them described by attributes like name, events, actions and thumbnail URL.

The *Rule Generator* is an interpreter that translates the user visual actions for rule creation into a JSON specification that describes the rule in terms of events, actions, logical operators and spatial and temporal constraints (see Fig. 2b). This is the module that actually manages the adopted interaction metaphor. The platform customization for specific domains thus principally requires modifying the way this module interprets the user visual actions to create the JSON rule specification.

```
{
    "name": "Bracelet",
    "url": "https://www.mybracelet.com/apidocs/en/api/v2"

    "body": {
        "appId": "VTnA9hAIsnGJ2OairDVv10KudZYwqLjhvsuil
        "appSecret": "Jokez2lH6hfnrXj6l7LgKeba28A5LDsvtell
        "restUri": "https://api.mybracelet.com/",
        "redirectUri": "https://localhost/callback/mybracelet",
        "tokenExpiredCode": 401,
        "authentication": "OAuth1",

        "functions": [
            {
                "type":"event",
                "name": "JustAwake",
                "path": "v2/awake_status/",
                "method": "GET"
                "response": "json"
            },

            {
                "type":"action",
                "name": "EmitVibration",
                "path": "v2/vibrate/",
                "method": "POST"
                "response": "json"
            }
        ]
    }
}
```

```
{
    "userId" : 2,
    "ruleId" : "21.json",
    "why" : "Beautify my wakeup",
    "triggers_logical_operator": "OR",
    "actions_logical_operator": "AND"
    "events" : [ {
        "who" : "Bracelet",
        "what" : "JustAwake",
        "when" : "0 0/1 9 ? * ?",
        "where" : "City, Address, number"
    },
    {
        "who" : "SmartAlarm",
        "what" : "Ringing",
        "when" : "0 0/1 9 ? * ?",
        "where" : ""
    }
    ],
    "actions" : [ {
        "who" : "Roll-upShutter",
        "what" : "Open",
        "when" : "",
        "where" : ""
    },{
        "who" : "CoffeMachine",
        "what" : "TurnOn",
        "when" : "",
        "where" : ""
    }
    ]
}
```

a   b

Fig. 2. (a) Service descriptor of the bracelet smart object; (b) JSON descriptor of a rule with 2 causes and 2 actions and

At the server side, the *Logic Layer* manages rules and services by means of respectively the *Rule Engine* and the *Service Engine* modules. The first one receives the rule JSON file (Fig. 2b) from the client (from the *Rule Generator* module) and instantiates the rule object based on a publish-subscribe, event-action model [8, 9]. This model is natively managed and handled by a Java Spring class[2] for tasks scheduling. Each rule object is characterized by a set of *Publisher* services, each of them associated with an event that can be complemented with temporal and spatial constraints, and by a set of *Subscriber* services, each of them associated to an action that can be complemented with temporal and spatial constraints. Moreover, details about the logical operators used among events or actions are stored in the rule object.

The Rule Engine acts as an event bus that mediates the communication between the different components. Components are decoupled: they do not need to be explicitly aware of each other or be blocked waiting for events from other components. Depending on the nature of the service, the Rule Engine can work as active or passive component. In the first case, it checks every N minutes if the publisher events are triggered (all of them or just one of them depending on the logical operator, respectively AND or OR). This check is performed by a *listener* associated to the rule. In the second case, it is notified by the service when an event is triggered. In both cases, if the events are triggered, the Rule Engine controls if there are temporal and spatial constraints on the events and, in case, if they are satisfied. If the events meet all the conditions, the Rule Engine runs all the subscribed actions associated with the rule or schedules the action execution according to the when constraint.

The *Service Layer* is located at the server side and stores service and rule descriptors by using JSON files. A *service descriptor* contains all the information useful to query an API and contributes to decouple the registered services from the rest of the platform. It is created when a new object is added to the platform. Different technology (e.g., RESTful) can be easily accommodated as the EFESTO service layer [14] is structured so that different types of adapters can be plugged in to manage the access to different API technologies. Alternatively, without developing further adapters, it is possible to adopt a dedicated middleware, as for example Azure IoT Suite[3], to mediate the access to additional service technologies [22]. The resulting platform is indeed open and each layer can be also implemented by external services.

An example of service descriptor is provided in Fig. 2a. It is divided into two main sections: header and body. The attributes *name* and *url* in the header specify respectively the service name and the API documentation URL. The body section includes a set of attributes (*appID*, *appSecret*, *restUri*, *redirectUri*, *tokenExpiredCode*, *authentication*) that the Service Engine uses to invoke the API. Moreover, the *functions* JSON array contains a list of *events* and *actions*, each of them characterized by the attributes *type*, *name*, *path*, *method* and *response*, which are respectively the type of function (event or action), the event/action name displayed to the users in the UI, the event/action path

---

[2] ThreadPoolTaskScheduler (http://docs.spring.io/spring-framework/docs/current/javadoc-api/org/springframework/scheduling/concurrent/ThreadPoolTaskScheduler.html).

[3] https://www.microsoft.com/en/server-cloud/internet-of-things/azure-iot-suite.aspx.

chained to the *restUri* URL to invoke the event/action, the type of API call (e.g., GET, POST) and the provider response format (e.g., JSON, XML).

3   Development and Customization of a Task-Automation System

In this section we describe a TAS called EFESTO-5 W we developed according to the proposed architecture. The separation of the UI layer from the other two layers allowed us to customize EFESTO-5 W by proposing three different composition paradigms. Each paradigm gives the name to the customized version of the platform, i.e., EFESTO-Free, EFESTO-Wizard and EFESTO-Wired, abbreviated to *E-Free*, *E-Wizard* and *E-Wired*, respectively. Lack of space prevents us to report further information about the prototype design and evaluation. Interested readers can refer to [15] for details about the design process.

E-Free and E-Wizard are based on two similar interaction paradigms. In both the prototypes, as shown in Fig. 3, the main screen where the rule is created presents two main areas, the left one to add the events and the right one to add the actions. To add an event, users have to click on the "+" button in the *Events* area, thus activating a wizard procedure that assists them in defining *Which* is the service to be monitored for detecting the triggering event, *What* service event has to be monitored and *When* and *Where* the event has to be triggered. Similarly, they can add an action by clicking the + button in the Action area to activate the wizard steps to define *Which* service will execute the action, *What* action the service has to perform and *When* and *Where* the action can be performed.

Fig. 3. E-Free: example of rule including two events and two actions.

The main difference between E-Free and E-Wizard is that in E-Wizard, before accessing the main screen, users are compelled to follow a wizard procedure to create a "basic rule" composed of one event and one action. Then, they can add further events and actions exploiting the main screen reported in Fig. 3. In E-Free the rule creation instead starts from the main screen, and here users may either define first all the events and then the actions, or define first a basic rule including one event and one action and later add new events and new actions. Events and actions can be added or removed at any time.

E-Wired implements an interaction paradigm based on the graph metaphor: nodes represent smart objects involved in a rule, while directed edges, i.e., arrows, represent cause-effect relationships between objects. As reported in Fig. 4, the E-Wired UI has two main areas. The sidebar on the left provides the list of all the available smart objects and Web services: Web services are light-yellow, while smart objects are light-green. In the workspace area, users build the rule. They first select one of the services in the left sidebar, which is added to the workspace and represented as a box augmented with two small circles, light-blue and purple, which represent the connection points for the arrows representing cause-effect relationships. As soon as the arrow is drawn, two pop-up windows in sequence allow the user to specify the parameters of the Event and of the Action in terms of *What, When,* and *Where*. A "Create Rule" button in the second pop-up window permits to save the rule, also specifying *Why*, i.e., a title shortly describing the rule.

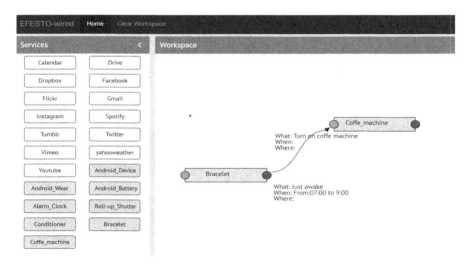

Fig. 4. E-Wired: example of rule including one event and one action. (Color figure online)

An experiment comparing the three EFESTO-5 W prototypes revealed that the E-Free composition paradigm outperforms the ones implemented in E-Wizard and E-Wired, both in terms of user performances and satisfaction [15]. Starting from E-Free, we recently extended its UI exploring three visual composition techniques to specify complex logical expressions [16]. The first technique proposes abstraction mechanisms to combine rule events by means of AND/OR logical operators, as well as to group set of conjunctive/disjunctive events, also recursively. The second technique constraints the creation of logic expressions taking into account a principle of the mental model theory [21] saying that people find easier the conceptualization of logical statements as a disjunction of conjunctions (Disjunctive Normal Form - DNF). The third technique is the opposite of DNF, since it allows the combination of rule events as a *conjunction of disjunction* (Conjunctive Normal Form - CNF). We are currently investigating pros and cons of each of these techniques in creating ECA rules.

4   Related Work

To bring close end users' desire to customize smart object behavior and the intrinsic complexity of programming languages, different solutions are emerging today. Since a smart object is remotely available as a Web service, in many cases such solutions are getting inspiration from the mashup research area. Mashup tools are Web platforms that permit to access and compose heterogeneous resources, including Web services, by exploiting visual mechanisms [13]. Starting from the mashup approaches, task-auto-mation systems [11] have been proposed as means for synchronizing services and smart objects. Such tools support users in the automation of their processes by establishing channels among smart objects (e.g., each time a user enters into his home, the Wi-Fi router switched on). A popular TAS is IFTTT (IF This Then That): it provides wizard mechanisms for creating automation rules, called *recipes*, to throw an action on a service when an event is triggered by another service [20]. For instance, when an intrusion is detected by the home alarm system, the Smartwatch shows a notification to the user.

The wizard paradigm fits very well the mental model of non-technical end users [3], and this is the reason why it is widely exploited also by other TASs. An example is *elastic.io,* a tool to create rule expressing data-flow chains [1]. It is more devoted to business aspects and offers the possibility to integrate custom services. Another example is *Zapier,* whose main features are *(i)* the possibility to create rules with multiple events and actions and *(ii)* the use of *filters* on the triggering events to control rules activation [11]. TASs implementing wizard approaches are also available as mobile apps. *Atooma* is one of the most popular; it allows the creation of rules with multiple events and actions, which put into communication device functions, Web services and smart objects [4]. A recent work demonstrated that, even if Atooma supports the creation of very expressive rules, the wizard approach guarantees similar performances between IFTTT (the mobile version) and Atooma with reference to time and accuracy [7]. Similarly to Atooma, tools like *AutomateIt* and *Tasker* support the creation of rules, but they simply enable the composition of apps and functions available on mobile devices [17, 24].

Besides wizard-based TASs, there are other different composition paradigms. For example, the graph metaphor is used to represent a Web service as a node and connec-tions among Web services as "wires". Users can define object communication/behavior by graphically sketching the wires among the objects. A popular tool implementing the wired paradigm is *Node-RED* [30]. Besides offering a set of pre-defined services, it allows users to register personal smart objects by invoking their RESTful interfaces. In addition, Node-RED supports the creation of complex automation rules characterized by: *(i)* multiple services that trigger events and multiple services that react by performing actions; *(ii)* special nodes, used for example to control the communication flow among services by means of custom JavaScript code; *(iii)* debug function to simulate and check the rules under creation. However, such features often require technical skills and thus they are not adequate for non-technical people [26, 27, 34]. The wire paradigm is implemented by tools typically devoted to more technical users, for example by *Bip.io* [33] and *Spacebrew* [19].

A completely different paradigm is implemented in *Zipato*, a platform specific for home-automation [35]. The rule creation occurs in a workspace where people can compose puzzle pieces representing components for control flow, sensors and actuators, logical operators, variables and other advanced elements. Despite the high degree of rule customization, the puzzle metaphor makes Zipato promising for non-technical users.

A recent systematic literature review identifies the best software tools that allow end users to manage and configure the behaviors of a smart home [18]. Some of the identified tools were also compared on the basis of seven design principles proposed for smart home control.

The analysis of the previous tools highlighted some lacks that make it difficult for non-programmers to use them effectively. In particular, very often the adopted graphical notations for rule specification do not match the mental model of most users [32]. Research on Web mashup composition paradigms – a field that has many aspects in common with smart object composition – showed that graph-based notations are suitable for programmers, while some issues concerning the conceptual understanding of such notations arise with laypeople who do not think about "connecting" services [27, 28, 34].

Another lack is related to the expressive power of the ECA rules that can be specified, which is limited to simple synchronized behaviours. In [6] authors discuss the importance of temporal and spatial conditions to create ECA rules to better satisfy users' needs. Specifying temporal conditions also emerged as an important requirement in home automation to schedule rule for appliance activation [29]. Some tools allow the definition of such conditions only by means of workarounds, for example by considering additional events to monitor the system time, or by creating filters on smart device data (e.g., in Zapier). Obviously, such workarounds complicate the rule creation, thus resulting into a scarce adoption of the available tools, especially by non-technical users, or in their adoption only for very simple tasks.

5   Conclusion

One key aspect in the future of the IoT will be to put in the hands of end user software tools offering natural and expressive paradigms to compose smart objects. Adequate tools can enable non-expert users to achieve this goal. Task-Automation Systems can suit very well the need for synchronizing different objects to program the behavior of smart spaces. The work presented in this paper goes in this direction, as it concentrates on specializing a generic TAS for the composition of services that enable accessing/

controlling smart things. The peculiarity of the presented platform is the possibility to adapt easily the composition paradigm. Through a series of user studies we indeed verified that, although in given situations a composition metaphor can result as the most fitting, adaptations might be required in different domains. Sometimes, even the combined provision of different paradigms can result effective.

The composition paradigm currently offered by EFESTO-5 W was elicited with the help of end users and then validated by means of controlled experiments. We are therefore very confident that this paradigm encounters the need and capabilities of non-expert programmers, letting them to take advantage of IoT technology. Of course, there are still several aspects to be investigated. First of all, to further extend the capability of EFESTO in supporting the EUD of smart spaces, we are planning future work to understand if and how the addition and the initial configuration of new objects into smart environments could be performed by non-technical users. Actually, our current prototype requires the intervention of expert programmers to define JSON-based object descriptors. We would like to understand whether there can be simple procedures, also based on natural (e.g., gesture-based, proximity-based) interaction paradigms that could (at least partially) enable non-technical users to perform these activities. This implies the identification of a "component model", i.e., a set of conceptual elements abstracting the underlying technology, which can mediate between the technical features to be addressed to program smart objects (the components) and the interaction layer supporting the customization by end users of objects by means of high-level programming constructs.

We also aim to understand how, using recent digital printing technologies, the "fabrication" of smart objects (including the design and production of the physical objects, and the definition of their programming interfaces) can be conducted interactively with the support of visual EUD environments.

References

1. ELASTIC.IO: GMBH. http://www.elastic.io/. Accessed 9 May 2017
2. Ardito, C., Costabile, M.F., Desolda, G., Lanzilotti, R., Matera, M., Piccinno, A., Picozzi, M.: User-driven visual composition of service-based interactive spaces. J. Vis. Lang. Comput. **25**(4), 278–296 (2014)
3. Ardito, C., Costabile, M.F., Desolda, G., Lanzilotti, R., Matera, M., Picozzi, M.: Visual composition of data sources by end-users. In: Proceedings of the International Conference on Advanced Visual Interfaces (AVI 2014), Como, Italy, 28–30 May. ACM, New York, pp. 257–260 (2014)
4. Atooma mobile App: https://www.atooma.com/. Accessed 9 May 2017
5. Atzori, L., Iera, A., Morabito, G.: The internet of things: a survey. Int. J. Comput. Comput. Netw. **54**(15), 2787–2805 (2010)
6. Barricelli, B.R., Valtolina, S.: Designing for end-user development in the internet of things. In: Díaz, P., Pipek, V., Ardito, C., Jensen, C., Aedo, I., Boden, A. (eds.) IS-EUD 2015. LNCS, vol. 9083, pp. 9–24. Springer, Cham (2015). https://doi.org/10.1007/978-3-319-18425-8_2
7. Cabitza, F., Fogli, D., Lanzilotti, R., Piccinno, A.: Rule-based tools for the configuration of ambient intelligence systems: a comparative user study. Multimed. Tools Appl. **75**(248), 1–21 (2016)

8. Cappiello, C., Matera, M., Picozzi, M.: A UI-centric approach for the end-user development of multidevice mashups. ACM Trans. Web **9**(3), 1–40 (2015)
9. Cappiello, C., Matera, M., Picozzi, M., Sprega, G., Barbagallo, D., Francalanci, C.: DashMash: a mashup environment for end user development. In: Auer, S., Díaz, O., Papadopoulos, G.A. (eds.) ICWE 2011. LNCS, vol. 6757, pp. 152–166. Springer, Heidelberg (2011). https://doi.org/10.1007/978-3-642-22233-7_11
10. Casati, F.: How end-user development will save composition technologies from their continuing failures. In: Costabile, M.F., Dittrich, Y., Fischer, G., Piccinno, A. (eds.) IS-EUD 2011. LNCS, vol. 6654, pp. 4–6. Springer, Heidelberg (2011). https://doi.org/10.1007/978-3-642-21530-8_2
11. Coronado, M., Iglesias, C.A.: Task automation services: automation for the masses. IEEE Internet Comput. **20**(1), 52–58 (2016)
12. Costabile, M.F., Fogli, D., Mussio, P., Piccinno, A.: Visual interactive systems for end-user development: a model-based design methodology. IEEE Trans. Syst. Man Cybern. - Part A: Syst. Hum. **37**(6), 1029–1046 (2007)
13. Daniel, F., Matera, M.: Mashups: Concepts, Models and Architectures. Springer, Heidelberg (2014)
14. Desolda, G., Ardito, C., Matera, M.: EFESTO: a platform for the end-user development of interactive workspaces for data exploration. In: Daniel, F., Pautasso, C. (eds.) RMC 2015. CCIS, vol. 591, pp. 63–81. Springer, Cham (2016). https://doi.org/10.1007/978-3-319-28727-0_5
15. Desolda, G., Ardito, C., Matera, M.: Empowering end users to customize their smart environments: model, composition paradigms and domain-specific tools. ACM Trans. Comput. Hum. Interact. (TOCHI) **24**(2), 52 (2017). Article 12
16. Desolda, G., Ardito, C., Matera, M.: Specification of complex logical expressions for task automation: an EUD approach. In: Barbosa, S., Markopoulos, P., Paternò, F., Stumpf, S., Valtolina, S. (eds.) IS-EUD 2017. LNCS, vol. 10303, pp. 108–116. Springer, Cham (2017). https://doi.org/10.1007/978-3-319-58735-6_8
17. Tasker: http://tasker.dinglisch.net/index.html Accessed 9 May 2017
18. Fogli, D., Lanzilotti, R., Piccinno, A.: End-user development tools for the smart home: a systematic literature review. In: Streitz, N., Markopoulos, P. (eds.) DAPI 2016. LNCS, vol. 9749, pp. 69–79. Springer, Cham (2016). https://doi.org/10.1007/978-3-319-39862-4_7
19. Spacebrew: http://docs.spacebrew.cc/. Accessed 9 May 2017
20. IFTTT: https://ifttt.com/. Accessed 9 May 2017
21. Johnson-Laird, P.N.: Mental Models: Towards a Cognitive Science of Language, Inference, and Consciousness. Harvard University Press, Cambridge (1983)
22. Li, S., Xu, L., Zhao, S.: The internet of things: a survey. Inf. Syst. Front. **17**(2), 243–259 (2015)
23. Lieberman, H., Paternò, F., Klann, M., Wulf, V.: End-user development: an emerging paradigm. In: Lieberman, H., Paternò, F., Wulf, V. (eds.) End User Development. Human-Computer Interaction Series, vol. 9, pp. 1–8. Springer, Netherlands (2006). https://doi.org/10.1007/1-4020-5386-X_1
24. AutomateIt - Smart Automation: http://automateitapp.com/. Accessed 9 May 2017
25. Lucci, G., Paternò, F.: Analysing how users prefer to model contextual event-action behaviours in their smartphones. In: Díaz, P., Pipek, V., Ardito, C., Jensen, C., Aedo, I., Boden, A. (eds.) IS-EUD 2015. LNCS, vol. 9083, pp. 186–191. Springer, Cham (2015). https://doi.org/10.1007/978-3-319-18425-8_14

26. Namoun, A., Nestler, T., Angeli, A.D.: Service composition for non-programmers: prospects, problems, and design recommendations. In: Proceedings of the IEEE European Conference on Web Services (ECOWS 2010), Lugano Switzerland, 14–16 September 2010. IEEE Computer Society, Washington DC, pp. 123–130 (2010)
27. Namoun, A., Nestler, T., De Angeli, A.: Conceptual and usability issues in the composable web of software services. In: Daniel, F., Facca, F.M. (eds.) ICWE 2010. LNCS, vol. 6385, pp. 396–407. Springer, Heidelberg (2010). https://doi.org/10.1007/978-3-642-16985-4_35
28. Namoun, A., Wajid, U., Mehandjiev, N.: Service composition for everyone: a study of risks and benefits. In: Dan, A., Gittler, F., Toumani, F. (eds.) ICSOC/ServiceWave -2009. LNCS, vol. 6275, pp. 550–559. Springer, Heidelberg (2010). https://doi.org/10.1007/978-3-642-16132-2_52
29. Rode, J.A., Toye, E.F., Blackwell, A.F.: The fuzzy felt ethnography—understanding the programming patterns of domestic appliances. Pers. Ubiquitous Comput. **8**(3–4), 161–176 (2004)
30. IBM Emerging Technology: http://nodered.org/. Accessed 9 May 2017
31. Tetteroo, D., Markopoulos, P., Valtolina, S., Paternò, F., Pipek, V., Burnett, M.: End-user development in the internet of things era. In: Proceedings of the Human Factors in Computing Systems (CHI 2015), Seoul, Republic of Korea. ACM, New York, pp. 2405–2408 (2015)
32. Wajid, U., Namoun, A., Mehandjiev, N.: Alternative representations for end user composition of service-based systems. In: Costabile, M.F., Dittrich, Y., Fischer, G., Piccinno, A. (eds.) IS-EUD 2011. LNCS, vol. 6654, pp. 53–66. Springer, Heidelberg (2011). https://doi.org/10.1007/978-3-642-21530-8_6
33. Bip.io: https://bip.io/. Accessed 9 May 2017
34. Zang, N., Rosson M.B.: What's in a mashup? and why? studying the perceptions of web-active end users. In: Proceedings of the IEEE Symposium on Visual Languages and Human-Centric Computing (VL-HCC 2008), Herrsching, Ammersee, Germany, 15–19 September 2008. IEEE Computer Society, pp. 31–38 (2008)
35. Zipato: https://www.zipato.com/. Accessed 9 May 2017

A Homemade Pill Dispenser Prototype Supporting Elderly

Paolo Buono⬤, Fabio Cassano⁽⊠⁾⬤, Alessandra Legretto⬤,
and Antonio Piccinno⬤

Dipartimento di Informatica, Università di Bari "Aldo Moro", Bari, Italy
{paolo.buono,fabio.cassanol,alessandra.legretto,
antonio.piccinno}@uniba.it

Abstract. People, and mainly elderly people, need a continuous support for different reasons. Recent technologies are offering many possibilities that was not possible to conceive in the past. In particular, the proliferation of IoT devices raise the need to standardize protocols and interaction languages. The aim of this work is to create a device for the management of pills according to the user's therapy, with Internet of things (IoT) devices and by allowing users to manage the pill dispenser by themselves. The work falls into two main areas of current research: the End-user development (EUD) and the Internet of things (IoT). The main issue we cope with such device is to allow the different therapies for each person and for each drug. We propose the EUDroid system, which provides the end user with the possibility to easily activate LEDs and buzzer related to pills from the users' smartphone. The user chooses the type of pill to be associated to each LED, the day and time of activation and some other property. A formal language to configure the device has been adopted in order to allow users to build complex conditions for remind to follow the therapy.

Keywords: Internet of Thing · End-user development · Elderly
Pill dispenser

1 Introduction

Computer users have rapidly increased in both number and diversity [1]. They include managers, accountants, engineers, teachers, scientists, health care workers, etc. Many of these people work on tasks that rapidly vary on a yearly, monthly, or even daily basis. Consequently, their software needs are different, complex, and frequently changing. Professional software developers cannot directly meet all of such needs because of their limited domain knowledge and slow development processes [2].

End-user Development (EUD) helps to solve this problem. EUD is defined as "a set of methods, techniques and tools that allow users of software systems, who are acting as non-professional software developers, at some point to create, modify, or extend a software artifact" [3], enabling end users to design or customize the user interface and functionality of a software. End users know both their own context and needs, better more than anybody else. Moreover, they often have real-time awareness of shifts in their respective domains. Through EUD, end users can adapt the software they are

© Springer International Publishing AG, part of Springer Nature 2018
I. Garrigós and M. Wimmer (Eds.): ICWE 2017, LNCS 10544, pp. 120–124, 2018.
https://doi.org/10.1007/978-3-319-74433-9_10

using to fit their requirements. A recent view of EUD extends the context of software systems to techniques, methodologies, situations, and socio-technical environments that allow end users to act as professionals in those domains in which they are not professionals, including IoT [4].

Our work address different situations in which a user might want to change the behavior of a software/hardware artifact. In this demo we address the need of many people to take one or more pills daily for a given period. We designed and developed an IoT device that allows the management and distributions of pills for the end users, who are often elderly, and by end users with no IT expertise.

The project EUDdroid has been developed into three parts: the first involves a smartphone app, the second is the pill dispenser that has the role of the "Internet of Things" (IoT) device and the third is a web server that manages the user's requests. IoT devices are objects to be sensed or controlled remotely across an existing network infrastructure, creating opportunities for more direct integration of the physical world into computer-based systems, and resulting in improved efficiency, accuracy and economic benefit in addition to reduced human intervention [5].

The main purpose of the project is to realize an Android application that allows the composition and customization of elementary events, such as the management of a pill for diabetes or cholesterol. The idea to use electronic devices to help elderly to take pills is well known in the literature. Many of the existing works, however, do not allow users to customize the behavior of the machine. As a matter of fact, commercial solutions allow users only to define what pill should be dropped according to the calendar. The final user is not allowed to deeply edit the parameters of the pills dispenser and, to the best of our knowledge, not any formal language has ever been defined to allow multiple users to customize the machine [6]. Moreover, it is not always possible for the end user, to control and edit the pills dispenser through the smartphone with an app. A similar solution like our pill dispenser is proposed in [7].

2   EUDroid Formal Language

A formal specification can describe unambiguously the behavior of a user interface and may help the designer to easily extend the functionalities of the app, making sure that such functionalities are not in contrast with the previous behavior. Once defined the behavior of the system (in terms of syntax and semantics), new widgets or features can be introduced, adding their semantics. In the following, is reported a formal description of the basic components and the logic of the system [4].

An elementary component (c) is an electronic device that receives an input or gives an output. The elementary components are divided into sensors and actuators. The first are electronic devices that mostly collect and analyze information; the latter are electronic devices that perform operations or "carry out a behavior".

The project includes five actuators: (a) red LED (LR), (b) blue LED (LB), (c) green LED (LG), (d) yellow LED (LY) and (e) Buzzer (B). All of them can assume the state of active (high level) or inactive (low level). The behavior of the buzzer is the opposite, the low level activates the buzzer, while the high level disables the buzzer. An Ethernet shield let the system communicate through the Internet. A button is the user's input. When the button is pressed, its state is low and all the actuators are turned off, when it is not pressed, its state is high. Another elementary component is the message (M). It belongs to the category of the actuators because it is an output component. In this work, the message is a text sent to a mobile phone. The goal is to build an app that composes elementary events in order to get composite events.

An elementary event (e) is composed of an action and a trigger. An Action (A) consists in the execution of operations, i.e. the turn on/off elementary components. A Trigger (TR) is the logical condition on one or more actions. In this demo, the trigger is the Calendar (CL) item. A calendar is composed by a start date (SD) and time (T). A Composite Event (CE) is the set of elementary events, so it is composed by more Trigger-Action relations. An elementary component can be any actuator of those provided in the project, listed above, that can carry information such as Delay (DY) and Duration (DU). AT defines the whole actuator's set. Given an actuator $AT = \{LR, LB, LG, LY, B, M\}$, an elementary component c is defined as:

$$c = \ <x, DY, DY> with\, x \in AT, DY \in N, DU \in N \tag{1}$$

For example, $c = \ <LR, 120, 60>$ means that the red LED will be on after 2 min (120″) compared to the activation of a given trigger, and will have a duration of 1 min (60″). We defined a sequence of elementary components form action as:

$$A = \ <c_1, c_2, \ldots, c_n> where\, c_i \in C, 1 \leq i \leq n \tag{2}$$

C is the set of elementary components. Therefore, as the elementary event is composed of the pair trigger-action we will write:

$$e = \ <CL, A>, where\, CL = \ <SD, T> \tag{3}$$

Consequently, given the set of elementary events E, a Composite Event (CE) is:

$$CE = \ <e_1, e_2, \ldots, e_n> where\, e_i \in E, 1 \leq i \leq n$$

The web server hosts a database with the pill dispenser location and the available commands for the specific device. Commands can be expressed in the form: $Cm = \ <p, s, DY, DU>$. Where p defines the pin position on the Arduino board, s defines the state (high or low) of the elementary component. In the demo the device, based on Arduino, has three tasks: (a) checks the Web Server if there is a command associated to its code; (b) if there is one it reads the event and run it according to the delay and duration; (c) if the user press the button it reset the status of the pill dispenser. As shown in Fig. 1, the physical prototype has currently four compartments for pills. At the bottom right there is the button to reset the current event. At the top right there is a small hole for the buzzer (Fig. 1).

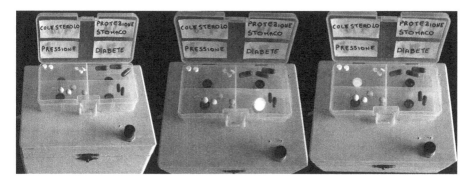

Fig. 1. Pill dispenser prototype in the status: off, diabetes pills, and pressure pills

3 Conclusions

This demo is intended to be an example of how to compose rules and apply them to a physical IoT device. In this demo we addressed a few elementary components. The final goal is to build a complete formal language that covers various user needs. Such language could be mapped to existing visual tools that allow users to compose rules, but lack of advanced operators, such as the composition operator. In the future, we will enhance the physical device allowing to perform EUD activities not only through a mobile device, but also manipulating physical devices [8] and allowing remote control from more generic automation platform, such as [9, 10].

References

1. Burnett, M., Scaffidi, C.: End-user development. In: Soegaard, M., Dam, R.F. (eds.) The Encyclopedia of Human-Computer Interaction, 2nd edn. The Interaction Design Foundation, Aarhus (2013)
2. Scaffidi, C., Shaw, M., Myers, B.: Estimating the numbers of end users and end user programmers. In: Proceedings of VL/HCC 2005. IEEE Computer Society, pp. 207–214 (2005)
3. Lieberman, H., Paternò, F., Klann, M., Wulf, V.: End-user development: an emerging paradigm. In: Lieberman, H., Paternò, F., Wulf, V. (eds.) End-User Development, vol. 9, pp. 1–8. Springer, Dordrecht (2006). https://doi.org/10.1007/1-4020-5386-X_1
4. Fischer, G., Fogli, D., Piccinno, A.: Revisiting and broadening the meta-design framework for end-user development. In: Paternò, F., Wulf, V. (eds.) New Perspectives in End User Development. Springer, Cham (2017). https://doi.org/10.1007/978-3-319-60291-2_4
5. Bartolomeo, M.: Internet of Things: Science fiction or business fact? Harvard Business Review (2004)
6. Crema, C., Depari, A., Flammini, A., Lavarini, M., Sisinni, E., Vezzoli, A.: A smartphone-enhanced pill-dispenser providing patient identification and in-take recognition. In: Proceedings of MeMeA 2015, pp. 484–489 (2015)

7. Yang, G., Xie, L., Mäntysalo, M., Zhou, X., Pang, Z., Xu, L.D., Kao-Walter, S., Chen, Q., Zheng, L.R.: A health-IoT platform based on the integration of intelligent packaging, unobtrusive bio-sensor, and intelligent medicine box. IEEE Trans. Ind. Inform. **10**(4), 2180–2191 (2014)
8. Ardito, C., Buono, P., Costabile, M.F., Lanzilotti, R., Simeone, A.L.: Comparing low cost input devices for interacting with 3D virtual environments. In: HSI 2009, pp. 292–297 (2009)
9. Desolda, G., Ardito, C., Matera, M.: EFESTO: a platform for the end-user development of interactive workspaces for data exploration. In: Daniel, F., Pautasso, C. (eds.) RMC 2015. CCIS, vol. 591, pp. 63–81. Springer, Cham (2016). https://doi.org/10.1007/978-3-319-28727-0_5
10. Desolda, G.: Enhancing workspace composition by exploiting linked open data as a polymorphic data source. In: Damiani, E., Howlett, R., Jain, L., Gallo, L., De Pietro, G. (eds.) Intelligent Interactive Multimedia Systems and Services. Smart Innovation, Systems and Technologies, vol. 40, pp. 97–108. Springer, Cham (2015). https://doi.org/10.1007/978-3-319-19830-9_9

Towards an Acceptance Testing Approach for Internet of Things Systems

Maurizio Leotta(✉)(iD), Filippo Ricca, Diego Clerissi, Davide Ancona,
Giorgio Delzanno, Marina Ribaudo, and Luca Franceschini

Dipartimento di Informatica, Bioingegneria, Robotica e Ingegneria dei Sistemi
(DIBRIS), Università di Genova, Genova, Italy
{maurizio.leotta,filippo.ricca,diego.clerissi,davide.ancona,
giorgio.delzanno,marina.ribaudo,luca.franceschini}@unige.it

Abstract. Internet of Things (IoT) applications and systems pervade our life increasingly and assuring their quality is of paramount importance. Unfortunately, few proposals for testing these complex—and often safety-critical—systems are present in the literature and testers are left alone to build their test cases.

This paper is a first step towards acceptance testing of an IoT system that relies on a smartphone as principal way of interaction between the user and a complex system composed by local sensors/actuators and a remote cloud-based system. A simplified mobile health (m-health) IoT system for diabetic patients is used as an example to explain the proposed approach.

1 Introduction

Internet of Things (IoT) is a network of interconnected physical objects and devices that share data through secure infrastructures and transmit to a central control server in the cloud. As the IoT technology continues to mature, we will see more and more novel IoT applications and systems emerging in different contexts. For example, trains able to dynamically compute and report arrival times to waiting passengers, cars able to avoid traffic-jam by proposing alternative paths and m-health systems able to determine the right medicament dose for a patient.

Ensuring that IoT applications are secure, reliable, and compliant is of paramount importance since IoT systems are often safety-critical. At the same time, testing these kinds of systems can be difficult due to the wide set of disparate technologies used to build IoT systems (hardware and software) and the added complexity that comes with Big Data (the three "V", huge volume, great velocity and big variety).

To the best of our knowledge, IoT software testing has been mostly overlooked so far, both by research and industry [14]. This is evident if one looks at the related scientific literature, where proposals and approaches in this context are extremely rare.

I. Garrigós and M. Wimmer (Eds.): ICWE 2017, LNCS 10544, pp. 125–138, 2018.
https://doi.org/10.1007/978-3-319-74433-9_11

In this work, we propose a novel approach for acceptance testing of IoT systems using a UI (in our specific case study, a smartphone) as principal way of interaction between the user and the system. The approach is performed at the system level and is based on two main ingredients: virtualization and the usage of automated visual testing tools that are able to drive the UI (i.e., the smartphone). We focus on acceptance testing, a type of black box testing based on the concept of test scenario, i.e., a sequence of actions performed on the system interfaces, which is considered by many organizations [13][1] the most effective way to ensure the quality of a fully deployed system. In fact, assembling the system and testing it as a whole is the most logical and effective way to ensure the quality. At the same time, this task can also be quite challenging for complex IoT applications.

This paper is organized as follows: Sect. 2 presents an invented but realistic testing scenario based on a mobile health IoT system. Section 3 describes our proposal for acceptance testing of IoT systems, with examples and a detailed description of the used testware. Finally, Sect. 4 presents the related works comparing them with our proposal, followed by conclusions and future work in Sect. 5.

2 The Testing Scenario: A Diabetes Mobile Health IoT System

We have chosen a diabetes mobile health IoT system as testing scenario for two reasons. First, these systems are incredibly difficult to test and no consolidated approaches have been proposed for them in literature. Second, many software apps for smartphones and IoT systems are now available for diabetes and are intended to assist patients to make decisions for themselves in real time [7].

This proliferation of apps and systems is due to the fact that diabetes is a very common disease that doubles a person's risk of early death. Just to give two estimates [2]: 422 million people have diabetes worldwide (2016) and the World Health Organization (WHO) reports that diabetes resulted in 1.5 million deaths in 2012, making it the 8th leading cause of death [1]. Insulin therapy is often an important part of diabetes treatment and it is injected to the patient to keep the blood glucose level low.

2.1 The Scenario

Let's suppose the following fictitious but realistic scenario. A *Company* has completed the implementation of its DiaMH system after several months of work and now it has to be tested. DiaMH is a Diabetes Mobile Health IoT system that: (1) monitors the patient's glucose level, (2) sends alerts to the patient and the doctor when a glucose level or a pattern of glucose levels is out of a pre-specified target range, and (3) regulates insulin dosing. DiaMH, sketched in Fig. 1, consists of the following components: a wearable glucose sensor, a wearable insulin pump,

---

[1] in [13] this kind of testing is called end-to-end testing.

a patient's smartphone, a doctor's smartphone and a cloud-based healthcare system. Glucose sensor and insulin pump are devices (respectively, the sensor and the actuator) connected to the smartphone that is used as a "bridge" between them and the cloud-based healthcare system. Moreover, the smartphone is used by the patient to visualize the glucose tendency and give commands to the system, e.g., to accept the novel dose of insulin suggested by DiaMH. The cloud-based healthcare system is the core of DiaMH and is able to process big data and turn it into valuable information (alerts and novel doses of insulin). The complete list of functionalities of DiaMH is explained in the next subsection.

Fig. 1. Components and actors of DiaMH

A thorough testing phase is required because the *Company* would like to request FDA (US Food and Drug Administration) to include DiaMH on its approved list. The boss of the *Company* is aware that it will be difficult because few treatment apps for any disease have been approved by the FDA to actually make decisions or treatment recommendations [7]. For this reason, she forms a team of testers and selects as project manager the best one in the *Company*. His fancy name is Jim.

The team has three months of time for: (1) selecting a testing approach, (2) producing a test plan, (3) implementing the testware, i.e., the testing infrastructure[2], and (4) testing the system. The challenge seems impossible because DiaMH is a complex, real-time, safety critical IoT system.

Jim knows that for convincing his boss to apply to the FDA he has to quickly realize a testware able to determine whether DiaMH satisfies the acceptance criteria (acceptance testing).

After having surfed the Internet and consulted the literature, Jim discovers that there are no well-documented approaches that can be used for acceptance

---

[2] Testware includes artifacts produced during the test process such as, test scripts, inputs, expected results, set-up and clear-up procedures, files, databases, environment, and any additional software or utilities used in testing.

testing purposes. He found only very general non-scientific papers concerning testing of IoT systems[3] and several proposals for testing bioinformatics software (e.g., [3]). Unfortunately, these works cannot be used for his purpose since they do not describe a specific solution for testing a complex m-health IoT system like DiaMH. Jim is desperate. What should he do? After a first moment of discouragement a possible idea "takes shape"[4] in his mind.

A possible way to determine whether DiaMH satisfies the acceptance criteria is using two ingredients: test automation tools/frameworks and mock devices (e.g., virtual or simulated ones). Test automation tools are used to execute test scripts in unattended way, report the results, and compare them with earlier test runs. Test automation tools/frameworks [9] control the execution of test scripts giving commands directly on the UI (e.g., the smartphone interface) and reading actual outcomes to be compared with predicted outcomes. Mock devices are pieces of software that mimic the behaviour of real devices (e.g., the glucose sensor) in controlled ways (e.g., providing glucose profiles of different kinds of diabetics patients). The idea taking shape in Jim's mind is building a set of acceptance test scripts for the acceptance criteria that, when executed, can drive the DiaMH system execution giving commands on the smartphone UI, as a real patient does, and verifying the correctness of the DiaMH system through the UI interface.

2.2 DiaMH Functionalities, Components and Protocols

This section specifies the functionalities of DiaMH, clarifies the role of the components, and sketches possible protocols to be used for implementing DiaMH. The following description has been inspired by two previous works: a Parasoft white paper [13] and the paper by Istepanian et al. [6].

The *glucose sensor* (e.g., SugarBeat®[5]) is a pain-free, non-invasive, needle-free sensor, that monitors the blood for detecting the glucose level, and performs measurements in timed intervals (sampling). The intervals can be set by the patient using the *smartphone* with a specific command (e.g., at 15 min intervals). Moreover, another command performs measurements on request. The glucose sensor is wirelessly connected to an app on the smartphone. The app stores the values locally and provides a UI so that the user can monitor the glucose levels in the blood and compare them with historical data. More precisely, glucose data are displayed on the smartphone screen with symbols that represent the *direction and value of glucose*. Other data displays include graphic representations indicating the *glucose pattern* over varying periods of time. The app running on the smartphone, in addition to provide simple analyses and charts to the user, transmits glucose level data to a cloud-based healthcare system for persistent storage and additional analyses.

---

[3] e.g., https://devops.com/functional-testing-iot/.

[4] note that since DiaMH is a safety critical system, also other verification techniques, not considered in this paper, should be applied (e.g., runtime verification [11], model checking [4]).

[5] http://www.nemauramedical.com/sugarbeat/.

The *insulin pump* follows a programmed schedule controlled wirelessly by the smartphone. Smartphone, glucose sensor and insulin pump use the Bluetooth Low energy technology[6] to communicate among them. MQTT[7] is the protocol used in the communication between smartphones, sensors, actuators, and healthcare system.

The *healthcare system* running on the cloud is the core of the DiaMH IoT system. It stores the data of all the patients, compares them to historical data, performs advanced analyses, computes the insulin quantities that should be injected by the insulin pump and sends alerts to the doctor and patient in case of danger, i.e., when problematic patterns are identified. To perform the analyses and control the insulin pump, the healthcare system uses cognitive computing, machine learning algorithms and, in general, artificial intelligence mechanisms. Indeed, establishing the "correct" dose of insulin is incredibly complex, since the insulin requirements are affected by the individual's physiology, the type and duration of daily activity, work schedule, exercise, illness and concomitant medications [12]. The alert sent to the patient contains some data, such as a guidance for the next steps and changes to the insulin dose (if any) to be delivered to the insulin pump. After the patient's approval, changes to the insulin dose are transmitted to the pump and set. When a problematic pattern is identified (i.e., something that requires immediate medical attention which cannot be solved only by injecting a certain quantity of insulin), the healthcare system sends an alert directly to the user's app and to the doctor's app. The alert sent to the doctor contains the GPS coordinates of the patient and a summary of her medical conditions.

3   Acceptance Testing for Healthcare IoT Systems: A Proposal

Testing the example system described in the previous section poses significant challenges, given that DiaMH is composed of several components (applications and devices containing logics) working together and with risk of individual fail. Moreover, further problems could derive by the integration of the components. Indeed, it is well-known that an "imperfect" integration can introduce a myriad of subtle faults.

In general, a complete test plan should include a combination of unit testing (components should be isolated and tested early), integration testing (components should be tested as a group, proceeding, e.g., bottom-up), and acceptance testing, and should be conducted at two different levels:

1. testing a *virtualized version of DiaMH*, where real hardware devices are not employed. In their place, Virtual devices (e.g., a mock glucose sensor) have to be implemented and used for stimulating the applications under test. At this level the goal is testing only the software produced by the *Company*,

---

[6] https://en.wikipedia.org/wiki/Bluetooth_low_energy.
[7] http://docs.oasis-open.org/mqtt/mqtt/v3.1.1/mqtt-v3.1.1.html.

i.e., the apps (for patients and doctors) running on the smartphones and the healthcare system running in the cloud. Thus, possible unwanted behaviours of DiaMH due to hardware or network problems cannot be detected in this setting.

2. testing the *real IoT DiaMH system* complete of applications and devices (i.e., glucose sensor and insulin pump). The goal here is testing the system in real conditions, i.e., under real world scenarios like communication of the application with hardware, network, and other applications.

Since the system is safety-critical, both testing phases should be conducted because the former (i.e., on the virtualized system) could favour earlier implementation problems detection and could potentially reveal more faults (timings of sensors and actuators can be made shorter and thus a huge quantity of tests can be run in a short time). Moreover, since DiaMH is a safety critical system, other useful verification techniques should be applied (e.g., runtime verification [11], model checking [4]), but these are out of the paper's goal. In this work, we mainly focus on phase (1) because: it is the first one that a test team has to face, it can be conducted without employing real sensors and actuators that can be complex to use/set and more expensive. Indeed, imagine how could be complex to test a dangerous life threatening scenario using a real glucose sensor. Moreover, since devices used in m-health systems are usually certified, they are not the main reason of failure of the entire system. Finally, we focus on acceptance testing because this phase seems to be neglected more than the others in the IoT domain, since the specific peculiarities of testing an IoT system (e.g., composed by different platforms, relying on various communication protocols, and including complex behaviours of smart-devices) are more evident when testing the whole system than when testing the single, isolated components.

Our proposal for facing the testing phase (1) is based on two concepts: virtualization (in particular simulation and emulation) and usage of automated visual testing tools. Simulation is used to model the devices. More precisely, the glucose sensor and the insulin pump are simulated via software, respectively, for stimulating the DiaMH system with selected inputs and for recovering the actual outputs of DiaMH to be compared with expected outputs. The real behaviour of each smartphone is emulated; that means that the real code of the smartphone will be executed on an emulator (e.g., Android Emulator[8]) able to mimic the real behaviour of the smartphone's app and visualize the UI of the smartphone on the PC screen. On the same PC an automated testing tool is installed. The testing tool will execute the test scripts that: – interact with the UI of the emulated smartphones, and – set the behaviour of the virtualized sensors (e.g., the glucose sensor should return a certain sequence of values representing a "problematic pattern"). Figure 2 reports an overview of the elements involved in our approach: the testware (i.e., the virtualized mocks for glucose sensor and insulin pump and the test scripts), the emulated smartphones, and the healthcare cloud system.

---

[8] https://developer.android.com/studio/run/emulator.html.

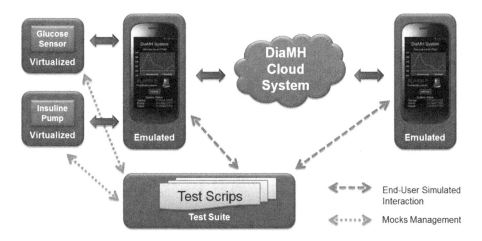

Fig. 2. Sketch of the testware used for testing `DiaMH`

3.1 Testware Implementation

Currently, our research group is working on the testware implementation, i.e., mocks for glucose sensor and insulin pump and the test suite for a sample system analogous, from a functional point of view, to the aforementioned `DiaMH` system.

For implementing the mocks we selected Node-RED[9], a flow-based visual programming language built on Node.js which has been expressly designed for wiring together hardware devices, APIs and online services by means of JavaScript nodes that can be easily created and combined with a rich browser-based flow editor. Moreover, Node-RED is also used to wire the mock devices with the emulated smartphones and with the healthcare cloud system using the MQTT protocol. All these software components (mock devices and emulated smartphones) will be uploaded on the IBM Bluemix[10] cloud, where the healthcare cloud system is already deployed. The execution of the emulated smartphones will allow to test the real implementation of the `DiaMH` mobile apps (i.e., one for the patients and one for the doctors). Note that since the `DiaMH` mobile apps implementation is done by relying on the Adobe PhoneGap cross-platform framework[11], iOS, Android and Windows Phone versions of the `DiaMH` mobile apps will be generated.

The second ingredient of our approach is the test suite and the corresponding testing tool. Several approaches can be employed to automate acceptance testing [9]. They can be classified using two main criteria:

1. *how test cases are developed.* It is possible to use the capture/replay or the programmable approach;

---

[9] https://nodered.org/.

[10] https://www.ibm.com/cloud-computing/bluemix/.

[11] http://phonegap.com/.

2. *how test scripts localize the UI elements to interact with*. There are three main approaches: visual (where image recognition techniques are used to locate UI elements), UI structure-based (a.k.a. DOM-based in the context of the web apps, where UI elements are located using the information contained in the Document Object Model and a locator is, for instance, an XPath expression [10]), and coordinates-based (where screen coordinates of the UI elements are used to interact with the app under test).

In our approach, we adopt the programmable approach for developing the test scripts since it provides a major flexibility over capture/replay for test development [9]. Programmable acceptance testing is based on manual creation of a test script. Test scripts can be written using ad-hoc languages and frameworks or general purpose programming languages (such as Java) with the aid of specific libraries. Usually, these libraries extend the programming language with user friendly APIs, providing commands to, e.g., click a button, fill a field and submit a form.

In this work we adopt the visual approach for interacting with the UI since test scripts have to interact with the UIs of mobile apps developed for different platforms (i.e., those supported by Adobe PhoneGap). In this case, the visual approach allows to create test scripts totally agnostic from the tested platform except, in some cases, for the locators since some UI elements are rendered differently among platforms.

Concerning the testing tool, we use Sikuli[12] that is based on the programmable and visual approaches, and developed as an open-source research project of the MIT User Interface Design Group. Sikuli is a visual technology able to automate and test graphical user interfaces using screenshot images. It provides image-based UI automation functionalities to Java programmers.

3.2   Test Cases, Test Scripts and Setup

In the context of this work, a *test case* is a list of actions performed on the DiaMH system followed by one or more assertions. A Sikuli *test script* is the implementation of a test case based on the Sikuli framework, and consists of a list of commands/instructions able to localize and interact with UI components, completed with JUnit assertions. Test cases must reflect the requirements of the system. To simplify the description, in the following of the paper we focus on test scripts concerning only the Android-based version of the patients mobile app. The app versions for the other platforms are functionally equivalent (unless cosmetic changes of the UIs).

We expect that the DiaMH system works correctly[13] when stimulated by the mock glucose sensor providing values taken from log files containing real glucose

---

[12] http://www.sikuli.org/.

[13] i.e., that it behaves as specified by the requirements in response to the currently observed glucose pattern. For instance, an alarm is displayed when a problematic pattern is detected (see Test case TC1).

patterns recorded from diabetic patients (see Fig. 3). Having realistic input data is fundamental in order to test the DiaMH system under realistic conditions.

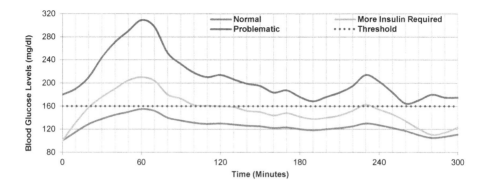

Fig. 3. Glucose patterns: Normal, More Insulin Required, and Problematic

The test suite will contain several test scripts for verifying the behaviour of the DiaMH system when different patterns are detected. For instance, when the test script that implements the test case TC1 (see below) will set the mock glucose sensor to "problematic pattern modality", we expect an alarm on the patient's smartphone. We speculate a pattern as problematic after 20 consecutive values over the threshold of 160 mg/dl of glucose in the blood (see Fig. 3).

Test case TC1

- **set** the mock glucose sensor to "problematic pattern modality" (i.e., 20 consecutive values over the threshold of 160 mg/dl)
- **set** the mock glucose sensor sampling rate at 1 read/sec[14]
- after 60 s, **assert** alarm displayed on the patient's smartphone[15]

Figure 4 shows what should be displayed on the smartphone screen in case a "problematic pattern" is detected by the DiaMH system (i.e., the interface of the DiaMH patient mobile app at the end of TC1, when the assertion is evaluated).

Figure 5 reports a simplified implementation of a Sikuli test script implementing TC1. The smartphone app interface is encapsulated by one (and in general more) Java classes as prescribed by the *Page Object* pattern (see DiaMH app = new DiaMH()).

---

[14] the log files plotted in Fig. 3 contain fictitious but realistic glucose level readings recorded every 10 min, thus using the mock of the glucose sensor at 1 read/sec allows to speed up the execution of the test of 600x.

[15] since the mock of the glucose sensor provides a new value every second, and all of them are above the 160 mg/dl threshold, after 20 s the system can, in theory, raise the alarm. However, some computations are required on the cloud system. For this reason, system requirements state that the alarm must be shown on the smartphone within 40 s the occurrence of a problematic pattern, thus the test verifies the presence of the alarm after 20 s + 40 s from the first read.

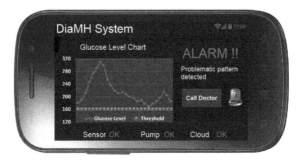

Fig. 4. Smartphone UI of the `DiaMH` app when a "problematic pattern" is detected

```
public void testProblematicPattern(){
 commonFunction.startApp("DiaMH");
 // wait => app loading
 wait(3);
 DiaMH app = new DiaMH();
 // check if DiaMH app is started
 assertTrue(app.isTitleDisplayed(new URL("Title.png")));
 // set mock glucose sensor in "problematic pattern" modality
 GlucoseSensor gs = new GlucoseSensor();
 gs.setPatternTo("Problematic");
 // set sampling at 1 sec
 gs.setSamplingRate(1);
 // wait => pattern "Problematic" should be detected after <= 60s
 wait(60);
 assertTrue(app.isAlarmDisplayed(new URL("Alarm.png")));
 }
```

Fig. 5. Test script for testing the display on the patient screen of an alarm raised in case of problematic pattern detection

The *Page Object*[16] pattern is a quite popular test design pattern, which aims at improving the test case maintainability and at reducing the duplication of code. A page object is a class that represents the UI elements as a series of class attributes and that encapsulates the features of the UI page into class methods. Adopting the *Page Object* pattern in test scripts implementation allows testers to follow the *Separation of Concerns* design principle, since the test scenario is decoupled from the implementation. Usage of *Page Object* pattern reduces the coupling between UI pages and test scripts, promoting reusability, readability and maintainability of the test suites [8] (note that Page Objects can be automatically generated [16] and transformed [17]). Similarly, the behaviours of the glucose sensor and the insulin pump are encapsulated in classes that contain methods implementing the commands required to execute specific actions on the mocks. For instance, the method "setPatternTo" (see Fig. 5) provides the mock glucose sensor with a glucose pattern recorded in an input file (i.e., a series of consecutive glucose levels).

---

[16] http://martinfowler.com/bliki/PageObject.html.

We can see in the example two visual interactions used for evaluating the two assertions: in one case verifying that the app has been correctly loaded (hence showing the DiaMH System string, see Fig. 5), while in the other verifying that the alarm message is displayed as expected. It is worth noting that Sikuli can be also used for simulating other kinds of interactions with the UI (e.g., clicking a button or typing in a field). Here, we have shown only an example of visual assertions for the sake of simplicity.

Similarly, also the other patterns can be tested by means of specific test cases. For instance, TC2 verifies the behaviour of the DiaMH system when the glucose levels are fine, while TC3 when an additional injection of insulin is required.

Test case TC2

– **set** the mock glucose sensor to "normal pattern modality" (slight changing values all near an optimal level of glucose and always below the threshold)
– **set** the mock glucose sensor sampling rate at 1 read/sec
– after 40, 60 and 120 s: **assert** NO alarm on the patient's smartphone

Test case TC3

– **set** the mock glucose sensor to "more insulin pattern modality" (in the last 20 reads there are at least 4 but not more than 15 values above the threshold of 160 mg/dl)
– **set** the mock glucose sensor sampling rate at 1 read/sec
– after 60 s: **assert** an increment of 2 units of insulin on the patient's smartphone

3.3 Strengths and Weaknesses of the Approach

In our opinion the major strengths of the proposed approach are the following: (1) the complexity of the entire IoT system is hidden, (2) test cases can be easily automated by adopting visual testing tools, (3) under certain conditions, test cases on a virtualized system can be executed in a fraction of the time required by the real settings.

On the other hand the weaknesses include: (1) tests are usually time consuming to develop, (2) tests are prone to non-determinism problems (i.e. the test outcomes could be influenced by factors that are outside the test control), (3) tests are prone to the fragility problem (i.e., a test that is broken when the application under test is slightly modified), (4) it is not easy to pinpoint the root cause of failure since anything in the entire flow could have contributed to the error, (5) visual test cases can verify only the functionalities of the system that provide a visible feedback on the GUI.

4 Related Work

To the best of our knowledge, this is the first paper concerning explicitly acceptance testing of IoT systems.

Rosenkranz *et al.* in [14] consider testing of IoT systems, but the goal is presenting a test system architecture for open-source IoT software instead of a general approach for acceptance testing of IoT systems as we propose. Before presenting a possible test architecture for open-source IoT systems, Rosenkranz *et al.* sketch some challenges that are specific to IoT systems. For example, heterogeneity of hardware and interoperability testing. With the Rosenkranz *et al.* proposal, we share two fundamental points: the importance of virtualization in IoT systems testing and the conviction that testing must be performed also on real devices to ensure that the combination of software and hardware works as requested.

Siboni *et al.* [15] propose a security testbed framework for testing wearable devices against external simulated attackers to cover different aspects of security design requirements. The testbed can emulate different environments (including mobile), can generate stimuli from simulated sensors, and can produce reports for data exploration and analysis. The testbed is then evaluated by a proof-of-concept. The goal of that work is different from ours: security testing for wearable devices instead of acceptance testing of a whole IoT system.

As already said, the case study used in this work has been inspired by a Parasoft white paper [13]. In that paper, the key ideas are: de-constructing the system into layers for effective testing, isolating components to improve automation and using a service testing solution for testing components. For testing the healthcare system, the service testing solution stimulates the virtualized glucose sensor and propagates to the system the obtained values. Then, the same service testing solution will be able to verify the alert irruption (if any). Our approach differs from the Parasoft's one in three respects. First, we explicitly envisage acceptance testing, while using the Parasoft's approach is difficult for a user to evaluate and accept the IoT system under test (because the interaction between the components is hidden in the service testing solution and not visible on the smartphone as in our case). Second, the solution proposed by Parasoft is more difficult to implement than ours without the commercial Parasoft tool. Third, our proposal is more complete: it tests together the smartphone's apps and the healthcare system (in particular the interactions between them), while the Parasoft proposal cannot test the software running on the smartphone (because that role is played by the Parasoft tool).

5   Conclusions and Future Work

In this work, we have presented an approach for acceptance testing of IoT systems. To explain the approach we used a realistic m-Health system composed by local sensors and actuators, a remote cloud-based healthcare system using artificial intelligence and two smartphones. However, the proposed approach is not limited to the m-health context, but can be applied to all the IoT systems that rely on smartphones as principal way of interaction between the user and the system.

As future work, we plan to complete the implementation of the testware sketched in this paper, write some test scripts and fine-tune the approach. Ongoing work is currently under-way to build up and integrate the Node-RED based mock sensors and the smartphone application. In the future, we also intend to experiment our testing approach with other IoT systems to verify its real applicability and scalability and extend our proposal to support also the acceptance test driven development of IoT systems [5]. A possible problem of the approach concerns the time for executing test scripts automatically; indeed we believe that in worst cases test suite execution could take long time.

Acknowledgements. This research was partially supported by Actelion Pharmaceuticals Italia and SEED 2015 grants.

References

1. The top 10 causes of death. World Health Organization (WHO), Geneva, Switzerland (2013). http://www.who.int/mediacentre/factsheets/fs310
2. Global Report on Diabetes, 1st edn. World Health Organization (WHO), Geneva (2016). http://www.who.int/diabetes/global-report/en/
3. Chen, T.Y., Ho, J.W., Liu, H., Xie, X.: An innovative approach for testing bioinformatics programs using metamorphic testing. BMC Bioinform. **10**(1), 24 (2009)
4. Clarke, E., Grumberg, O., Peled, D. (eds.): Model Checking, pp. 67–114. MIT Press, Cambridge (1997). https://doi.org/10.1007/978-3-319-10575-8
5. Clerissi, D., Leotta, M., Reggio, G., Ricca, F.: Test driven development of web applications: a lightweight approach. In: Proceedings of 10th International Conference on the Quality of Information and Communications Technology, QUATIC 2016, pp. 25–34. IEEE (2016)
6. Istepanian, R., Hu, S., Philip, N., Sungoor, A.: The potential of internet of m-health things "m-IoT" for non-invasive glucose level sensing. In: 33rd International Conference of the IEEE Engineering in Medicine and Biology Society, EMBC 2011, pp. 5264–5266 (2011)
7. Klonoff, D.C.: The current status of mHealth for diabetes: will it be the next big thing? J. Diab. Sci. Technol. (JDST) **7**(3), 749–758 (2013)
8. Leotta, M., Clerissi, D., Ricca, F., Tonella, P.: Capture-replay vs. programmable web testing: an empirical assessment during test case evolution. In: Proceedings of 20th Working Conference on Reverse Engineering, WCRE 2013, pp. 272–281. IEEE (2013)
9. Leotta, M., Clerissi, D., Ricca, F., Tonella, P.: Approaches and tools for automated end-to-end web testing. Adv. Comput. **101**, 193–237 (2016)
10. Leotta, M., Stocco, A., Ricca, F., Tonella, P.: ROBULA+: an algorithm for generating robust XPath locators for web testing. J. Softw. Evol. Process **28**(3), 177–204 (2016)
11. Leucker, M., Schallhart, C.: A brief account of runtime verification. J. Logic Algebraic Program. **78**(5), 293–303 (2009)
12. McAdams, B.H., Rizvi, A.A.: An overview of insulin pumps and glucose sensors for the generalist. J. Clin. Med. 5(1) (2016)
13. Parasoft. End-to-end testing for iot integrity. Technical report. https://alm.parasoft.com/end-to-end-testing-for-iot-integrity

14. Rosenkranz, P., Wählisch, M., Baccelli, E., Ortmann, L.: A distributed test system architecture for open-source IoT software. In: Proceedings of 1st Workshop on IoT Challenges in Mobile and Industrial Systems, IoT-Sys 2015, pp. 43–48. ACM (2015)
15. Siboni, S., Shabtai, A., Tippenhauer, N.O., Lee, J., Elovici, Y.: Advanced security testbed framework for wearable IoT devices. ACM Trans. Internet Tech. (TOIT) **16**(4), 26 (2016)
16. Stocco, A., Leotta, M., Ricca, F., Tonella, P.: APOGEN: automatic page object generator for web testing. Softw. Qual. J. **25**(3), 1007–1039 (2017). https://doi.org/10.1007/s11219-016-9331-9
17. Leotta, M., Stocco, A., Ricca, F., Tonella, P.: PESTO: Automated migration of DOM-based web tests towards the visual approach. J. Softw. Test, Verification Reliab. (STVR) (2018, to appear)

International Workshop on the Practice of the Open Web

Preface

The aim of this workshop has been to bring together researchers, practitioners, stakeholders and users of the *Open Web*, meant as a huge and easily accessible source of data, information and services. The focus of the workshop has been therefore on practical engineering approaches *(i)* to design and develop open data and services on the Web (i.e., the Web seen as an output media of an organization's information system), on the one side, and *(ii)* to design and develop open source intelligence and retrieval techniques on the other side (i.e., the Web seen as input media of an organization's information system). Submitted papers described practical engineering approaches, case studies, and lessons learned.

PRACTI-O-WEB 2017, the International Workshop on the Practice of the Open Web, was held on June 5, 2017 in Rome, Italy, in conjunction with the 17th International Conference on Web Engineering (ICWE 2017), and consisted of five papers and a keynote talk. Those five accepted papers, out of several submissions, exactly provide a good overview of the above mentioned topics. Some of them, namely "Using Ontologies for Official Statistics: the Istat Experience" by Scannapieco et al., "Towards a UML and IFML mapping to GraphQL" by Rodriguez-Echeverria et al., and "Accessing Government Open Data through Chatbots" by Porreca et al., focus on the point *(i)*, i.e., on the Open Web seen as the output of an information system. Others, namely "Ontology Population from Raw Text Corpus for Open-Source Intelligence" by Ganino et al., and "ABC Algorithm for URL Extraction" by Lalit Mohan et al., conversely focus on the Web seen as an input to the organization's information system, addressing the interesting topics of harvesting, crawling and intelligence from the Web in the larger meaning. Each paper was reviewed by three members of the internationally renowned Program Committee. The program was completed by a keynote talk by Domenico Fabio Savo (Sapienza Università di Roma) on "Introducing Ontology-based Open Data Publishing".

We would like to thank all the Program Committee members for their valuable work in selecting the papers, and the ICWE 2017 consulting agency Consulta Umbria for the organization of this successful event.

June 2017

Evangelos Kalampokis
Francesco Leotta
Massimo Mecella

Organization

Chairs

Francesco Leotta	Sapienza Università di Roma, Italy
Evangelos Kalampokis	University of Macedonia and Centre for Research & Technology-Hellas, Greece
Massimo Mecella	Sapienza Università di Roma, Italy

Program Committee

Yu Asano	Hitachi, Japan
Peter Haase	Metaphacts, Germany
Armin Haller	Australian National University, Australia
Paul Hermans	ProXML, Belgium
Marijn Janssen	TUDelft, Netherlands
Sabrina Kirrane	Vienna University of Economics and Business - WU Wien, Austria
Domenico Lembo	Sapienza Università di Roma, Italy
Nikos Loutas	PwC, Belgium
Fadi Maali	SAP, Ireland
Peyman Nasirifard	Volkswagen AG, Germany
Vassilios Peristeras	International Hellenic University, Greece
Bill Roberts	Swirrl, UK
Domenico Fabio Savo	Sapienza Università di Roma, Italy
Monica Scannapieco	ISTAT, Italy
Efthimios Tambouris	University of Macedonia, Greece

ABC Algorithm for URL Extraction

Lalit Mohan Sanagavarapu$^{(\boxtimes)}$ ⓘD, Sourav Sarangi, and Y. Raghu Reddy

International Institute of Information Technology, Gachibowli, Hyderabad, India
lalit.mohan@research.iiit.ac.in, sourav.sarangi@students.iiit.ac.in,
raghu.reddy@iiit.ac.in

Abstract. Seed URLs, Content Classification, Indexing and Ranking are key factors for search results relevance. Domain specific search engines (DSSE) provide more relevant search results as they have lesser ambiguity issues. For wide usage of DSSEs, identification of seed URLs and related child URLs is required. Identification of seed URLs has been manual and takes longer duration for building/decisioning on URL availability for DSSE. We propose nature inspired Artificial Bee Colony algorithm for identification and scoring of seed and child URLs. We implemented the algorithm on 'Security' domain and extracted 34,007 seed URLs from Wikipedia data dump and 323,488 child URLs using the seed URLs. Based on the volume and the relevance of the extracted URLs, a decision for building a DSSE can be made easily.

Keywords: ABC algorithm · URL extraction
Domain specific search · Crawler

1 Introduction

There are 1+ Billion websites with more than 3+ Billion internet users. Google, Bing, Baidu, etc. continue to be popular generic search engines with some estimates stating that they indexed more than one exabyte of data and consumed a million+ computing hours for crawling and indexing. The relevance of search results is still an area of concern. For improved search relevance, Domain Specific Search Engines also referred as Vertical Search Engines are gaining wider acceptance. Some of the popular Domain Specific Search Engines (DSSE) are Google Scholar, Yahoo Finance, PubMed, etc. Relevant seed URLs and the related child URLs are required for DSSE. Most of the DSSEs have a manual approach for identification of seed URLs and this would delay the process of building DSSEs. Also, for someone to make a decision to build DSSE, they have to perform a guess work on the number of URLs available in the domain, this could impede the decision process. We propose an automated approach for URL (seed and child) identification of a domain. Our proposed approach draw's inspiration from Artificial Bee Colony (ABC) algorithm because of its exploration and exploitation capability.

© Springer International Publishing AG, part of Springer Nature 2018
I. Garrigós and M. Wimmer (Eds.): ICWE 2017, LNCS 10544, pp. 143–148, 2018.
https://doi.org/10.1007/978-3-319-74433-9_12

Artificial Bee Colony (ABC) and other nature inspired algorithms[1] are used for Vehicular design, Computer virus detection, Optimization for higher dimensional problems, etc. ABC [8] is an optimization algorithm based on intelligent foraging behaviour of honey bee/agent swarm. ABC algorithm is being used in combinatorial and functional optimization, routing and wavelength assignment in all-optical networks, etc. In ABC algorithm, Scout Agent (Bee) finds location of seed URL (flower patches) for extraction of webpage content (food). Employee Agents (Bee) extracts content (food) from identified child URLs (flowers) of the seed URL (flower patch) and evaluates neighbour source. After extraction, Employee Agent (Bee) provides direction (IP address) similar to Bee dances in the hive and the number of URLs (flowers) available for webpage content extraction (food). Onlooker Agents (Bees) moves in IP address direction for further webpage content (food) extraction. Completed seed URLs (food sources) are determined and new seed URL (flower patches) are identified by Scout Agents (Bees). Best seed URL (food source) is registered based on number of relevant child URLs (nectar carrying flowers).

There is growing interest and concern among IT users on 'Security' with increased internet and IT adoption. We propose the implementation of ABC algorithm for 'Security - Information and Cyber' domain URL extraction. In the following sections of the paper, the literature survey on seed URL extraction, proposed approach, results and analysis and followed by conclusion are presented.

2   Related Work

Seed URL identification and extraction is a manual process for most of the DSSEs. We look at the existing work on seed URL extraction, crawlers algorithms and focused crawlers. Zheng et al. [12] proposed a graph based framework for seed selection and compares it with algorithms such as $Maxout$, $MaxWeight$, $MaxSCC$ (strongly connected components), etc. Zheng's work describes how the crawlers can use existing seed URLs but does not contain literature on seed URLs identification. Du et al. [4] uses ontology created by domain experts for obtaining seed URLs. However, the work does not establish coverage across subdomains. Pappas et al. [11] identifies topics using dynamic seed URLs and evaluates topic relevance. In this work, the identification of seed URLs is manual. As available literature on seed URL is limited, we looked at focused crawlers literature.

Focused crawlers use Anchor text [2], Content text classification [9], Reinforcement learning, Ontology, Context graph [3], Page properties, Key word base [5], Clickstream [1], etc. for obtaining domain content. Generic search engines that seek to cover as much proportion of web as possible usually implement a Breadth-First Search or Depth-First Search algorithm [10] for content extraction. However, the research for optimizing URL extraction process except for threading and queuing is limited. Most of the scalable opensource crawlers implement threading and queuing. However, in any of these (generic or focused crawler) approaches,

---

[1] http://www.algorithmsinnature.org/.

there isn't an optimized way for determining number of runtime agents/threads based on existing/newly identified seed URLs. Also, the division of labour for seed URL identification, providing information on additional threads and direction to crawl, content extraction has not been implemented.

While there are controversies in terms of borrowing nature's behaviour for optimization, Bee algorithms continue to be adopted and considered for situations requiring collective intelligence, optimization and routing [7].

3 Approach

The scouts in the algorithm perform the initial exploration process of identifying the source of seed URL. Onlookers and employed agents/threads extract the webpage content of the URLs for relevance, thus performing an exploitation action. Generally, the initial count of scouts in ABC algorithm is a random number, however, we have fixed it as 11 - these are subdomains of 'Security' domain. The 11 subdomains of 'Security' are identified from 'Information Security' - ISO 27001:2013 standards ('Access', 'Management', 'Operations Control', 'Physical', 'Network', 'Application', 'Endpoint', 'Hardware' and 'Cloud Computing'). We also included 'Cyber Security' and 'Attacks' to represent the 'Security' domain as there is an overlap between 'Information Security' and 'Cyber Security' in the form of attacks. The ABC algorithm for extraction of seed and child URLs is shown in Algorithm 1.

Algorithm 1. Extract URLs of a Domain

Data: Domain Name, Subdomains[]
Result: Seed and Child URLs of a Domain
  Initialize WikiAPI;
  Initialize subdomain.maxCycle, subdomain.runtime;
  Open WikiDump;
  while *Subdomains of Domain* **do**
    subdomain.KeyPhrases[] = Extract from WikiDump;
    subdomain.runtime = Size of subdomain.KeyPhrases[];
    for *run=0 ; run < subdomain.runtime ; run++* **do**
      | subdomain.initialize();
    end
    subdomain.maxCycle = subdomain.maxCycle + subdomain.runtime;
  end
  for *iter=0;iter < subdomain.maxCycle;iter++* **do**
    subdomain.SendURLThreads();
    subdomain.CalculateSimilarity();
    subdomain.SendOnlookerThreads();
    subdomain.MemBestSeed();
    subdomain.SendScoutTheads();
  end

For each of these subdomains, we used Wikipedia datadump and *Wiki Python API* for extracting the keyphrases of the subdomains and the seed URLs. The implementation of the algorithm is available at Github[2]. Scouts, Employee and Onlookers agents/threads are implemented as threads in our Python implementation. The various functions in ABC algorithm are described below

- **subdomain.KeyPhrases[]**: Array contains the Keyword phrases of 11 'Security' subdomains.
- **subdomain.initialize()**: Number of seed URLs are initialized randomly and fitness of each seed URL of a subdomain is computed. This task is performed by the initial scout thread of a subdomain and hence supports exploration.
- **subdomain.runtime**: Number of Threads based on the Keyword phrases in the Wikipedia text.
- **subdomain.maxCycle**: Total number of threads based on the Keyword phrases of all subdomains.
- **subdomain.MemBestSeed()**: The best seed URL is memorized by the thread. The scoring for best seed URL is based on the number of out-of-domain links (links that do not belong to the same URL domain) and text similarity of the webpage with the sub-domain.
- **subdomain.SendURLThreads()**: In this function, thread generates a random score that is a mutant of the original solution. If the new URL contains more similarity value to the subdomain, the earlier URL is replaced with the new URL otherwise the earlier URL is retained.
- **subdomain.CalculateSimilarity()**: The Onlooker thread chooses a URL based on the similarity value associate with the seed URL.
- **subdomain.SendOnlookerThreads()**: IP addresses of URLs are used for providing the direction for URL content extraction, clusters are formed based on sorted IP Address. IP routing algorithms are standardized and optimizated for faster fetch. We do not make any claim in crawling time reduction based on IP address.
- **subdomain.SendScoutTheads()**: The trial parameter is defined for those solutions that are exhausted and not changing. This function determines those seed URLs and abandons them.

We implemented this approach as against other nature inspired collective intelligence algorithms as threads to be initialized can vary based on the availability of child URLs and there is no requirement of leaving a trace of the path to the food source (URL). The number of parameters to control and the scalability of the ABC algorithm makes it a better fit as compared to other approaches [6]. Also, the capability of self-organization and division of labor is necessary and sufficient condition for ABC algorithm that makes it efficient.

---

[2] https://github.com/souravsarangi/SeedURLWork.

4 Results and Analysis

Our approach extracted 34,007 seed and 400,726 child URLs[3] of 'Security' domain as shown in Table 1 with an average number of 12 child URLs per seed URL. 'Network' and 'Attacks' subdomain has higher number of seed and child URLs. However, 'Endpoint' has higher average child URLs per seed. For similarity, we use Phrase2Vec[4] similarity method on extracted content and keyword phrases of the subdomain. Phrase2Vec is trained on Google NewsArchives (100 Billion Words) and provides literal and semantic similarity and is considered as a robust Neural Networks based algorithm. We use metadata description of a webpage instead of entire webpage content for obtaining similarity score so that the processing time for identification of URL relevance is shorter and storage space requirement is also less. We executed the algorithm on 8 GB RAM Quadcore machine for a period of 18 h to extract the URLs (Seed and Child) and the metadata of Child URLs representing 11 subdomains of 'Security'. The Table 1 shows the results of URLs extracted for each of the subdomains and the count of child URLs per seed URL.

Table 1. URL coverage across subdomain using ABC

Subdomain	Seed	Child	URLs/Seed
Access	638	8,240	13
Application	2,417	27,006	11
Attacks	9,381	78,719	8
Cloud Computing	1,526	18,519	12
Cyber	1,884	14,253	8
Endpoint	3,825	63,101	16
Hardware	409	5,389	13
Management	2,327	30,453	13
Network	6,159	88,256	14
Operations Control	907	11,716	13
Physical	4,534	54,374	12

In the exploitation process, we implemented zero depth (metadata extraction only in the URL page and we did not go into each of the in-domain webpages of the website) for algorithm demonstration; threads initiation and content download are limited by machine capability and internet bandwith. In the extracted URLs, we realized that 77,238 URLs had 'HTTP 404' error or could also have been obstructed due to robots.txt. These URLs did not provide any insight into seed URL relevance in some of the cases and have been excluded in similarity calculation.

---

[3] http://tinyurl.com/URLData.
[4] https://radimrehurek.com/gensim/models/phrases.html.

5   Conclusions

Usage of ABC algorithm optimized the number of threads required for identification of seed and child URLs and extraction of metadata from child URLs. Through our proposed approach, we extracted 323,428 URLs that can be used for building 'Security' Search Engine. In our algorithm, we plan to implement other crawler functionalities such as re-visit, politeness, selection, etc. and other parallelization goals for minimizing overheads and maximizing download rate. This implementation can be used to benchmark our results with existing open-source crawlers. We plan to experiment our approach for other domains such as Agriculture, Banking, etc. to establish generality.

References

1. Ahmadi-Abkenari, F., Selamat, A.: An architecture for a focused trend parallel web crawler with the application of clickstream analysis. Inf. Sci. **184**(1), 266–281 (2012)
2. Chakrabarti, S., Punera, K., Subramanyam, M.: Accelerated focused crawling through online relevance feedback. In: Proceedings of the 11th International Conference on World Wide Web, pp. 148–159. ACM (2002)
3. Diligenti, M., Coetzee, F., Lawrence, S., Giles, C.L., Gori, M., et al.: Focused crawling using context graphs. In: VLDB, pp. 527–534 (2000)
4. Du, Y., Hai, Y., Xie, C., Wang, X.: An approach for selecting seed urls of focused crawler based on user-interest ontology. Appl. Soft Comput. **14**, 663–676 (2014)
5. Frank, E., Paynter, G.W., Witten, I.H., Gutwin, C., Nevill-Manning, C.G.: Domain-specific keyphrase extraction. In: 16th International Joint Conference on Artificial Intelligence (IJCAI 99), vol. 2, pp. 668–673. Morgan Kaufmann Publishers Inc., San Francisco (1999)
6. Karaboga, D., Akay, B.: A comparative study of artificial bee colony algorithm. Appl. Math. Comput. **214**(1), 108–132 (2009)
7. Karaboga, D., Akay, B.: A survey: Algorithms simulating bee swarm intelligence. Artif. Intell. Rev. **31**(1–4), 61–85 (2009)
8. Karaboga, D., Gorkemli, B., Ozturk, C., Karaboga, N.: A comprehensive survey: artificial bee colony (abc) algorithm and applications. Artif. Intell. Rev. **42**(1), 21–57 (2014)
9. McCallum, A., Nigam, K., Rennie, J., Seymore, K.: A machine learning approach to building domain-specific search engines. In: IJCAI, vol. 99, pp. 662–667. Citeseer (1999)
10. Najork, M.: Web crawler architecture. In: Encyclopedia of Database Systems, pp. 3462–3465. Springer (2009)
11. Pappas, N., Katsimpras, G., Stamatatos, E.: An agent-based focused crawling framework for topic-and genre-related web document discovery. In: IEEE 24th International Conference on Tools with Artificial Intelligence, vol. 1, pp. 508–515. IEEE (2012)
12. Zheng, S., Dmitriev, P., Giles, C.L.: Graph-based seed selection for web-scale crawlers. In: Proceedings of the 18th ACM Conference on Information and Knowledge Management, pp. 1967–1970. ACM (2009)

Towards a UML and IFML Mapping to GraphQL

Roberto Rodriguez-Echeverria[1]([✉]), Javier Luis Cánovas Izquierdo[2], and Jordi Cabot[3]

[1] Quercus SEG, Universidad de Extremadura, Cáceres, Spain
rre@unex.es
[2] UOC, Barcelona, Spain
jcanovasi@uoc.edu
[3] ICREA – UOC, Barcelona, Spain
jordi.cabot@icrea.cat

Abstract. Web APIs have become first-class citizens on the Web, in particular, to provide a more unified access to heterogeneous data sources that organizations want to make publicly available. While REST APIs have become the norm to structure web APIs, they can be regarded as a server-side solution, offering default limited query capabilities and therefore forcing developers to implement ad-hoc solutions for clients requiring to perform complex queries on the data. Lately, GraphQL has gained popularity as a way to simplify this work. GraphQL is a query language for Web APIs specially designed to build client applications by providing an intuitive and flexible syntax for describing their data schema, requirements and interactions. In this paper we propose an approach for the generation of GraphQL schemas from UML class diagrams and IFML interaction models, two well-known standard modeling languages in the web engineering field, to facilitate the creation of web applications relying on this new GraphQL paradigm following a model-based approach. While UML is used to generate the GraphQL schema, IFML is used to derive the set of queries and modifications to be performed on that schema.

Keywords: GraphQL · UML · IFML · Web APIs

1 Introduction

To design and develop open data and services on the Web, organizations may rely on model-driven engineering (MDE) approaches [2]. These kind of approaches have been widely used in the web engineering community to model and (semi)automatically generate many types of web applications [7,11,12].

This work has been supported by the Spanish government (ref. TIN2016-75944-R).

© Springer International Publishing AG, part of Springer Nature 2018
I. Garrigós and M. Wimmer (Eds.): ICWE 2017, LNCS 10544, pp. 149–155, 2018.
https://doi.org/10.1007/978-3-319-74433-9_13

Typical languages used in this context are UML (or ER and its variations) for the definition of the domain models or data structures and IFML-like languages (that generalizes many other languages proposed by the web engineering community in the past) to express the user interactions.

With the push of Web APIs, which are increasingly becoming first-class citizens on the Web, some MDE approaches have been extended to support organizations looking to publish their data sources online, specially as Representational State Transfer (REST) APIs [5].

Still, we believe this is not enough to really enable the publication and consumption of open data on the Web. While REST APIs offer many benefits, they can be regarded as, mainly, server-side solutions offering very limited default query capabilities. Therefore, MDE tools can only very partially cover the generation of complete web applications on top of REST APIs, specially if the web application needs to integrate several kinds of (possibly heterogeneous) backends. In those cases, an ad-hoc integration of the external sources is always required [8–10].

The recent popularization of GraphQL is a very good opportunity to solve this problem. GraphQL is a query language for Web APIs developed by Facebook and released in 2015 for describing the capabilities and requirements of data models for Web applications. A GraphQL document comprises two declarations: a schema declaration defining the types of the objects that can be queried, and the actual queries/modifications to be performed on them. The language has been designed to build client applications by providing an intuitive and flexible syntax and system for describing their data requirements and interactions, offering a seamless and uniform language description to access the data, no matter where this data resides. It is up to the web application server to translate/execute the requests.

Therefore, extending current MDE tools to generate GraphQL specifications from UML and IFML models can be a key tool to facilitate the exploitation of online data sources. To advance in this direction, in this paper we present a set of mappings between both sets of languages. The mapping covers the main UML and IFML elements, which are transformed into GraphQL types and queries respectively.

The rest of the paper is structured as follows. Section 2 presents GraphQL and a running example. Section 3 describes the mapping between UML and GraphQL while Sect. 4 explores the IFML to GraphQL mappings. Section 5 concludes the paper and presents some future work.

2   Background and Running Example

GraphQL includes two different sublanguages: query and schema. The former, specified by Facebook[1], is intended for the definition of query and mutation requests on the data, which follows the specific schema defined with the latter.

---

[1] http://facebook.github.io/graphql/.

Then the GraphQL server will execute the requests on the backend where the data actually resides.

UML class diagrams may be used to represent the static data organization of GraphQL schemas. To represent the dynamic aspects (queries and modifications) several alternatives exist, including UML behavioral diagrams (sequence diagrams, state machines), OCL expressions (e.g. as part of query operations or contracts) or interaction languages like IFML [3], the preferred option to express basic user interaction patterns with the data, specially in a web context. Therefore, in this paper we will focus on the UML and IFML mapping to GraphQL, covering the schema and query sublanguages respectively.

To illustrate our approach, we use a running example based on the reference example provided in GraphQL documentation[2]. Figure 1a shows the UML model of our running example, which models the cast of the first trilogy of Star Wars. The model includes classes to represent characters (see **Character** hierarchy), starships piloted by human characters and reviews for the films. Note that films are modeled as an enumeration type according to the example provided by GraphQL (which also help us to illustrate some mapping specificities). Figure 1b shows a IFML model which illustrates two kind of interaction scenarios involving (1) listing the casting of an episode and the details of a particular character of Star Wars (queries), and (2) adding a review to one of the films (mutation). Given these models, our objective is to obtain the corresponding GraphQL schema. Listing 1.1 shows the GraphQL schema for our example.

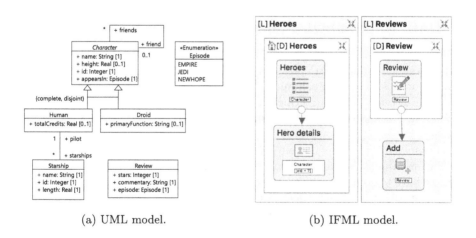

(a) UML model.   (b) IFML model.

Fig. 1. Running example.

---

[2] http://graphql.org/learn.

Listing 1.1. GraphQL schema.

```
scalar Date

enum Episode {
  NEWHOPE
  EMPIRE
  JEDI
}

interface Character {
  id: ID!
  name: String!
  friends: [Character]
  appearsIn: [Episode]!
}

type Human implements Character {
  id: ID!
  name: String!
  friends: [Character]
  appearsIn: [Episode]!
  starships: [Starship]
  totalCredits: Int
}

type Droid implements Character {
  id: ID!
  name: String!
  friends: [Character]
  appearsIn: [Episode]!
```

```
  primaryFunction: String
}

type Starship {
  id: ID!
  name: String!
  length: Float
}

input ReviewInput {
  id: ID!
  stars: Int!
  commentary: String
  episode: Episode!
}

type Query {
  casting(episode: Episode): [Character]
  character(id:ID!): Character
}

type Mutation {
  createReview(episode: Episode,
   review: ReviewInput): ReviewInput
}

schema{
  query: Query
  mutation: Mutation
}
```

In the following, we show the mappings to generate the GraphQL schema an query documents from the UML and IFML models, respectively.

3   UML to GraphQL Mapping

UML class diagrams are used to drive the generation of the GraphQL schema definition. Table 1 (upper part) presents an excerpt of the main mappings we have defined for this. The first column indicates the UML metaclass to be mapped while the second column describes the GraphQL snippet to be generated. Due to space limitations, we only comment in detail the transformation of class hierarchies.

Class hierarchies are not supported in GraphQL. Therefore, similarly to UML to relational database implementations [6], which suffer the same limitation, we have to come up with a strategy to flatten these hierarchies. Among the possible strategies, in this paper we generate an object type from every concrete class in the hierarchy. Each object type must explicitly contain all the fields inherited or defined by the source class. In addition to the types, we create a set of GrahpQL interfaces that then allows us to manipulate homogeneously all objects of the same "superclass". Interfaces are generated for every class, including abstract ones. Same as before, each interface must explicitly contain all the fields inherited or defined by the UML element (note that a GraphQL interface is just a collection of field definitions, no explicit operations are defined). Finally, **implement** relationships are set among the object types generated and their corresponding interfaces, i.e. interfaces generated from every class along its path to the root.

Table 1. UML (class diagram) and IFML to GraphQL mapping.

UML METACLASS	GRAPHQL	LANGUAGE
c : Class	type c.name {...}	Schema
i : {Abstract Class, «Interface»}	interface i.name {...}	Schema
c : Class.implements -> i : «Interface»	type c.name implements i.name {...}	Schema
a : {attrs., assocs. max. mult. 1}	a.name : a.type (field)	Schema
a : assocs. max. mult.>1	a.name : [a.type] (field)	Schema
e : «Enumeration»	enum e.name {...}	Schema
el : Enum Literal	el.name (enum value)	Schema
f : structural feature min mult. 1	f.name : f.type! (type marker)	Schema
t : Type not in GraphQL scalar types	scalar t.name	Schema
Hierarchy	Interface(s) & Object Type(s)	Schema
IFML METACLASS	GRAPHQL	LANGUAGE
f : ViewComponent «form»	input f.name	Schema
db : ViewComponent Part «DataBinding»	db.name: db.type (input field)	Schema
View Container (most external)	schema	Schema
v : ViewComponent «details», «list»	query v.name	Query
v : ViewComponent «form» + Action	mutation v.name	Query
db : ViewComponentPart «DataBinding»	db.name : db.type (field)	Query
p : ParameterBinding	(p.name: p.type) (argument)	Query
ce : ViewComponent Part «ConditionalExpression»	@include(if: ce) (directive)	Query

In our example presented at Fig. 1, the UML class hierarchy comprising the abstract class **Character** and the concrete classes **Human** and **Droid** is transformed into the interface **Character** and the types **Human** and **Droid** in the GraphQL schema (see Listing 1.1). Note that both types implements the **Character** interface and define their own fields together with the ones from the interface.

4   IFML to GraphQL Mapping

Every GraphQL Web API has a query type and may have an additional mutation type as root types. They are defined as regular object types, but they are special because they define the entry point of every GraphQL query or mutation. Indeed, those types collect, in form of fields with arguments, all the different queries (or mutations) defined over the schema, as the types **Query** and **Mutation** in Listing 1.1. In our approach, these special GraphQL types are created from the collection of every query (or mutation) definition generated from the IFML model.

In particular, GraphQL queries and mutations can be generated out of View Component definitions in the IFML model. *«list»* and *«details»* stereotypes become queries since they define a view over a data entity by filtering which data objects to show (parameter binding) and which attributes to present (fields). In our example, *«list»* view component **Heroes** is transformed into the query **casting** which is listed in the **Query** type (root query) of the resulting GraphQL schema. At the same time, the query **character** with the argument **id** is created from the *«details»* **Hero details** and the parameter binding (id) represented by the navigation flow.

Additionally, *«form»* stereotyped view components would be transformed into mutations and input types, which collects the data fields parameterizing the invoked mutation. In our example, the *«form»* view component and its associated action `Add` are transformed into the mutation `createReview` which is listed in the `Mutation` type (root mutation) of the resulting GraphQL schema.

Mappings sketched in Table 1 have been implemented as a model-to-model transformation between the UML metamodel and the GraphQL metamodel[3] generated thanks to XText [1].

5   Conclusion and Future Work

In this paper we have presented an approach to generate GraphQL schemas and queries out of UML class and IFML models, respectively. We believe our approach properly aligns with current MDWE approaches enabling designers to deploy their applications into GraphQL-enabled infrastructures. The generated GraphQL document (including both schema and queries/mutations) can be used in any Web application to provide an uniform access to the data.

As future work, we would like to continue expanding our approach to support additional modeling capabilities, like arbitrary query expressions specified in OCL (Object Constraint Language) or other similar languages. We also plan to consider reverse engineering scenarios, where developers want to make existing web applications GraphQL-enabled. Reverse engineering scenarios would require analyzing the current data schema (and querying facilities) to provide the corresponding support in GraphQL. In these scenarios UML and IFML models could play the role of a pivot intermediate representation between the current platform and the new GraphQL interface. Finally, we would like to explore how to integrate our approach with other tools to create Web applications combining different technologies (e.g., based on REST API generation or OData [4]).

References

1. Bettini, L.: Implementing Domain-Specific Languages with Xtext and Xtend. Packt Publishing, Birmingham (2013)
2. Brambilla, M., Cabot, J., Wimmer, M.: Model-Driven Software Engineering in Practice. Synthesis Lectures on Software Engineering. Morgan & Claypool Publishers, San Rafael (2012)
3. Brambilla, M., Fraternali, P.: Interaction Flow Modeling Language. Morgan Kaufmann, San Francisco (2014)
4. Ed-douibi, H., Cánovas Izquierdo, J.L., Cabot, J.: A UML profile for OData web APIs. In: Cabot, J., De Virgilio, R., Torlone, R. (eds.) ICWE 2017. LNCS, vol. 10360, pp. 420–428. Springer, Cham (2017). https://doi.org/10.1007/978-3-319-60131-1_28
5. Fielding, R.T.: Architectural styles and the design of network-based software architectures (2000)

---

[3] https://github.com/SOM-Research/graphQL-xtext-grammar/releases/tag/0.1.

6. Fowler, M.: Patterns of Enterprise Application Architecture. Addison-Wesley Longman Publishing Co., Inc., Boston (2002)
7. Fraternali, P.: Tools and approaches for developing data-intensive web applications: a survey. ACM Comput. Surv. **31**(3), 227–263 (1999)
8. Herzig, D.M., Tran, T.: Heterogeneous web data search using relevance-based on the fly data integration. In: World Wide Web Conference, pp. 141–150 (2012)
9. Preda, N., Kasneci, G., Suchanek, F.M., Neumann, T., Yuan, W., Weikum, G.: Active knowledge: dynamically enriching RDF knowledge bases by web services. In: International Conference on Management of Data, pp. 399–410 (2010)
10. Quarteroni, S., Brambilla, M., Ceri, S.: A bottom-up, knowledge-aware approach to integrating and querying web data services. TWEB **7**(4), 19:1–19:33 (2013)
11. Rossi, G., Pastor, O., Schwabe, D., Olsina, L. (eds.): Web Engineering: Modelling and Implementing Web Applications. Human-Computer Interaction Series. Springer, Heidelberg (2008)
12. Valderas, P., Pelechano, V.: A survey of requirements specification in model-driven development of web applications. TWEB **5**(2), 10 (2011)

Accessing Government Open Data Through Chatbots

Simone Porreca[1], Francesco Leotta[1(✉)], Massimo Mecella[1], Stavros Vassos[2,3], and Tiziana Catarci[1]

[1] Dipartimento di Ingegneria Informatica Automatica e Gestionale Antonio Ruberti, Sapienza Università di Roma, Rome, Italy
porreca.1673726@studenti.uniroma1.it,
{leotta,mecella,catarci}@diag.uniroma1.it
[2] Helvia, Athens, Greece
[3] Helvia, Tallinn, Estonia
stavros@helvia.io

Abstract. In this paper, we propose to employ chatbots as an interface for open data published by organizations, specifically focusing on public administrations. Open data are especially useful in e-Government initiatives but their exploitation is currently hampered to end users by the lack of user-friendly access methods. On the other hand, current UX in social networks have made people used to chatting. Building on cognitive technologies, we prototyped a chatbot on top of the OpenCantieri dataset published by the Italian Ministero delle Infrastrutture e Trasporti, and we argue that such a model can be extended as a generally available access method to open data.

1 Introduction

Open data generally refers to the idea that some data should be freely available to everyone to use and republish as they wish, without restrictions from copyright, patents or other mechanisms of control. In particular, according to the Open Definition, "a piece of data is open if anyone can freely access, use, modify, and share for any purpose (subject, at most, to requirements that preserve provenance and openness)"[1]. Some characteristics should be granted to provide open data, namely *(i)* accessibility – all the users can freely access to data, mostly free or at a very low cost, *(ii)* machine readability – data can be naturally "understood" and processed by machines, *(iii)* rights – data are released under certain licenses that bound softly the usage, the transformation and the distribution of those data.

Much related to open data, *open government* is the governing doctrine that supports the right of citizens to access the documents and proceedings of the government for an effective public oversight. Enabling interested citizens to get more directly involved in the legislative process, making government information

---

[1] cf. http://opendefinition.org/.

© Springer International Publishing AG, part of Springer Nature 2018
I. Garrigós and M. Wimmer (Eds.): ICWE 2017, LNCS 10544, pp. 156–165, 2018.
https://doi.org/10.1007/978-3-319-74433-9_14

available to the public as machine readable open data, can facilitate government transparency, accountability and public participation. Opening up official information can support technological innovation and economic growth by enabling third parties to develop new kinds of digital applications and services. Notably, the first speech and memo of Barack Obama as US President in 2009 was about open government and transparency: "More citizens are petitioning their governments online, and more citizens are participating directly in policymaking. More entrepreneurs are using open data to innovate and start new businesses. More sunlight is shining on how tax dollars are spent. And more governments are partnering with civil society to find new ways to expose corruption and improve good governance"[2].

Several national governments have created sites to distribute a portion of the data they collect, e.g., the European Commission has created two portals for the European Union: the EU Open Data Portal[3] giving access to open data from the EU institutions, agencies and other bodies, and the Public Data portal[4] providing datasets from local, regional and national public bodies across Europe. In October 2015, the Open Government Partnership (OGP) launched the International Open Data Charter, a set of principles and best practices for the release of governmental open data formally adopted by seventeen countries (including Italy[5]) during the OGP Global Summit in Mexico.

Despite all these initiatives, access from citizens to such open data is not always as large as expected. Technical issues often inhibit easy access from citizens, if no specific user-friendly applications are built on top of such open data for easy access and navigation. Currently the most of these applications consist in tables or some other kind of visual representations, which can be constructed directly from the data or through a preliminary normalization, in order to increase the homogeneity of the presented information. The main drawback of this approach is that it is not so easy to consult, especially when the amount of data is particularly large. In addition, when the diversity of data is elevated, the visualization might result messy, affecting the user's capability of performing comparisons and evaluations. This results in a decrease in the system's usability and, thus, in a not large diffusion among consumers. The most natural way for an user to interact is through the natural language.

In this, we present the disruptive idea of adopting chatbots as user-friendly access and querying method to open data. Nowadays persons are used to chat with friends over popular applications (e.g., WhatsApp or Facebook Messenger), and the typical interaction is indeed based on the paradigm ask – get a response. Citizens accessing open data would appreciate the same paradigm in querying the data, for which a chatbot can be a much more natural way of interaction than traditional web applications.

---

[2] cf. B. Obama, Memorandum of January 21, 2009. Transparency and Open Government. Federal Register, 2009. https://federalregister.gov/a/E9-1777.

[3] cf. http://data.europa.eu/euodp/en/data/.

[4] cf. http://publicdata.eu/.

[5] cf. https://www.opengovpartnership.org/country/italy.

Developing chatbots over open data poses many challenges, such as inter-preting the natural language adopted by users in querying the dataset, and translating into effective queries over the dataset. In this paper, we present a prototype of such a system built using the cognitive platform by IBM, namely Bluemix and related APIs, in order to evaluate the technical feasibility of the proposed idea.

The following of this paper is organized as it follows: Sect. 2 provides some background information and relevant work; Sect. 3 describes the architecture used to build a chatbot over the Open Cantieri dataset, published by the Italian Ministero delle Infrastrutture e Trasporti at http://opencantieri.mit.gov.it, by using a cognitive platform, and Sect. 4 describes the realization aspects. Finally Sect. 5 concludes the paper, by remarking future work, including a user evalua-tion to assess the argued simplicity of use.

2   Background and Relevant Work

Chatbots are computer programs able to hold up a conversation with a user, either in textual or vocal form. Given the growing complexity of information systems, chatbots are specifically designed to support the user interaction and to make it as natural as possible. They do not only represent a faster and more natural way to access information, but they will also be a significant key factor in the process of humanizing machines in the near future [1,2]. Gartner Group estimates that "by 2020, customers will manage 85% of their relationship with the enterprise without interacting with a human". A chatbot is able to simulate a human conversation, which is the most familiar way by which a user could interact with anything, as he is using the natural language; the user does not need to be trained in how to use the interface with the system, as it is some-thing which he is used to. This represents a shift from Graphic User Interfaces (GUIs) to Conversational User Interfaces (CUIs, [7]). Notably it represents a significant advance in human-computer interaction, as it perfectly fits some of Jakob Nielsen's 10 Usability Heuristics[6]. The second one states: "match between system and the real world: the system should speak the users's language, with words, phrases and concepts familiar to the user, rather than system-oriented terms. Follow real-world conventions, making information appear in a natural and logical order"; indeed a chatbot is a perfect example of this principle, as the user can interact with the system through the natural language, which perfectly represents a real-world experience.

In order to correctly and efficiently design a chatbot, many techniques have to be not trivially combined, including pattern matching, parsing, artificial intel-ligence, machine learning, and ontologies. There are numerous approaches and methodologies proposed for this; in this work, we followed the approach that divides the chatbot architecture in three parts: *responder*, *classifier* and *graph-master* [1]. The responder is the interface by which users access the system. It is responsible for taking the input and validate the output. The classifier is

---

[6] cf. https://www.nngroup.com/articles/ten-usability-heuristics/.

located between the responder and the graphmaster. It is dedicated to normalize the input to pass to the graphmaster and processing the output coming from the latter (e.g., interacting with a database). Finally, the graphmaster is the agent responsible to elaborate the correct output to the corresponding input. It represents the pattern matching element of the chain.

Tim Berners-Lee suggested a 5-star deployment scheme for open data[7], being a star when an organization makes data available on the Web (whatever format) under an open license, 2 stars when it makes data available as structured data (e.g., Excel file instead of image scan of a table), 3 starts when data are available in a non-proprietary open format (e.g., CSV as well as of Excel), 4 stars by using URIs to denote things, so that people can point at them and 5 stars when data are linked to other data to provide context [3]. Technologies supporting this vision of linked open data are those ones commonly referred as Semantic Web, including RDF/RDFS, OWL (ontologies) and SPARQL (for querying). In Italy, the AgID - Agenzia per l'Italia Digitale, publishes every year guidelines for Public Administrations on how to publish their data as open, including a model for metadata consisting of 4 levels[8]. In this work, we have built our prototype on the basis of a dataset which can be ranked at most at level 3 of the above classification.

During the last years, some attempts to apply chatbots to query and retrieve data have been made. In [4], a chatbot was constructed on top of some open data. Here the first step is to extract plain text from documents stored as PDF files by employing an optical character recognition (OCR) software. At this point, a set of possible questions about the extracted contents were constructed using a "Overgenerating Transformations and Rankings" algorithm, which was implemented using the question generation framework presented in [5]. Finally, the matching patterns, essential to the chatbot's answering capability, are defined through Artificial Intelligence Markup Language (AIML).

Authors in [6] presents a system, called OntBot, which employs a mapping technique to transform an ontology into a relational database and then uses that knowledge to construct answers. Therefore, likewise our solution, OntBot does not need to handwrite all the knowledge base that stands behind the system. The main drawback of traditional chatbots, implemented for example through AIML, is the fact that the knowledge base has to be constructed ad-hoc by handwriting thousands of possible responses. OntBot, likewise our system, does not construct answers by looking for a matching one inside the database. Instead, it retrieves information from the database, which will be then used to build up the response.

3   Case Study and Proposed Architecture

Open Cantieri, offered by the Italian Ministero delle Infrastrutture e dei Trasporti (MIT), is an open, complete and up-to-date repository about the realization status and history of the public infrastructures. All the available data

---

[7] cf. http://5stardata.info/en/.

[8] cf. http://www.agid.gov.it/agenda-digitale/open-data.

are generated and published by public sources. Open Cantieri offers a unified platform, with specific views, in which all these different datasets are collected together. The platform is a collection of open data in a very raw form: datasets can be downloaded as single CSV files, sometimes grouped in archives. Very often, unfortunately, different files do not employ the same keys to represent concepts (e.g., cities are represented using their code in some files whereas their names is used in others) and manual mapping between different representations was needed. More generally, the files do not follow any standard on field names and reported values.

The system can be accessed through the Facebook Messenger platform just by search its name, which, in this example, is "TestBot01". According to the main HCI principles, it is the user that, on the basis of his/her willingness, start or not the conversation. The system is not sending messages if the user is not currently interacting with it or she/he does not asking for anything. Once the user is ready, he could start the conversation. Figure 1 shows how an interaction with the chatbot. The user starts by greeting the system. As this is the very first interaction of the user and so she/he is not confident with it, she/he asks for help (cf. the *Aiuto* message), in order to understand what can be asked. The system responds by shortly explaining what is known and what it is able to answer to (the balloon tells that *"You can ask me about the public funding*

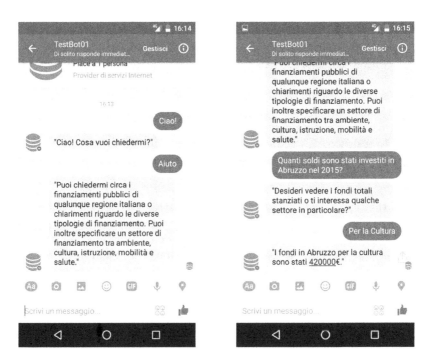

Fig. 1. Some screenshots of the chatbot. The language is Italian in the current prototype

of any Italian region or clarifications regarding the different types of financing. You can also specify a funding sector among environment, culture, education, mobility and health"). Now that the user realizes what the system does, she/he asks for a more specific question, regarding the Italian region *Abruzzo* and the amount of public funding invested in the culture area. From now on, she/he can continue the conversation as she/he prefers, by asking, e.g., about other regions, areas or financing types.

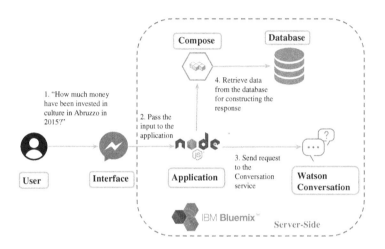

Fig. 2. Architecture

Figure 2 shows the architecture of the proposed solution. The user interface to the system is implemented as a Facebook Messenger application. The back-end core of the system is deployed on the IBM Bluemix cloud computing platform. In particular, a Node.js server-side application handles the requests and constructs the corresponding responses by orchestrating two Bluemix service instances: *(i)* an instance of Watson Conversation, specifically created and trained, which is responsible for processing, and *(ii)* an instance of Compose for MySQL, which handles the connection and the query to the back-end database. In particular, the user interacts through the chat interface, e.g., issuing a question as "How much money have been invested in culture in Abruzzo in 2015?" (step 1). The sentence is forwarded to the Node.js application, which handles it in order to construct the appropriate response (step 2). The Watson Conversation instance receives a request constructed starting from the user input, and generates the corresponding response (step 3). According to the provided response, the Node.js application defines an SQL query to be issued to the database through Compose (step 4). Once all the elements needed to construct the output are collected, the application will proceed to generate the response to be shown through the Facebook Messenger chat.

In order to generate the response, Watson Conversation performs the following operations (the reader should also refer to following subsections): intents and entities extraction; verification of which node, within the Dialog Tree, has conditions satisfied by these information; and, finally, return of the node response. In our specific case, the intent is triggered by "How much money", which is associated to the intention of knowing the investment, and is concerning the intent "#Investment". The entities are: "Abruzzo", which is a specific value of the entity "@Geographical_Region", "culture", which is a specific value of the entity "@Type", and "2015", which is a value of "@Year". In the Conversation response, the application is able to find all the essential information for constructing the output. First of all, a flag, called "DB_Search", is retrieved from the Conversation response in order to understand if a database search is required. This is achieved by constructing the SQL query, starting from the information obtained from Watson Conversation, and by send it to Compose for MySQL, which will retrieve the desired data from the database. The SQL query is specifically constructed with the "Text" included into the Conversation response, which is one of many JSON variables returned with the response itself. Once all the elements needed to construct the output are collected, the application will proceed to generate the users output and send it back through the interface.

In the following, we describe the single components.

3.1 Watson Developer Cloud and Conversation

IBM Watson Developer Cloud (WDC) offers a set of services for developing Cognitive Applications, which consists of programs able to take advantage of the most modern technologies in artificial intelligence, machine learning, and natural language processing. Each WDC service provides a REST API for interacting with it, and most of these services also includes Software Development Kits (SDKs) for various programming languages. In our work we used the Java one.

Inside IBM WDC, the Watson Conversation service allows to create an application that understands natural language input and uses machine learning to respond to users in a way that simulates a conversation between humans. When an instance of this service is created, it is able to contains several *workspaces*. A workspace is a container for all the artifacts that define the conversation flow and it is responsible for the natural language processing operations. A workspace includes the following elements:

Intents. An intent represents the intention and the purpose behind user input. It could be associated with the "goal" the user wants to achieve with every request and thus it is important to define one intent for each type of user request the application has to support. Each intent is prefixed with the character "#" and, during its creation, the developer is encouraged to provide "positive examples", in order to allow the system to construct the corresponding model. A positive example is a sentence that clarifies the way in which the intent could be presented to the system. By collecting at least five positive examples, the instance of the Conversation service will be able to perform a deep learning process, which will train the service itself to recognize that specific intent. The most important fact is to distinctly define each intent from the others. The "borders" between intents should be clear in order to allows the system to correctly recognize them inside user requests. If there is the need for an intent to have more "interpretations", depending on a particular user request, it is possible to make use of another Watson Conversation's element: the Entity.

Entities. An entity is an element, corresponding to a term or an object, that could be used in order to better specify the intention behind a user request. They are frequently used in combination with intents to increase their range of possible interpretations and meanings. Each entity is prefixed with the character "@" and is associated with a set of values. Each value of a specific entity represents an object or a term that belongs to the same category defined by the entity itself. In this way, an entity called "day of the week", could be include values as "Monday", "Thursday", etc. Associated with each value, the developer has the possibility to insert synonyms, in order to be sure that the system will recognize a specific value of the entity even if the user provides it with a different word.

Dialog. The dialog represents the flow of the conversation, divided in several branches, which defines how the application responds when it recognizes the defined intents and entities. The dialog is composed by several nodes, structured in a tree-like graph. At a very basic level, each node is defined by two main elements: the condition and the response. When the condition, composed by elements like intents and entities, is satisfied, the node is considered "activated" and hence its response will be returned as output. The response could be a sentence, another node, or it can be defined by the developer. In order to maintain the state of the conversation through each interaction with the user, the instance service keeps a JSON variable called "context". In this element there are several variables, which can be customized by the developer, and, among them, there is the "Dialog Stack", which contains the stack of all the nodes visited during the conversation and the first one, the "Contextual Node", is the ID of the node that should be returned when the user will start another interaction, within the same session, with the instance of the service Watson Conversation.

3.2 Compose for MySQL

IBM Compose for MySQL is a platform able to simplify the maintenance and the management of a MySQL database; it automatically executes some common operations as backups, scaling and health check. Even though the database can be accessed as a normal MySQL database, the main benefit offered by Compose is that no management aspects (such as security issues or scaling) has to be manually handled.

4 Realization Aspects

As seen in the previous sections, at a certain point of the interaction with the user, the system (through the Compose component) requires to retrieve data from a database in order to build answers. As stated above, the Open Cantieri dataset does not follow any standard, thus a database schema able to rationalize the information contained in the different CSVs has been defined. The result of this operation is a schema that does not match anymore in terms of tables and columns with the original file, making it necessary to proceed to an ETL (Extract, Transform and Load) operation.

Once the database was set up, we had to configure the Watson Conversation service to be able *(i)* to understand user requests, *(ii)* to find out if a database search is needed to fulfill the request, and *(iii)* to present a response template to the user. The response template is filled by the JSP using the data retrieved from the database through the Compose component.

In order to define and create a Watson Conversation instance, we need to define intents and entities useful for our purposes. An intent, in our case, represents an argument the user is interested to, e.g., the highway management or the airport system. In order to correctly define them, we have collected all the possible ways in which a user could refer to them, and then we passed these ones as positive examples in the intent's creation process. An entity, on the other hand, corresponds to the values that may concern a specific intent, e.g., the concessionaire societies for the highway management or the airports of the airport system. All these elements were then used in order to construct the dialog of the Watson Conversation instance. Here, we had to figure out all the possible questions the user might ask and the ways in which he might do it. The user may, for example, specify an argument, and then ask for more specific data about it through other questions. He may specify, as argument, the highway s management and then asks for the name of all the concessionaire societies. The user may, at anytime, specify a new argument or asks for more questions, in a human-like conversation. The system can also recognize when the user insert an invalid input and it will help him to correct it.

5   Concluding Remarks

We have presented our preliminary idea of combining a chatbot with open data. It involves the employment of several novel instruments and services that are increasingly employed by the researchers and practitioners involved in the development of smart services. Our intent was to take advantage of these new technologies in order to make something new, able to improve the accessibility of open government data.

Open data should be accessible to the public; with our prototype, we would like to showcase a new mean to consult them, in such a way that allows the user to easily retrieve and analyze them.

Future work will include an extensive validation of the approach on a sample of users. This evaluation is going to test the usability and functionality of the system. Through the users' participation, the effectiveness of the interaction will be tested. Since the chatbot can be accessed just by using a smartphone, we are going not to distinguish between laboratory or field studies, taking also into account its mobile nature and usage non-specific of a location. The evaluation will be conducted by using some well-known techniques, as think aloud. With this kind of approach, the evaluator will design a set of tasks, which could be related to obtaining some specific information from the system, like "How many routes XYZ is actually managing". The experiment could be repeated as many times as necessary, with a different user each time. Once the hypothesis are set, the user is then invited to sequentially perform the designed tasks, commenting what she/he is doing and what she/he thinks is happening. The evaluator will take notes about the user impressions, without helping her/him to accomplish the tasks. Then, all these information will help to improve the system in its ability to let the user accomplish its tasks.

Additionally, structured data represents only a face of government complexity. Next steps will also include automatic analysis of procedures in order to provide users with a mean to explore bureaucracy in a simpler manner. The conjunction of structured data with unstructured ones may provide public administrations a useful tool to turn open data into something directly usable by citizens.

References

1. Abdul-Kader, S.A., Woods, J.: Survey on chatbot design techniques in speech conversation systems. Int. J. Adv. Comput. Sci. Appl. **6**(7), 72–80 (2015). https://thesai.org/Downloads/Volume6No7/Paper_12-Survey_on_Chatbot_Design_Techniques_in_Speech_Conversation_Systems.pdf
2. Yang, Y.P.: An innovative distributed speech recognition platform for portable personalized and humanized wireless devices. Comput. Linguist. Chin. Lang. Process. **9**(2), 77–94 (2004)
3. Bizer, C., Heath, T., Berners-Lee, T.: Linked data the story so far. Int. J. Semant. Web Inf. Syst. **5**(3), 1–22 (2009)
4. Pichponreay, L., Choi, C.H., Cho, W.S., Kim, J.H., Lee, K.H.: Smart answering chatbot based on OCR and overgenerating transformations and ranking. In: Proceedings of ICUFN 2016. IEEE (2016). https://doi.org/10.1109/ICUFN.2016.7536948
5. Heilman, M., Smith, N.A.: Question generation via overgenerating transformations and ranking. Language Technologies Institute, Carnegie Mellon University, Technical report CMU-LTI-09-013 (2009). http://www.cs.cmu.edu/~ark/mheilman/questions/papers/heilman-smith-qg-tech-report.pdf
6. Al-Zubaide, H., Issa, A.A.: OntBot: Ontology based ChatBot. In: Proceedings of ISIICT 2011. IEEE (2011). https://doi.org/10.1109/ISIICT.2011.6149594
7. McTear, M.F.: Spoken Dialogue Technology: Toward the Conversational User Interface. Springer, London (2004). ISBN 978-0-85729-414-2

Using Ontologies for Official Statistics:
The Istat Experience

Raffaella M. Aracri, Roberta Radini, Monica Scannapieco,
and Laura Tosco[(✉)]

Istat - Italian National Institute of Statistics, Rome, Italy
{raffaella.aracri, roberta.radini, monica.scannapieco,
laura.tosco}@istat.it

Abstract. In this paper, we illustrate some experiences by the Italian National Institute of Statistics (Istat) on using ontologies for the purpose of both data integration and data dissemination. The shown data integration project is based on the Ontology Based Data Management (OBDM) paradigm, proposed for integrating multiple and heterogeneous data sources. The dissemination experience exploits the Linked Data paradigm and led to the publication of the Istat's Linked Open Data portal.

Keywords: OBDM · OBDA · LOD · Ontology-driven data integration
Linked Data

1 Introduction

National Statistical Institutes (NSIs) play an important role as data producers, by publishing Official Statistics in the service of citizens and policy-makers. Statistical production processes are indeed intended to produce "data" as their final output.

A statistical production pipeline mainly consists of: (i) a data collection phase, where both direct data collections, like surveys, and secondary ones, like administrative data acquisitions, are performed; (ii) a data processing and analysis phase where data are corrected, integrated and analyzed and (iii) a data dissemination phase where data are published in accordance to final users' requirements.

In this paper, we will show the current efforts by Istat to address the (macro) phases (ii) and (iii) by exploiting the powerful instrument of ontologies.

In Sect. 2, we will address how the emerging Ontology Based Data Management (OBDM) paradigm is being used to design and implement the new Integrated System of Statistical Registers, which will serve as a pillar of Istat's statistical production.

Section 3, instead, will focus on the use of ontologies to disseminate Istat's data and metadata.

Finally, Sect. 4 will draw some conclusions.

© Springer International Publishing AG, part of Springer Nature 2018
I. Garrigós and M. Wimmer (Eds.): ICWE 2017, LNCS 10544, pp. 166–172, 2018.
https://doi.org/10.1007/978-3-319-74433-9_15

2   Ontology-Based Data Integration System: The New Integrated System of Statistical Registers

Istat has engaged a modernization programme that includes a significant revision of statistical production processes. The focal point of such an important change is the adoption of a system of integrated statistical registers as a base for all the production surveys; this system will be in the following referred to as the Italian Integrated System of Statistical Registers (ISSR). A system of statistical registers consists of a number of registers that can be linked to each other, specifically:

- Base Statistical Registers (BSRs): (i) Persons, Families and Cohabitations; (ii) Economic Units; (iii) Places; (iv) Activities.
- Extended Statistical Registers (ESRs), which extend the information available for a population of a specific BSR with other variables i.e. reproductive stories of women register.
- Thematic Statistical Registers (TSRs), which are not bound to a specific population, but rather they have the objective of supporting statistics referred to more than one statistical population, i.e. labour relationships.

A first initial effort toward the modeling of the ontology for the BSR of Persons, Families, and Cohabitations, is shown in Fig. 1. The ontology is expressed in OWL2 and is represented through Graphol, a notation equivalent to OWL2 [2, 3]. The main concepts of the ontology are:

- **Person**: represents single person for which we describe gender, date of birth, citizenship, place of birth, educational level and other features;
- **Family**: represents a group of persons bound by marriage, kinship, affinity, adoption, guardianship, or affection, cohabiting and having their usual residence in the same municipality. A family can also be made by one person.
- **Nuclear Family**: represents a group of persons forming a couple relationship or parent-child type; namely married or cohabiting couple without children or with never-married children, or a single parent with one or more children never married.
- **Cohabitation**: represents a group of persons who, without being bound by marriage, kinship, affinity, lead life together for religious reasons, care, assistance, military, prisons and others.

All these concepts are linked by several roles, examples of relevant ones are:

- **Relationship**: represents all kind of relations linking two Persons. It is detailed in sub-properties i.e. relativeOf as marriedOf, parentOf (and its inverse son/daughterOf), and affectiveRelationship as cohabitant.
- **Stays**: links a Person to the concept StayingPlace. This role is detailed in the followings: usualResidence, livesIn and residence, each describing the different reason why a Person stays in a place.

The design and implementation of the information architecture of the ISSR relies on the Ontology Based Data Management (OBDM) paradigm [1]. The main reasons underlying the choice of this paradigm are:

- The complexity of the metadata asset (structural metadata asset or intensional data representation) in terms of hugeness and lack of a direct control (several sources are administrative ones that come with their own semantics). The use of ontologies, which permits a formalization and a machine-actionable representation of such metadata, looks promising in order to deal with such a complexity.
- National Statistical Institutes have a long experience in dealing with metadata. However, OBDM has a major difference with respect to approaches typically used within NSIs for designing and implementing metadata management systems, namely: ontologies permit to represent metadata "coupled" with data, so they are not only limited to a "documentation" role but they do permit to "govern" the data integration step by ensuring the quality of integrated data.
- The need for having an integration layer permitting to virtualize data resources and performing "on-the fly" query answering. We think that OBDM can properly answer to such a requirement of the ISSR as an alternative to rigid and materialized traditional data integration approaches like traditional data warehousing.

Figure 2 shows an excerpt of mapping assertions, expressed through a notation introduced in [17], that maps the tuples of three relations of a relational database to the corresponding instances of classes and properties of the ontology showed in Fig. 1.

3   The Ontology-Based Dissemination Channel: datiopen.istat.it

Being "data" the final output of a statistical production process, that is data are the final product that Istat supplies to its end-users, it is very important that released data are semantically enriched. In this respect, the Linked Data paradigm [4], based on ontologies to model data, proved to be extremely suitable as part of the dissemination strategy of Istat.

Istat has published a LOD Portal, available at the URL: http://datiopen.istat.it/index.php?language=eng. The initial set up was for the purpose of disseminating the 15th Italian Population and Housing Census Data [5]. This project started in 2012, much earlier than the project described in Sect. 2. So far, there is still the need to integrate the dissemination system with the integration one, which is however among our main objectives.

Data are conceptually modeled through two ontologies expressed according to OWL (Ontology Web Language) [6]:

- The Territorial Ontology that describes the administrative and the geographical organization of the Italian territory. More in detail, the Territorial Ontology describes the administrative organization of the territory, namely: region, province, municipality and geographical-statistical organization of the territory as location, Census section, special areas or special units (like, e.g., abbeys or hospitals).

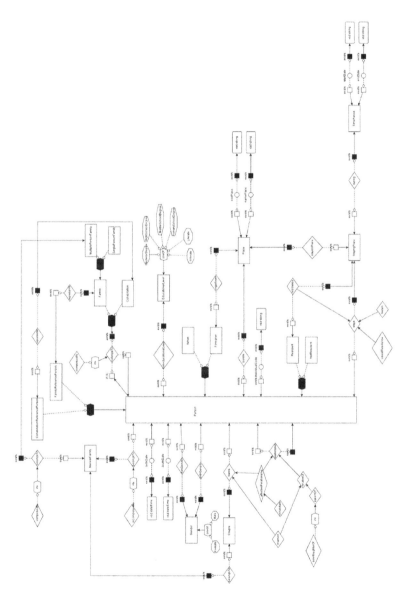

Fig. 1. Ontology for the base statistical register of persons, families and cohabitations

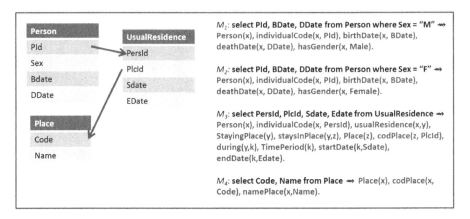

Fig. 2. Excerpt of mapping rules

- The Census Data Ontology that models the actual aggregated Census data. We used the Data Cube Vocabulary [7] to describe the Population and Households census data in terms of measures (e.g., number of residents) and dimensions (e.g., sex or age classes).

Figure 3 shows an example of an observation expressed with the Data Cube Vocabulary.

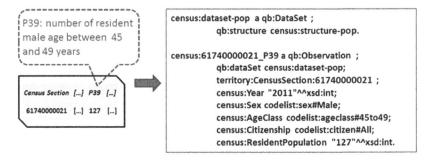

Fig. 3. Example of a Data Cube observation

Both ontologies make use of meta ontologies as: (i) SKOS [8] for the description of classifications, (ii) ADMS [9] for the description of interoperability assets, and (iii) PROV ontology [10] for the description of the provenance of the data in terms of information about entities, activities, and people involved in the data production process.

The Linked Data paradigm results to be relevant also for metadata dissemination: global uniform naming and addressing are crucial for structural metadata like classifications, code lists, cube dimensions, etc. Istat moved several steps towards the conceptual modeling of classifications [11] to be disseminated through its LOD portal.

Moreover, the statistical community develops metadata standard of good quality, but these standards are "not" represented in formal languages; indeed, such models are mainly described in MS Word documents, XLS files, or UML diagrams that is they are not available internally or for other users in open and machine-actionable formats. Important efforts have been paid to the definition of ontologies for such models (e.g. General Statistical Information Model - GSIM ontology [12], General Statistical Business Process Model - GSBPM ontology [13] and Common Statistical Production Architecture - CSPA ontology [14]). In addition, the need for integrating such models among each other and resolve inconsistencies brought to a specific UNECE project "Implementing ModernStats Standards - Linked Open Metadata" [15]. It is nice to observe how the OWL representation of GSIM, GSBPM and CSPA highlighted some inconsistencies among them (and even within each model) [16].

4 Conclusions

The use of ontologies within an NSI can be relevant for both integration and dissemination purposes.

The integration usage is mainly intended for internal statistical users that can benefit from having:

- Access to integrated data: for instance the "labour" concept has different definitions according to different statistical domains like National Accounts, Structural Business Statistics and Labour Force Survey. Ontologies permit that such different definitions can coexist and underlying data can be accessed consistently.
- Reasoning capability: even if some concepts are not "explicitly" linked, reasoning over ontologies allows to "infer" new knowledge (e.g. new relationships). In this way, statistical users can "discover" implicit patterns that can help in understanding data for their analyses.

The dissemination users, mainly external users of Official Statistics, can greatly benefit from the Linked Open Data portal by (i) exploiting services built on machine-to-machine accessible data, and (ii) retrieving data in a transparent way with respect to their physical location (e.g. by accessing simultaneously multiple publication endpoints).

References

1. Lenzerini, M.: Ontology-based data management. In: Proceedings of the 20th International Conference on Information and Knowledge Management (CIKM 2011), pp. 5–6 (2011)
2. Graphol. http://www.dis.uniroma1.it/∼graphol
3. Console, M., Lembo, D., Santarelli, V., Savo, D.F.: Graphol: ontology representation through diagrams. In: Proceedings of the 27th International Workshop on Description Logic (2014)
4. Linked Data. http://linkeddata.org/

5. Aracri, R., De Francisci, S., Pagano, A., Scannapieco, M., Tosco, L., Valentino, L.: Publishing the 15th Italian population and housing census in linked open data. In: The Proceedings of the 2nd International Workshop on Semantic Statistics (2014)
6. Ontology Web Language (OWL), 10 February 2004. http://www.w3.org/TR/owl-ref/
7. Data Cube Vocabulary, 25 June 2013. http://www.w3.org/TR/2013/CR-vocab-data-cube-20130625/
8. Simple Knowledge Organization System (SKOS), 18 August 2009. http://www.w3.org/TR/2009/REC-skos-reference-20090818/
9. Asset Description Metadata Schema (ADMS). https://joinup.ec.europa.eu/asset/adms/home
10. PROV Ontology, 30 April 2013. http://www.w3.org/TR/2013/NOTE-prov-overview-20130430/
11. Lodi, G., Maccioni, A., Scannapieco, M., Scanu, M., Tosco, L.: Publishing official classification in linked open data. In: The Proceedings of the 2nd International Workshop on Semantic Statistics (2014)
12. Scannapieco, M., Tosco, L., Gillman, D., Dreyer, A., Duffes, G.: An OWL ontology for the generic statistical information model (GSIM): design and implementation. In: The Proceedings of the 4th International Workshop on Semantic Statistics (2016). http://ceur-ws.org/Vol-1654/article-03.pdf
13. Cotton, F., Gillman, D.: Modeling the statistical process with linked metadata. In: The Proceedings of the 3rd International Workshop on Semantic Statistics (2015). http://ceur-ws.org/Vol-1551/article-06.pdf
14. Dreyer, A., Duffes, G., Cotton, F.: An OWL ontology for the common statistical production architecture. In: The Proceedings of the 4th International Workshop on Semantic Statistics (2016). http://ceur-ws.org/Vol-1654/article-06.pdf
15. IMS – Implementing ModernStats Standard Project. http://www1.unece.org/stat/platform/pages/viewpage.action?pageId=122323917
16. Implementing ModernStats Standards Linked Open Metadata Design Guidelines. http://www1.unece.org/stat/platform/download/attachments/129172661/HLG-MOS%20-%20IMS%20Design%20Guidelines_Jan2017.docx?version=1&modificationDate=1483969944574&api=v2
17. Poggi, A., Lembo, D., Calvanese, D., De Giacomo, G., Lenzerini, M., Rosati, R.: Linking data to ontologies. J. Data Semant. **10**, 133–173 (2008)

Ontology Population from Raw Text Corpus for Open-Source Intelligence

Giulio Ganino, Domenico Lembo[(⊠)], and Federico Scafoglieri

Sapienza Università di Roma, DIAG, Rome, Italy
{ganino,lembo,scafoglieri}@diag.uniroma1.it

Abstract. Open-Source INTelligence (OSINT) is intelligence based on publicly available sources, such as news sites, blogs, forums, etc. The Web is the primary source of information, but once data are crawled from it, they need to be interpreted and structured. Ontologies may play a crucial role in this process, but due to the vast amount of documents available, automatic mechanisms for their population starting from the crawled text are needed. In this paper, we present an approach for the automatic population of pre-defined ontologies based on the General Architecture for Text Engineering (GATE) system. We present some experimental results, which are encouraging in terms of extracted correct instances of the ontology. Finally, we describe an alternative approach and additional experiments for one of the phases of our pipeline, which requires the use of pre-defined dictionaries for relevant entities. Thanks to such variant, we were able to reduce the manual effort required in this phase, still obtaining promising results.

1 Introduction

Open-Source INTelligence (OSINT) is intelligence based on publicly available resources, such as news sites, blogs, forums, etc. OSINT is nowadays used in many application scenarios, like, for instance, security (e.g., identifying lone wolfs and weak signal on the Web [3]), market intelligence (understanding user profiles and trends), or statistics (to cross-check and complement data collected with traditional methods [13]). A major issue in using *Internet as a data source* is that Web data come mainly in the form of free text, thus with no structure and precise semantics. This therefore requires that two problems have to be faced, that is, how to derive structured information from unstructured text, and how to interpret the derived information according to a clear semantics.

To provide a comprehensive solution to this, in the present work we investigate how to populate a domain ontology using the information extracted from a given cluster of raw data crawled from the Web. Ontologies are indeed nowadays recognized as the best means to represent domain knowledge at the conceptual level, and thus are particularly suited to define the concepts and relationships of interest for an application [8]. Thus, structuring Web data according to the predicates and axioms defined in an ontology turns out particularly effective

© Springer International Publishing AG, part of Springer Nature 2018
I. Garrigós and M. Wimmer (Eds.): ICWE 2017, LNCS 10544, pp. 173–186, 2018.
https://doi.org/10.1007/978-3-319-74433-9_16

to our aims, even in the light of the reasoning abilities ontologies allow for [2]. It is worthwhile however to point out that we do not consider here the task of extracting (the intensional/schema level of) ontologies in an automatic way from text documents. Domain ontologies indeed have usually a very complex intensional structure, and their design is typically carried out manually, since automatic ontology construction approaches are in general not able to deal with all the needs of the specific application domain at hand [1,8]. In this work we instead pursue an approach for information extraction from text that assumes that a domain ontology is already available, and that text should be mined to extract instances of ontology predicates.

In order to solve this task, *Named Entity Recognition* (NER) [5] can be initially adopted, but this approach is mainly focused on recognizing specific types of concepts (persons, places, or organizations), without considering relationships among them; *Relational Information Extraction* attempts in addition to identify the relationships existing among concepts, as allowed by, e.g., SystemT[1], an IBM-developed commercial tool that is used in order to derive rich information from documents and emails. In this paper we will adopt both approaches, by relying on open-source technologies.

Among various open-source instruments available (e.g., LingPipe[2] or OpenNLP[3]), we decided to adopt GATE[4], given its ability to customize and shape the underlying architecture components, and to incorporate other external components developed by third parties. The extraction activity in GATE is carried out through different stages, each depending on the contingent needs of the user, who can either adopt existing dictionaries (a.k.a. Gazetteers) or create different extraction rule sets through the adoption of Java Annotation Patterns Engine (JAPE) language [6]. GATE has becoming very popular over the last years, especially in relation to the information extraction from English documents. To some extent, it also supports other languages, primarily thanks to the dictionaries created and then shared on the platform by different users over time.

We have tested our techniques within the XASMOS and RoMA projects, involving the Leonardo company and the Sapienza research center on Cyber Intelligence and Information Security. In the project we have considered the case study "Mafia Capitale", from the name of an important inquiry of 2015 that received a lot of attention by the Italian media, thus it turned out to be a valid testbed (for both number of available documents from the Web and significance of the domain). For this work, we have created specific dictionaries and JAPE rules for the Italian language to instantiate an ontology created for our case study through the information acquired from text documents. To provide some insights on the possibilities offered by our approach, we present the case study successfully applied to more than 2600 documents crawled from the Web.

---

[1] http://researcher.watson.ibm.com/researcher/view_group_subpage.php?id=5577.
[2] http://alias-i.com/lingpipe/.
[3] https://opennlp.apache.org/.
[4] https://gate.ac.uk/.

In our case study we have experienced that some of the tasks we conducted, such as dictionaries or JAPE rule definition, are rather domain specific and time-consuming, since require a lot of manual intervention. We thus started to investigate how to refine our approach so that the time needed for these tasks is reduced and the solution adopted can be reused in different contexts. In particular, in this paper, after describing our complete solution and the use case, we focus on dictionary construction, and propose a general approach for it, which relies on the simple extraction thorough SPARQL queries of dictionaries from the open knowledge base Wikidata[5].

2 Background

In this Section, we recall some basic notions and tools that we will use in the following sections and that constitute the main background of our approach.

Natural Language Processing (NLP). NLP aims at solving problems related to the automatic generation and understanding of human language. It addresses, through computational linguistic techniques, the most peculiar challenges related to the ambiguity of the language (since the same statement may have more than one meaning), its flexibility (given by the different ways in which a fact can be described), and the stream of updates (given by continuous creation of new words) [12]. The process carried out by NLP is made up of several critical steps:

- *Tokenization*: This process starts with breaking down the raw text in tokens, which can be words, spaces or dots [10]. At this stage, words are not classified into grammatical categories, and there is a very limited indication of the syntactic structure of the text, but still a reasonable amount of meta-information is added to the documents [4].
- *Part of Speech (POS)*: A further stage in analysing text is to associate every token with a grammatical category or part of speech. This phase aims at labeling each word with a unique tag indicating its syntactic role, i.e. Noun, Verb, or Pronoun.
- *Named Entity Recognition*: It labels atomic elements in the sentence into categories (such as "Person" or "Location") through the application of specific rules or statistical machine learning techniques [5]. In order to identify and classify the entities three approaches are adopted [9]:
  - *Lookup lists and Gazetteers*: This approach resorts to pre-computed lists of entities divided by categories;
  - *Rule-based (pattern-matching)*: The entities are pinpointed through rules that analyse the context and/or the key characteristics of the studied entities, such as the orthography, the POS classification, etc.;
  - *Machine-trainable*: Machine learning techniques are used in this approach, such as those based on Hidden Markov Models (HMM).

---

[5] https://www.wikidata.org/.

– *Semantic Role Labelling (SRL)*: It aims at giving a semantic role to a syntactic constituent of a sentence, and add further labels to word in the documents with respect to those identified by the previous steps. In other words, SRL aims at understanding the meaning of an entire sentence starting from the meaning of each word taken in isolation and the relationship existing among all the words [16].

General Architecture for Text Engineering (GATE). GATE, is an architecture, a framework and a development environment for Language Engineering (LE) [7]. As an architecture, it defines the organisation of a LE system and the assignment of responsibilities to different components, and ensures that the component interactions satisfy the system requirements. As a framework, it provides a reusable design for a LE software system and a set of prefabricated software building blocks that language engineers can use, extend and customise for their specific needs. As a development environment, it helps its users to minimize the time they spend for building new LE systems or modifying existing ones, by aiding overall development and providing a debugging mechanism for new modules [7]. GATE has a component-based model, which allows for easy coupling and decoupling of the processors, thereby facilitating comparison of alternative configurations of the system or different implementations of the same module (e.g., different parsers). GATE comprises a core library and a set of reusable LE modules. The framework implements the architecture and provides (among other things) facilities for processing and visualising resources, including representation, import and export of data. The provided reusable modules are able to perform basic language processing tasks such as POS tagging and semantic tagging. This eliminates the need for users to keep recreating the same kind of resources, and provides a good starting point for new applications. The modules used in this work are described in more detail in Sect. 3.

Ontologies. An ontology is commonly defined as a formal description of an abstract, simplified view of a certain portion of the world [8]. By virtue of their characteristics ontologies can be naturally used to represent knowledge on the web, where they are mainly adopted to add semantics to data. This also enables the usage of the reasoning mechanisms ontologies are equipped with [2]. The importance of ontologies to interpret and structure Web data is testified also by the huge standardization effort carried out by the W3C, which led to the definition of OWL, the standard web ontology language[6].

As usual in ontologies, OWL distinguishes between *intensional* and *extensional* knowledge. Intensional knowledge is given in terms of logical axioms involving classes (a.k.a. concepts) and properties, which are of two types, objectproperties (a.k.a. binary relationships or roles) and dataproperties (a.k.a. attributes). Classes denote sets of objects, objectproperties denote binary relations between objects, whereas dataproperties denote binary relations between objects and values from predefined datatypes. Person, livesIn and personAge are

---

[6] https://www.w3.org/TR/owl2-primer/.

examples, of class, objectproperty, and dataproperty, respectively. At the extensional level, an OWL ontology is a set of assertions about its instances. For example ClassAssertion(Person John) indicates that the individual John is an instance of Person, whereas ObjectPropertyAssertion(livesIn John NY) specifies that the pair of individuals (John, NY) is an instance of livesIn.

3 Approach

Our GATE-based approach for ontology population from text documents is divided in two main phases, namely *Semantic Annotation* and *Ontology Population*. In the following we describe in detail each such phase.

3.1 Semantic Annotation

In this stage we create annotations, i.e., metadata that indicate properties of the text contained in the analyzed documents. At the end of this phase, the annotations will allow us to identify in the text those entities that are indeed instances of the classes and properties of the ontology given as input to our pipeline. In our GATE-based approach, this phase relies on several Processing Resources (PRs), which are available as GATE plugin-ins, possibly provided by third-party organizations[7]. Such resources are described below.

1. *GATE Unicode Tokeniser*: This component is used to split the text in *Tokens* and so-called *Space Tokens*, where the latter denote spaces among single terms, whereas the former are of four kinds, i.e., number, punctuation, symbol, and word. The use of this component is essential for introducing in the document those annotations that will be exploited in the next phases by JAPE rules, which we describe later.
2. *RegEx Sentence Splitter*: This component divides the processed document into *sentences*, which are chunks of text that make sense taken in isolation. It is essentially language-independent, in the sense that it can be used as is for very many common languages, such as, English, German, Italian, etc. This component is implemented in Java, and it is based on regular expressions that define syntactic rules for sentence identification. At the end of this phase two new annotations are added to the document, i.e., *Sentences* and *Splits*, the latter being annotations that separate.
3. *TreeTagger POS*[8]: It is a component for document annotation with POS and lemma information, developed at the Institute for Computational Linguistics of the University of Stuttgart. It is a Markov Model tagger which makes use of a decision tree to get more reliable estimates for contextual parameters [14]. It can be used with various languages, including Italian. At the end of this phase we have a set of annotations providing POS and lemma information.

---

[7] https://gate.ac.uk/gate/doc/plugins.html.
[8] http://www.cis.uni-muenchen.de/~schmid/tools/TreeTagger.

4. *Gazetteer* [6]: This component annotates the documents on the basis of a set of lists containing names of entities, such as cities or organisations, or practical indicator names, such as types of companies (e.g., ltd., Corp., Inc.), noble titles (e.g., King, Duke, Baron), etc. Each list can be associated with a so-called major and minor type. These types correspond to categories, such that minor types are more specific than the corresponding major types. If the document contains a string matching with an element of a Gazetteer list, the component annotates the string with the major and minor type of this list. In case the string has more than one match, major and minor types of all the matching lists are added.

5. *JAPE Transducer (Semantic)*: This component is used to import user-written JAPE rules into the GATE platform. A JAPE program is constituted by a set of pattern/action rules, such that the left-hand side of a rule consists of an annotation pattern description, and the right-hand side consists of annotation manipulation statements. The JAPE language allows to recognize regular expressions among the annotations produced from the PRs that run before the JAPE Transducer. Once the expression is found, a further annotation referring to the searched patterns/entities is added to the document [6].

3.2   Ontology Population

Ontology population is the process of inserting instances into an existing domain ontology. It makes use of three PRs:

1. *JAPE Transducer (MuNPEx)*[9]: This component is implemented in JAPE, and is used for (multi-lingual) noun phrase (NP) extraction, i.e., identification of elements in a sentence having a noun as head word, which is the word determining the syntactic function of the phrase. MuNPEx requires a POS tagger to work and can additionally use detected named entities to improve chunking performance. Currently the supported languages are English, German, and French, with additional Spanish support in beta. Thus we had to adapt it for the Italian language. For each detected NP, an annotation *NP* is added to the document.

2. *JAPE Transducer (Mapping)*: It converts the annotations created in the Semantic Annotation phase and by the MuNPEx, to make them compatible with the OwlExporter, the PR that realizes the actual ontology population. The format conversion is realized through JAPE rules. The user needs to create the following two new annotations declaring the mapping between the annotations created by the above PRs and the domain ontology [15]:
   - *OwlExportClass*: This annotation records which document annotations referring to entities that have to be exported as instances of a certain class, with some associated the dataproperties.
   - *OwlExportRelation*: Similar to OwlExportClass, but relative to the instantiation of OWL objectproperties.

---

[9] http://www.semanticsoftware.info/munpex.

3. *OwlExporter*[10]: This is an application-independent PR that allows for exporting as OWL assertions document annotations created by the previous PRs. The OwlExporter manages two ontologies: the first one is a domain specific ontology, whereas the second one is a domain independent NLP ontology, which contains concepts commonly used in language engineering, like paragraphs, sentences, or noun phrases [15]. When OwlExporter terminates, we obtain the population of the domain ontology with the information obtained from the analysed text documents.

4 Case Study

As said in the introduction, we tested our solution within the XASMOS project, where we considered the domain of "Mafia Capitale", which is the name of a judicial inquiry that involved the city council of Rome, in 2015. This investigation received a lot of attention by the media, thus we could retrieve from the Web a large number of newspaper articles for our tests. We started our project development from the Web crawling phase, and after that we have defined a domain ontology to represent some aspects of interest for the domain at hand. Our ontology is defined on a alphabet of 21 Classes, 9 Relationships and 14 Data Properties. We have then manually created specific Gazetteer lists and JAPE rules used for document annotation by the GATE PRs described in Sect. 3. We remark that the extracted documents from the web are all written in the Italian.

As for the crawling, we used Web Content Extractor[11] to retrieve articles appeared on the Web portals of some major Italian newspapers between June 16, 2015, and February 29, 2016. The crawling phase generated 2657 articles.

In order to estimate the quality of our approach, we used evaluation metrics adopted in Ontology-based Information Extraction [11], i.e., *Precision*, which is the fraction of correctly identified items over the total number of identified items, and *Recall*, which is the fraction of the correctly identified items over the total number of correct items. Formally, $Precision = \frac{Correct}{Correct+Spurious}$, whereas $Recall = \frac{Correct}{Correct+Missing}$, where *Correct* and *Spurious* indicate how many correct and wrong items are identified, respectively, and $Missing$ is the number of correct items not identified.

We carried out two different tests:

1. In the first test, we have chosen 10 documents, in a random way among those produced by the crawling phase, and have asked a domain expert to annotate them, according to the domain ontology we specified. The manual annotations aimed to identify all and only the instances of the ontology predicates that can be extracted by the documents (on the basis of the document content and the knowledge of the expert). We have then processed these documents through our GATE-based pipeline, and we have compared the annotations produced by our pipeline with the manual annotations of the domain expert, in order to calculate the Precision and Recall.

---

[10] http://www.semanticsoftware.info/owlexporter.

[11] http://www.newprosoft.com/web-content-extractor.htm.

2. In the second test we have processed in our pipeline all the 2657 articles obtained by the crawling phase. Due to the large number of documents, obviously no previous reference annotation could be done, and also checking Precision for all annotations has been impossible. We thus used this test to measure the total number of Class, ObjectProperty and DataProperty assertions, and to verify the Precision on a portion of the analyzed documents.

Table 1. Results of test #1

Words	Annotations	CA	OPA	DPA	Correct	Missing	Precision	Recall
6.084	414	404	10	1.140	403	98	97%	78%

Table 2. Results of test #2

Words	CA	OPA	DPA	Exec. time (sec.)
1.285.290	38.452	419	99145	1.948,88 (−30 mins)

Both the experiments were performed on a MacBook Pro 9.2, with Intel Core i7 2,90 GHz and 8GB RAM. The results of the the above tests are shown in Table 1 and in Table 2, respectively, where *Words* indicate the number of words contained in the document, and *CA*, *OPA*, *DPA* respectively denote the number of class, objectproperty, and dataproperty assertions extracted. In Table 2 the execution time represents the running time of the entire pipeline in order to process 2657 documents.

For the first experiment, we soon notice excellent Precision and good Recall, a very high number of dataproperty assertions added to the ontology, a good number of class assertions, but few objectproperty assertions. As for the precision, we point out that the errors we obtained are mainly due to the wrong annotations associated to the word "Marino", which is both a city (close to Rome) and the last name of a Rome ex-mayor. Indeed, in our pipeline disambiguation is done through the JAPE rules we defined, which however are able to identify the correct annotation only when the last name is coupled in the text with the first name of the mayor, which is often not the case in the selected documents. As for the number of dataproperty assertions, we observe that it might be substantially increased by adding the two following PRs to our pipeline:

1. *Pronominal Coreference (PC)*: This PR provides an annotation on pronouns whereby they are referred to an annotated entity. For example, in the sentence "Marco Rossi lives in Bolzano, he is a successful lawyer", our solution recognizes that an individual named Marco Rossi is associated by the objectproperty *linvesIn* to an individual representing the city of Milano, but it is not able to understand that the first individual is a lawyer. By using PC we can instead obtain the missing annotation. Currently GATE provides this PR only for English language, and thus we could not directly introduce it in our pipeline.

2. *OrtoMatcher*: It provides an annotation on entities that are indeed denoted in the text with abbreviations of expressions denoting an already identified entity. For instance, in the sentence "Marco Rossi lives in Bolzano. Rossi is a successful lawyer" our solution is not able to understand that Marco Rossi is a lawyer, since the full name is abbreviated into the last name only. OrtoMatcher would be able instead to find such annotation. Unfortunately, OrthoMatcher provided by GATE needs an exhaustive list of abbreviations for each non-abbreviated denotation of an entity, similar to Gazetteer lists. This approach is clearly impossible to pursue for cases with very many possible abbreviations (as for persons). In the current release of our approach this resource is actually used only for the most common abbreviations for the names of some famous organizations in the world. A more extensive usage of such resource needs some further investigation, which is part of our future work.

We point out that the insertion in our pipeline of the above resources would also allow to augment the recall in our experiments, since its current value is mainly due to missed objectproperty assertions.

In the second test, as said, we could not measure precision and recall for all documents, but we mainly used this test to evaluate the impact of our approach on a large text corpus. Nonetheless, to get an idea of the quality of the result, we measured the Precision on the 1% of the data in the output and we have got a value of 94%.

5 Simplifying Gazetteer Lists Generation

In this section we describe a new case study, focusing in particular on the design and development of the Gazetteer lists. As said in Sect. 3, Gazetteer annotates the documents on the basis of a set of lists containing names of entities. These lists are used to find occurrences of these names in text (e.g., for the task of named entity recognition). In our project, it was crucial to create all the Gazetteer lists used for document annotation, because all the articles we analyzed are written in the Italian, and when we started our project no reusable support for Gazetteer lists for Italian was available. To create the lists related to the domain entities of "Mafia Capitale", we use two methods:

- based on *Human-Knowledge*: This approach is used to write the lists containing words that identify certain categories entities belong to, e.g., containing all the words identifying lawyers. In order to create this list, we have read some articles from newspapers about the domain of interest, to better understand the terms which identify a specific category, as "Lawyer", "Advocate", "Barrister" and "Attorney" for the category of "Lawyer". Then we have written the terms in the gazetteer lists in both uppercase and lowercase letter, as GATE has a case sensitive approach.
- based on *Open Data Sources*: This approach is used to find the first and last name of individuals belonging to a specific category, e.g. the members

of the Government of the city of Rome, with the information of their role in the Government, as well. To this aim we have downloaded specific lists of interest from open data sites, e.g., as OpenPolitici[12] for the lists of Politicians currently in charge, and also by other data sources such as DBpedia. After the downloads, we needed to do some manual cleaning of the lists, and to convert them in the right format accepted by GATE.

The construction of such lists through this approach was non-trivial and required a significant amount of time to obtain good quality results. We thus investigated alternative methods for Gazetteer lists generation that could reduce the manual effort required, and could be easily replicable in different domains, thus augmenting the generality of our approach. To this aim, we focused on Wikidata as informative source for Gazetteer.

Wikidata is a collaboratively edited knowledge base, which organizes a large amount of data in a structured way according to a general reference ontology. It is an openly accessible resource, following the Semantic Web standards for exporting, interconnecting and querying data, which can be edited and read by both machine and humans. Our idea has been therefore to take advantage of the mass knowledge provided by Wikidata to annotate text documents, and in particular to exploit such resource to partially automate the process of Gazetteer lists generation. We have thus downloaded a Wikidata RDF dump (specifically we used the version of March 3, 2017), and have loaded it on a graph database management system with RDF/SPARQL support, namely Blazegraph[13]. This has enabled us to access Wikidata information through standard SPARQL queries. By virtue of this approach it is possible to avoid tedious and time-consuming development of ad hoc solutions for each wanted Gazetteer list. Indeed, once the setup of the system is completed, a user just need to define and execute a set of SPARQL queries to obtain the lists of interest. Such queries have to specified taking into account the set of lists to populate, the Wikidata ontology structure, and its data model. In Wikidata, every resource is classified as *item*, and every item is associated with statements defining its properties. For example, the Item *Democratic Party* is associated with the statement *Istance Of: Political Party*. To complete the picture, below we report the structure of the *Democratic Party* item[14]:

```
Democratic Party (Q47563)
Instance of(31) Political Party(Q7278)
Country(P17) Italy(Q38)
```

Then if we want to obtain a list of items, characterized by the same interesting features, we need to create a specific SPARQL query. For example, to obtain the list of the names of Italian political parties, it is possible to use the property wdt:P31, which represents *instance of* (corresponding to the predicate rdf:type),

---

[12] http://politici.openpolis.it/.

[13] https://www.blazegraph.com/.

[14] https://www.wikidata.org/wiki/Q47729.

and the property wdt:P279, which represents *subclass of* (corresponding to the predicate rdfs:subclassOf), and to reference the class wd:Q7278, which represents *political party*. Finally we need to filter this statement through the property wdt:P17, which represents *country of belonging*, referencing the class wd:Q7278, which represents *Italy*. Below we give the exact structure of the SPARQL query that returns the names of Italian political parties from Wikidata:

```
SELECT ?element
WHERE {
    ?item wdt:P31/wdt:P279* wd:Q7278.
        ?item wdt:P17 wd:Q38.
        ?item rdfs:label ?element. }
```

The result of the SPARQL query is a CSV file, that is not directly acceptable by the Gazetteer PR, but that has to be simply renamed into a .lst format file to be processed by the Gazetteer. In the next paragraph we test the quality of the lists obtained through the two defined approaches, comparing the quality of annotations produced by them.

To test the two different approaches, we have decided to compare five lists, obtained with these approaches and identifying the entities of Italian Politicians, Italian Journalists, Italian First Names, Italian Criminal Organizations and Italian Political Parties. The evaluation process is performed on 15 articles and is based on the same criteria of the first test of Sect. 4, so a hand-based annotations of the five chosen entities has been performed by an expert user on the 15 articles. The same articles have been then annotated through the Gazetteer component of our pipeline by using the two different sets of lists generated by the two approaches, i.e., the manual one and the Wikidata based one, and finally we have compared the annotations produced, in order to calculate Precision and Recall. The results are shown in Table 3.

We first notice that on average, the number of entries in the lists created with Wikidata is 9 times greater than the other, manual approach. As for the precision, we analyzed the lists created by Wikidata and noticed that they contain various entries with typos and flaws. For example, the Political Parties list contains the entry """PSDI""" (with wrong additional quotation marks). Thus, if in an analysed text document there is the word PSDI (which is an acronym of a political party), it will not be annotated as Political Party. The presence of more errors in the Wikidata generated lists with respect to those contained in the lists manually realized was some how expected. Our experiments however show that the Precision value for annotation with Wikidata lists in most cases reach good levels, similar to the manual approach. For several Wikidata lists, also the Recall is close to the one measured for the corresponding manually realized list. For the cases of Criminal Organizations and Political Parties we instead initially got very low values for the Recall. We noticed that this mainly was due to problems with uppercase/lowercase letters (remember that GATE is case sensitive). We have thus refined the two lists by adding for each term the thee versions: all uppercase letters, all lowercase letters, and capitalize words. In Table 3 these new lists are denoted as *Wikidata Mod*. We can observe that with

Table 3. Results of test #1

List	Entries	Annotations	Spurious Ann.	Missing Ann.	Precision	Recall
First Names Opensource	8913	322	83	0	74%	100%
First Names Wikidata	2517	262	31	5	88%	98%
Criminal Organizations Hand-Based	25	37	21	0	43%	100%
Criminal Organizations Wikidata	68	20	19	13	5%	7%
Criminal Organizations Wikidata Mod.	273	30	24	9	20%	40%
Politicians Opensource	1083	11	0	40	100%	22%
Politicians Wikidata	7778	17	0	34	100%	33%
Italian Journalists Opensource	369	4	0	0	100%	100%
Italian Journalists Wikidata	3727	8	0	0	100%	100%
Political Parties Opensource	131	23	0	2	100%	92%
Political Parties Wikidata	447	4	0	21	100%	16%
Political Parties Wikidata Mod.	1293	26	7	6	73%	76%

this fix the value of Recall become greater than that of the original Wikidata lists. However, in Political Parties Wikidata Mod. this approach has generated a decrease of Precision caused by the introduction of new entries, e.g., the word *si* (which is the lowercase version of the acronym SI, an Italian Political Party). This word is indeed used in Italian as reflexive pronoun, thus leading to some wrong annotations. In the Political Parties Wikidata list, the entries are only in initial capitalize word and for this reason the ambiguity between Political Parties and other concepts is not present. Although the decrease of Precision, we notice that the modification of the Political Parties list increase the Recall of 60%, not far from the Recall of the manual approach.

Finally, we focus on Precision and Recall for the Italian Journalists lists. As we can observe in Table 3, the number of annotations produced by the two lists is different, but the value of Precision and Recall is 100% for both. This is caused by the presence of entities into the articles annotated as Italian Journalists by the Wikidata list, but for which it is not possible to classify them as such only from a reading of the article. In other to take into account the bias introduced by the knowledge of the domain expert, which is unavoidable, we manually verified all the annotations produced by means of the Wikidata lists that were not expected according to the domain expert annotation, and considered correct those for which we could verify that the information obtained from Wikidata is indeed exact. From the data present in Table 3, we can conclude that our experiments have been quite been successful, since the Wikidata based approach has adequate values in terms of number of annotations, Precision and Recall. Realistically, these values keep unchanged when the number of analysed articles increases. We believe that this confirms that resorting to Wikidata for producing lists to be used by the Gazetteer PR allows for both time savings and good results.

6   Conclusions

Automatic ontology population from text documents is a very useful task, as it can provide semantic annotations about the domain of interest and the identification of the relevant concepts to be finally exported into a reference ontology. Once this process is finished, the user can perform query answering on the populated ontology to obtain specific information. This is especially useful in OSINT applications, in which large amount of texts are crawled from the Web, which could not be processed manually.

Future improvements our approach include the insertion of the Pronominal Coreference and the OrtoMatcher components discussed in Sect. 4 in our pipeline. Also, we are working on further refinement of our approach in order to automatize some of the phases that now require a manual intervention, in the spirit of the work done on Gazetteer lists described in Sect. 5. In particular, we are currently investigating a way to automatize the definition of JAPE rules.

Acknowledgments. This work has been partly supported by Leonardo Company (formerly Selex ES) in the context of the *XASMOS* initiative, and by the Italian project *RoMA* (SCN_00064). The work of Giulio Ganino has been supported by the FILAS grant *Laboratori teorico-sperimentali a supporto delle applicazioni spaziali delle industrie laziali* (FILAS-RU-2014-1058).

References

1. Antonioli, N., Castanò, F., Coletta, S., Grossi, S., Lembo, D., Lenzerini, M., Poggi, A., Virardi, E., Castracane, P.: Ontology-based data management for the Italian public debt. Proceedings of FOIS **2014**, 372–385 (2014)
2. Baader, F., Calvanese, D., McGuinness, D., Nardi, D., Patel-Schneider, P.F. (eds.): The Description Logic Handbook: Theory, Implementation and Applications, 2nd edn. Cambridge University Press, New York (2007)
3. Baldoni, R., Nicola, R.D.: The White Book on Cyber-security (2015)
4. Bird, S., Klein, E., Loper, E.: Natural Language Processing with Python: Analyzing Text with the Natural Language Toolkit. O'Reilly, Beijing (2009)

5. Collobert, R., Weston, J., Bottou, L., Karlen, M., Kavukcuoglu, K., Kuksa, P.: Natural language processing (almost) from scratch. J. Mach. Learn. Res. **12**, 2493–2537 (2011)
6. Cunningham, H.: Developing Language Processing Components with GATE Version 8. University of Sheffield Department of Computer Science (2014)
7. Cunningham, H., Maynard, D., Bontcheva, K., Tablan, V.: GATE: A framework and graphical development environment for robust NLP tools and applications. In: Proceedings of ACL 2002 (2002)
8. Guarino, N.: Formal ontology in information systems. In: Proceedings of FOIS 1998, Frontiers in Artificial Intelligence, pp. 3–15. IOS Press (1998)
9. Johnson, M., Khudanpur, S., Ostendorf, M., Rosenfeld, R.: Mathematical Foundations of Speech and Language Processing. Springer, New York (2004)
10. Kibble, R.: Introduction to Natural Language Processing. University of London (2013)
11. Maynard, D., Li, Y., Peters, W.: NLP techniques for term extraction and ontology population. In: Ontology Learning and Population: Bridging the Gap between Text and Knowledge, pp. 107–127. IOS Press (2008)
12. Navigli, R.: Word sense disambiguation: a survey. ACM Comput. Surv. **41**(2), 1–69 (2009)
13. Scannapieco, M., Barcaroli, G., Summa, D., Scarnò, M.: Using internet as a data source for official statistics: a comparative analysis of web scraping technologies. In: Proceedings of NTTS 2015 (2015)
14. Schmid, H.: Probabilistic part-of-speech tagging using decision trees. In: Proceedings of the International Conference on New Methods in Language Processing, pp. 44–49 (1994)
15. Witte, R., Khamis, N., Rilling, J.: Flexible ontology population from text: the OwlExporter. In: Proceedings of LREC 2010. May 2010
16. Zhao, H., Zhang, X., Kit, C.: Integrative semantic dependency parsing via efficient large-scale feature selection. J Artif. Intell. Res. **46**, 203–233 (2013)

3rd International Workshop on Natural Language Processing for Informal Text

Preface

It is our great pleasure to welcome you to the *3rd International Workshop on Natural Language Processing for Informal Text (NLPIT 2017)*, associated with ICWE 2017. The rapid growth of Internet usage in the last two decades adds new challenges to understand the informal user generated content (UGC) on the Internet. Textual UGC refers to textual posts on social media, blogs, emails, chat conversations, instant messages, forums, reviews, or advertisements that are created by end-users of an online system. A large portion of language used on textual UGC is informal. Informal text is the style of writing that disregards language grammars and uses a mixture of abbreviations and context dependent terms. The straightforward application of state-of-the-art Natural Language Processing approaches on informal text typically results in a significantly degraded performance due to the following reasons: the lack of sentence structure; the lack of enough context required; the seldom entities involved; the noisy sparse contents of users' contributions; and the untrusted facts contained. The NLPIT workshop hopes to bring opportunities and challenges involved in informal text processing under the attention of researchers. In particular, we are interested in discussing informal text modeling, normalization, mining, and understanding in addition to various application areas in which UGC is involved. The workshop is a follow-up of the first NLPIT workshop that was held in conjunction with ICWE 2015: the International Conference on Web Engineering held in Rotterdam, The Netherlands, from 23rd to 26th of July 2015 and the 2nd NLPIT workshop that was held in conjunction with WWW 2016: the International Conference on World Wide Web held in Montreal, Canada, from 11th to 15th of April 2016. The call for papers attracted 6 submissions from 6 different countries. Each paper received at least 3 reviews. The program committee reviewed and accepted 3 papers with an acceptance rate of 50%.

The workshop program started with a keynote presentation given by Roberto Navigli[1] from the Sapienza University of Rome entitled "*Overcoming the Language Barrier with BabelNet and Multilingual Disambiguation of Text*". The keynote is followed by 3 research presentations. The first paper discussed the characteristics of the Egyptian dialect. The second paper presented a multi-level novel architecture to classify named entities in tweets that uses features extracted from images and text. Finally, the last paper studied the positive impact of online expectation maximization methods for estimating language distributions and improving per-document language identification from those estimates.

---

http://wwwhome.cs.utwente.nl/~badiehm/nlpit2017/.

[1] http://wwwusers.di.uniroma1.it/~navigli/.

We thank all authors for enabling us to offer an attractive program. We also thank the program committee for reviewing the papers and writing extensive reports with feedback for the authors. Finally, we would like to thank the ICWE 2017 workshop chairs for support in organizing the workshop.

Mena B. Habib
Florian Kunneman
Maurice van Keulen

Organization

Program Committee

Alexandra Balahur	The European Commission's Joint Research Centre (JRC), Italy
Barbara Plank	University of Copenhagen, Denmark
Chenliang Li	Wuhan University, China
Claudia Hauff	Delft University, The Netherlands
Dolf Trieschnigg	My Data Factory, The Netherlands
Erik Tjong Kim Sang	Meertens Institute, The Netherlands
Gerasimos Spanakis	Maastricht University, The Netherlands
Heba Elfardy	Columbia University, USA
Kevin Gimpel	Toyota Technological Institute, USA
Malvina Nissim	University of Groningen, The Netherlands
Orphee De Clerq	Ghent University, Belgium
Robert Remus	ExB Group, Germany
Sabine Bergler	Concordia University, Canada
Wang Ling	Carnegie Mellon University, USA
Yannis Korkontzelos	Edge Hill University, UK
Zhemin Zhu	Elsevier, The Netherlands

Named Entity Recognition in Twitter Using Images and Text

Diego Esteves[1] , Rafael Peres[2] , Jens Lehmann[1] ,
and Giulio Napolitano[3](✉)

[1] University of Bonn, Bonn, Germany
{Esteves,Lehmann}@cs.uni-bonn.de
[2] Federal University of Rio de Janeiro, Rio de Janeiro, Brazil
rafaelperes@ufrj.br
[3] Fraunhofer IAIS, Sankt Augustin, Germany
giulio.napolitano@iais.fraunhofer.de

Abstract. Named Entity Recognition (NER) is an important subtask of information extraction that seeks to locate and recognise named entities. Despite recent achievements, we still face limitations with correctly detecting and classifying entities, prominently in short and noisy text, such as Twitter. An important negative aspect in most of NER approaches is the high dependency on hand-crafted features and domain-specific knowledge, necessary to achieve state-of-the-art results. Thus, devising models to deal with such linguistically complex contexts is still challenging. In this paper, we propose a novel multi-level architecture that does not rely on any specific linguistic resource or encoded rule. Unlike traditional approaches, we use features extracted from images and text to classify named entities. Experimental tests against state-of-the-art NER for Twitter on the *Ritter* dataset present competitive results (0.59 F-measure), indicating that this approach may lead towards better NER models.

Keywords: NER · Short texts · Noisy data · Machine learning
Computer vision

1 Introduction

Named Entity Recognition (NER) is an important step in most of the natural language processing (NLP) pipelines. It is designed to robustly handle proper names, which is essential for many applications. Although a seemingly simple task, it faces a number of challenges in noisy datasets and it is still considered an emerging research area [2,5]. Despite recent efforts, we still face limitations at *identifying* entities and (consequently) correctly *classifying* them. Current state-of-the-art NER systems typically have about 85–90% accuracy on news text - such as articles (*CoNLL03 shared task* data set) - but they still perform poorly (about 30–50% accuracy) on short texts, which do not have implicit linguistic

© Springer International Publishing AG, part of Springer Nature 2018
I. Garrigós and M. Wimmer (Eds.): ICWE 2017, LNCS 10544, pp. 191–199, 2018.
https://doi.org/10.1007/978-3-319-74433-9_17

formalism (e.g. punctuation, spelling, spacing, formatting, unorthodox capitalisation, emoticons, abbreviations and hashtags) [5,10,12,19]. Furthermore, the lack of external knowledge resources is an important gap in the process regardless of writing style [18]. To face these problems, research has been focusing on microblog-specific information extraction techniques [19,22].

In this paper, we propose a joint clustering architecture that aims at minimizing the current gap between world knowledge and knowledge available in open domain knowledge bases (e.g., Freebase) for NER systems, by extracting features from unstructured data sources. To this aim, we use images and text from the web as input data. Thus, instead of relying on encoded information and manually annotated resources (the major limitation in NER architectures) we focus on a multi-level approach for discovering named entities, combining text and image features with a final classifier based on a decision tree model. We follow an intuitive and simple idea: some types of images are more related to people (e.g. faces) whereas some others are more related to organisations (e.g. logos), for instance. This principle is applied similarly to the text retrieved from websites: keywords for search engines representing names and surnames of people will often return similarly related texts, for instance. Thus, we derive some indicators (detailed in Sect. 3 which are then used as input features in a final classifier.

To the best of our knowledge, this is the first report of a NER architecture which aims to provide *a priori* information based on clusters of images and text features.

2   Related Work

Over the past few years, the problem of recognizing named entities in natural language texts has been addressed by several approaches and frameworks [15,20]. Existing approaches basically adopt look-up strategies and use standard local features, such as *part-of-speech tags*, *previous and next words*, *substrings*, *shapes* and *regex expressions*, for instance. The main drawback is the performance of those models with noisy data, such as Tweets. A major reason is that they rely heavily on hand-crafted features and domain-specific knowledge. In terms of architecture, NER algorithms may also be designed based on *generative* (e.g., Naive Bayes) or *discriminative* (e.g., MaxEnt) models. Furthermore, *sequence* models (HMMs, CMM, MEMM and CRF) are a natural choice to design such systems. A more recent study proposed by Lample et al. [11] used neural architectures to solve this problem. Similarly in terms of architecture, Al-Rfou et al. [1] had also proposed a model (without dependency) that learns distributed word representations (word embeddings) which encode semantic and syntactic features of words in each language. Chiu and Nichols [4] proposed a neural network architecture that automatically detects word and character-level features using a hybrid bidirectional LSTM and CNN. Thus, these models work without resorting to any language-specific knowledge or resources such as *gazetteers*. They, however, focused on *newswire* to improve current state-of-the-art systems and not on the *microblogs* context, in which they are naturally harder to out-perform due to the aforementioned issues. According to Derczynski et al. [5] some approaches have been proposed for Twitter, but they are mostly still in development and often not freely available.

3   Conceptual Architecture

The main insight underlying this work is that we can produce a NER model which performs similarly to state-of-the-art approaches but without relying on any specific resource or encoded rule. To this aim, we propose a multi-level architecture which intends to produce biased indicators to a certain class (LOC, PER or ORG). These outcomes are then used as input features for our final classifier. We perform clustering on images and texts associated to a given *term* t existing in complete or partial sentences S (e.g., "new york" or "einstein"), leveraging the *global context* obtained from the Web providing valuable insights apart from standard *local features* and hand-coded information. Figure 1 gives an overview of the proposed architecture.

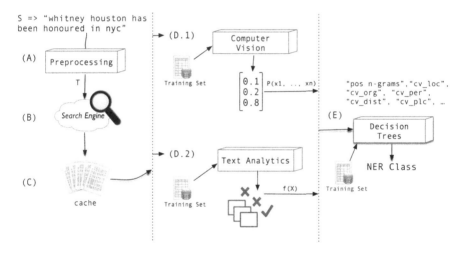

Fig. 1. Overview of the approach: combining computer vision and machine learning in a generic NER architecture

In the first step (A), we simply apply *POS Tagging* and *Shallow Parsing* to filter out tokens except for those[1] tagged as *propn* or *nouns* and their *compounds* (*local context*). Afterwards, we use the search engine (B) to query and cache (C) the top N texts and images associated to each term $t \in T$, where T is the set resulting of the pre-processing step (A) for each (partial or complete) sentence S.

---

[1] State-of-the-art POS tagging systems still do not have exceptional performance in short texts.

This resulting data (composed of excerpts of texts and images from web pages) is used to predict a possible class for a given term. These outcomes are then used in the first two levels (D.1 and D.2) of our approach: the *Computer Vision* and *Text Analytics* components, respectively, which we introduce as follows:

Computer Vision (CV): Detecting Objects: Function Description (D.1): given a set of images $\mathcal{I}$, the basic idea behind this component is to detect a specific object (denoted by a class c) in each image. Thus, we query the web for a given term t and then extract the features from each image and try to detect a specific object (e.g., logos for ORG) for the top N images[2] retrieved as source candidates. The mapping between objects and NER classes is detailed in Table 1. Training (D.1): we used SIFT (Scale Invariant Feature Transform) features [13] for extracting image descriptors and BoF (Bag of Features) [17,21] for clustering the histograms of extracted features. The clustering is possible by constructing a large vocabulary of many visual words and representing each image as a histogram of the frequency words that are in the image. We use *k-means* [14] to cluster the set of descriptors to k clusters. The resulting clusters are compact and separated by similar characteristics. An empirical analysis shows that some image groups are often related to certain named entities (NE) classes when using search engines, as described in Table 1. For training purposes, we used the *Scene 13* dataset [8] to train our classifiers for *location* (LOC), "faces" from *Caltech 101 Object Categories* [7] to train our *person* (PER) and logos from *METU dataset* [16] for *organisation* ORG object detection. These datasets produces the training data for our set of supervised classifiers (1 for ORG, 1 for PER and 10 for LOC). We trained our classifiers using Support Vector Machines [9] once they generalize reasonably enough for the task[3].

Table 1. NER classes and respective objects to be detected in a given image. For LOC we trained more models due to the diversity of the object candidates.

NER	Images candidates (number of trained models)
LOC	Building, Suburb, Street, City, Country, Mountain, Highway, Forest, Coast and Map (10)
ORG	Company Logo (1)
PER	Human Face (1)

Text Analytics (TA): Text Classification - Function Description (D.2): analogously to (D.1), we perform clustering to group texts together that are "distributively" similar. Thus, for each retrieved web page (title and excerpt of its content), we perform the classification based on the main NER classes. We extracted features using a classical sparse vectorizer (Term frequency-Inverse document frequency - TF-IDF. In experiments, we did not find a significant performance gain using *HashingVectorizer*) - Training (D.2): with

---

[2] We set $N = 10$ in our experiments and used Microsoft Bing as the search engine.

[3] *scikit-learn*: svm.NuSVC(nu = 0.5, kernel = 'rbf', gamma = 0.1, probability = True).

this objective in mind, we trained classifiers that rely on a bag-of-words technique. We collected data using *DBpedia* instances to create our training dataset ($N = 15000$) and annotated each instance with the respective MUC classes, i.e. *PER*, *ORG* and *LOC*. Listing 1.1 shows an example of a query to obtain documents of organizations (ORG class). Thereafter, we used this annotated dataset to train our model.

```
SELECT ?location, ?abstract FROM <http://dbpedia.org>
WHERE {?location rdf:type dbo:Location .
       ?location dbo:abstract ?abstract .
FILTER (lang(?abstract) = 'en')} LIMIT 15000
```

Listing 1.1. SPARQL: an example of querying DBPedia to obtain LOC data for training

Final Classifier (E) - Function Description (E): we use the outcomes of (D.1 and D.2) as part of the input to our final model. The final set of indicators is defined as follows: let W_s be a set of *tokens* existing in a given sentence $s \in S$. We extract the POS tag (using Stanford POS Tagger) for each token w and filter out any token classified other than *PROP-NOUN* and existing *compounds* as entity candidates ($t \in S'$). The result is a simple structure:

$$M_i = \{j, t, ng_{pos}, C_{loc}, C_{per}, C_{org}, C_{dist}, C_{plc}, T_{loc}, T_{per}, T_{org}, T_{dist}\} \quad (1)$$

where i and j represent the ith and j^{th} position of $s \in S$ and $w \in W_s$, respectively. ng_{pos} represents the n-gram[4] of POS tag. C_k and T_k ($k \in \{loc, per, org\}$) represent the total objects found by a classifier Φ for a given class k ($\sum_{n=1}^{N} \Phi(k, img_n)$)[5] (where N is the total of retrieved images $\mathcal{I}$). C_{dist} and T_{dist} represent the distance between the two higher predictions ($\mathcal{P} = \{C_k \forall K\}$), i.e. $\max(\mathcal{P}) - \max(\mathcal{P}')|\mathcal{P}' = \mathcal{P} - \{\max(\mathcal{P})\}$. Finally, C_{plc} represents the sum of all predictions made by all *LOC* classifiers $\mathcal{CL}$ ($\sum_{l=1}^{L} \sum_{n=1}^{N} \mathcal{CL}_l(loc, img_n)$)[6]. Training (E): the outcomes of D.1 and D.2 (M) are used as input features to our final classifier. We implemented a simple *Decision Tree*[7] (non-parametric supervised learning method) algorithm for learning simple decision rules inferred from the data features (since it does not require any assumptions of linearity in the data and also works well with outliers, which are expected to be found more often in a noisy environment, such as the Web of Documents).

4   Experiments

In order to check the overall performance of the proposed technique, we ran our algorithm without any further rule or *apriori* knowledge using a gold standard

---

[4] *bigram*, in our experiments.
[5] $pos = +1$, $neg = -1$.
[6] $pos = +1$, $neg = 0$.
[7] *scikit-learn*: criterion='entropy', splitter='best'.

Table 2. Performance measure for our approach in Ritter dataset: 4-fold cross validation

NER class	Precision	Recall	F-measure
Person (PER)	0.86	0.53	0.66
Location (LOC)	0.70	0.40	0.51
Organisation (ORG)	0.90	0.46	0.61
None	0.99	1.0	0.99
Average (PLO)	0.82	0.46	**0.59**

Table 3. Performance measures (PER, ORG and LOC classes) of state-of-the-art NER for short texts (Ritter dataset). Approaches which do not rely on hand-crafted rules and *Gazetteers* are highlighted in gray. Etter et al. [6] trained using 10 classes.

NER System	Description	Precision	Recall	F-measure
Ritter et al., 2011 [19]	LabeledLDA-Freebase	0.73	0.49	0.59
Bontcheva et al., 2013 [3]	Gazetteer/JAPE	0.77	0.83	0.80
Bontcheva et al., 2013 [3]	Stanford-twitter	0.54	0.45	0.49
Etter et al., 2013 [6]	SVM-HMM	0.65	**0.49**	0.54
our approach	Cluster (images and texts) + DT	**0.82**	0.46	**0.59**

for NER in microblogs (Ritter dataset [19]), achieving 0.59 F1. Table 2 details the performance measures per class. Table 3 presents current state-of-the-art results for the same dataset. The best model achieves 0.8 F1-measure, but uses encoded rules. Models which are not rule-based, achieve 0.49 and 0.56. We argue that in combination with existing techniques (such as linguistic patterns), we can potentially achieve even better results.

As an example, the sentence *"paris hilton was once the toast of the town"* can show the potential of the proposed approach. The token *"paris"* with a LOC bias (0.6) and *"hilton"* (global brand of hotels and resorts) with indicators leading to LOC (0.7) or ORG (0.1, less likely though). Furthermore, *"town"* being correctly biased to LOC (0.7). The algorithm also suggests that the *compound* *"paris hilton"* is more likely to be a PER instead (0.7) and updates (correctly) the previous predictions. As a downside in this example, the algorithm misclassified *"toast"* as LOC. However, in this same example, Stanford NER annotates (mistakenly) only *"paris"* as LOC. It is worth noting also the ability of the algorithm to take advantage of search engine capabilities. When searching for *"miCRsOft"*, the returned values strongly indicate a bias for ORG, as expected ($C_{loc} = 0.2$, $C_{org} = 0.8$, $C_{per} = 0.0$, $C_{dist} = 6$, $C_{plc} = -56$, $T_{loc} = 0.0$, $T_{org} = 0.5$, $T_{per} = 0.0$, $T_{dist} = 5$). More local organisations are also recognized correctly, such as *"kaufland"* (German supermarket), which returns the following metadata: $C_{loc} = 0.2$, $C_{org} = 0.4$, $C_{per} = 0.0$, $C_{dist} = 2$, $C_{plc} = -50$, $T_{loc} = 0.1$, $T_{org} = 0.4$, $T_{per} = 0.0$, $T_{dist} = 3$.

5   Discussion

A disadvantage when using web search engines is that they are not open and free. This can be circumvented by indexing and searching on other large sources of information, such as Common Crawl and Flickr[8]. However, maintaining a large source of images would be an issue, e.g. the Flickr dataset may not be comprehensive enough (i.e. tokens may not return results). This will be a subject of future work. Besides, an important step in the pre-processing is the classification of part-of-speech tags. In the Ritter dataset our current error propagation is 0.09 (107 tokens which should be classified as NOUN) using NLTK 3.0. Despite good performance (91% accuracy), we plan to benchmark this component. In terms of processing time, the bottleneck of the current implementation is the time required to extract features from images, as expected. Currently we achieve a performance of 3–5 seconds per sentence and plan to also optimize this component. The major advantages of this approach are: (1) the fact that there are no hand-crafted rules encoded; (2) the ability to handle misspelled words (because the search engine alleviates that and returns relevant or related information) and incomplete sentences; (3) the generic design of its components, allowing multilingual processing with little effort (the only dependency is the POS tagger) and straightforward extension to support more NER classes (requiring a corpus of images and text associated to each desired NER class, which can be obtained from a Knowledge Base, such as DBpedia, and an image dataset, such as METU dataset). While initial results in a gold standard dataset showed the potential of the approach, we also plan to integrate these outcomes into a Sequence Labeling (SL) system, including neural architectures such as LSTM, which are more suitable for such tasks as NER or POS. We argue that this can potentially reduce the existing (significant) gap in NER performance on microblogs.

6   Conclusions

In this paper we presented a novel architecture for NER that expands the feature set space based on feature clustering of images and texts, focused on microblogs. Due to their terse nature, such noisy data often lack enough context, which poses a challenge to the correct identification of named entities. To address this issue we have presented and evaluated a novel approach using the Ritter dataset, showing consistent results over state-of-the-art models without using any external resource or encoded rule, achieving an average of 0.59 F1. The results slightly outperformed state-of-the-art models which do not rely on encoded rules (0.49 and 0.54 F1), suggesting the viability of using the produced metadata to also boost existing NER approaches. A further important contribution is the ability to handle single tokens and misspelled words successfully, which is of utmost importance in order to better understand short texts. Finally, the architecture of the approach and its indicators introduce potential to transparently support multilingual data, which is the subject of ongoing investigation.

---

[8] http://commoncrawl.org/ and https://www.flickr.com/.

Acknowledgments. This research was supported in part by an EU H2020 grant provided for the HOBBIT project (GA no. 688227) and CAPES Foundation (BEX 10179135).

References

1. Al-Rfou, R., Kulkarni, V., Perozzi, B., Skiena, S.: Polyglot-NER: massive multilingual named entity recognition. In: Proceedings of the 2015 SIAM International Conference on Data Mining, Vancouver, British Columbia, Canada. SIAM (2015)
2. Basave, A.E.C., Varga, A., Rowe, M., Stankovic, M., Dadzie, A.-S.: Making sense of microposts (#msm2013) concept extraction challenge. In: Cano, A.E., Rowe, M., Stankovic, M., Dadzie, A.-S. (eds.) CEUR Workshop Proceedings, #MSM, vol. 1019, pp. 1–15. CEUR-WS.org (2013)
3. Bontcheva, K., Derczynski, L., Funk, A., Greenwood, M.A., Maynard, D., Aswani, N.: Twitie: an open-source information extraction pipeline for microblog text. In: RANLP, pp. 83–90 (2013)
4. Chiu, J.P., Nichols, E.: Named entity recognition with bidirectional LSTM-CNNs. arXiv preprint arXiv:1511.08308 (2015)
5. Derczynski, L., Maynard, D., Rizzo, G., van Erp, M., Gorrell, G., Troncy, R., Petrak, J., Bontcheva, K.: Analysis of named entity recognition and linking for tweets. Inf. Process. Manage. **51**(2), 32–49 (2015)
6. Etter, D., Ferraro, F., Cotterell, R., Buzek, O., Van Durme, B. Nerit: named entity recognition for informal text. The Johns Hopkins University, The Human Language Technology Center of Excellence, HLTCOE, 810 Wyman Park Drive, Baltimore, Maryland 21211, Technical report (2013)
7. Fei-Fei, L., Fergus, R., Perona, P.: Learning generative visual models from few training examples: an incremental Bayesian approach tested on 101 object categories. Comput. Vis. Image Underst. **106**(1), 59–70 (2007)
8. Fei-Fei, L., Perona, P.: A Bayesian hierarchical model for learning natural scene categories. In: 2005 IEEE Computer Society Conference on Computer Vision and Pattern Recognition, CVPR 2005, vol. 2, pp. 524–531. IEEE (2005)
9. Fletcher, T.: Support vector machines explained (2009). http://sutikno.blog.undip. ac.id/files/2011/11/SVM-Explained.pdf. Accessed 6 June 2013
10. Gattani, A., Lamba, D.S., Garera, N., Tiwari, M., Chai, X., Das, S., Subramaniam, S., Rajaraman, A., Harinarayan, V., Doan, A.: Entity extraction, linking, classification, and tagging for social media: a wikipedia-based approach. Proc. VLDB Endow. **6**(11), 1126–1137 (2013)
11. Lample, G., Ballesteros, M., Subramanian, S., Kawakami, K., Dyer, C.: Neural architectures for named entity recognition. arXiv preprint arXiv:1603.01360 (2016)
12. Liu, X., Zhou, M., Wei, F., Fu, Z., Zhou, X.: Joint inference of named entity recognition and normalization for tweets. In: Proceedings of the 50th Annual Meeting of the Association for Computational Linguistics: Long Papers, vol. 1, pp. 526–535. Association for Computational Linguistics (2012)
13. Lowe, D.G.: Object recognition from local scale-invariant features. In: The Proceedings of the Seventh IEEE International Conference on Computer Vision 1999, vol. 2, pp. 1150–1157 (1999)
14. MacQueen, J., et al.: Some methods for classification and analysis of multivariate observations. In: Proceedings of the Fifth Berkeley Symposium on Mathematical Statistics and Probability, Oakland, CA, USA, vol. 1, pp. 281–297 (1967)

15. Nadeau, D., Sekine, S.: A survey of named entity recognition and classification. Lingvisticae Investigationes **30**(1), 3–26 (2007)
16. Tursun, O., Sinan, K.: A challenging big dataset for benchmarking trademark retrieval. In: IAPR Conference on Machine Vision and Applications (2015)
17. Philbin, J., Chum, O., Isard, M., Sivic, J., Zisserman, A.: Object retrieval with large vocabularies and fast spatial matching. In: 2007 IEEE Conference on Computer Vision and Pattern Recognition, pp. 1–8. IEEE (2007)
18. Ratinov, L., Roth, D.: Design challenges and misconceptions in named entity recognition. In: Proceedings of the Thirteenth Conference on Computational Natural Language Learning, pp. 147–155. Association for Computational Linguistics (2009)
19. Ritter, A., Clark, S., Etzioni, O., et al.: Named entity recognition in tweets: an experimental study. In: Proceedings of the Conference on Empirical Methods in Natural Language Processing, pp. 1524–1534. Association for Computational Linguistics (2011)
20. Roberts, A., Gaizauskas, R.J., Hepple, M., Guo, Y.: Combining terminology resources and statistical methods for entity recognition: an evaluation. In: LREC (2008)
21. Sivic, J., Zisserman, A.: Video Google: a text retrieval approach to object matching in videos. In: Proceedings Ninth IEEE International Conference on Computer Vision 2003, pp. 1470–1477. IEEE (2003)
22. Van Erp, M., Rizzo, G., Troncy, R.: Learning with the web: spotting named entities on the intersection of NERD and machine learning. In: #MSM, pp. 27–30 (2013)

Online Expectation Maximization for Language Characterization of Streaming Text

Jonathan Wintrode[(⊠)], Nhat Bui, Jan Stepinski, and Chris Reed

Raytheon Applied Signal Technology, Sunnyvale, CA 94085, USA
jonathan.c.wintrode@raytheon.com

Abstract. This work examines the effect of online Expectation Maximization (EM) methods for learning language distributions of unlabeled text data in a streaming environment and its impact on language identification (ID). We show that unsupervised estimation of the language distribution over the test environment improves ID error by up to 40% relative to a mismatched prior scenario. EM-based strategies also improve distribution estimates over a simple maximum likelihood baseline by up to 75% on our largest test set. By introducing online approaches we can achieve maximal ID performance after only a single pass over the data, and achieve our best distribution estimate when compared to the batch approach while processing no more than 25% of the data.

1 Introduction

In the world of high-volume social media data streams, online processing with statistical Natural Language Processing (NLP) tools is now commonplace. Tweets, blogs, news, status updates, ads: all are uploaded, scanned, tagged, filtered, characterized, or routed to the desired audience. Keeping these algorithms, or more precisely their underlying classifiers, properly calibrated is a critical task, not only to the user experience, but also, in the case of ads, the bottom line.

In this work, we consider textual language identification (ID) as our core task. Language ID is useful both in the labeling of individual messages and also in characterizing of broad segments of a data stream. For example, a public health organization might want to know the distribution of languages for tweets containing the hashtags #zika or #ebola.

A key component of any well-calibrated statistical Language ID system is well-tuned prior probability estimates. Work by McCree in spoken Language ID [7] and Carter et al. [3] illustrate the impact of accurate priors on the task. The other face of prior estimation is language characterization, and McCree showed that this is accomplished in a straightforward, unsupervised manner with an EM-based (expectation maximization) approach.

The downside to traditional EM (batch) techniques is the necessity to make multiple passes over the entire data set during optimization. In a high-volume

© Springer International Publishing AG, part of Springer Nature 2018
I. Garrigós and M. Wimmer (Eds.): ICWE 2017, LNCS 10544, pp. 200–208, 2018.
https://doi.org/10.1007/978-3-319-74433-9_18

setting, we cannot assume we can retain the entirety of the data stream during prior estimation. Therefore we consider online unsupervised techniques for this setting.

Using Twitter's public language-annotated corpus of tweets (cf. [10]), we can show online EM techniques improve Language ID performance more effectively than a batch approach on most if not all tests drawn from this corpus. Online distribution estimation also achieves equivalent or better estimates of the true priors, while processing an order of magnitude less data.

2   Language ID of Text

State of the art textual Language ID systems typically employ classifiers based on character or byte N-gram features. Two of the top performing systems on micro-blogs (Twitter) are Naive Bayes classifiers with well-tuned feature sets: langid.py from [5] and Google's Compact Language Detector, CLD2 [9]. The usefulness of well-tuned prior estimates is suggested directly by the Bayesian formulation for predicting language label $\hat{l}$ for document d:

$$\hat{l} = \underset{i}{\operatorname{argmax}} P(d|l_i) \cdot P(l_i) \tag{1}$$

Typically the priors $P(l)$ are estimated based on the language distribution of the training corpus. An off-the-shelf model, in most scenarios, will be mis-calibrated. Re-training the system would require additional labeled data, time, and compute to do so (a challenge for browser-based installations, such as the CLD2 system).

Yet without additional labeled data, the unsupervised method of [7] reduced error rates over the uniform prior scenario from 10% to 70% relative. Although not focusing specifically on the prior estimation task, Carter et al. [3] looked at the impact of priors on a smaller 5-language Twitter corpus and found similar but smaller magnitude improvements of roughly 5%.

For this work, we use the `langid.py` system because it is fully open source and allows us to train new models or to modify only the prior probability estimates for an existing model. Other techniques besides Naive Bayes have been studied and shown to be effective at the basic identification task, including Prediction by Partial Matching [1] as well as deep learning approaches [6]. Whether priors are used directly, as in Naive Bayes, or applied as a second calibration step, we believe the conclusions presented here are applicable regardless of the particular classifier.

3   Online EM for Distribution Estimation

The Expectation Maximization algorithm (EM) has been the workhorse for estimation of probabilistic models from unlabeled data. As described by McCree [7], the estimation of the underlying language distribution in an unlabeled data setting is best described by an EM process. In the E step for iteration k, expected

---

Algorithm 1. Batch EM

$P_1 \leftarrow 1/|L|$
for iteration $k \leftarrow 1 \ldots N$ **do**
   $C \leftarrow \mathbf{0}$
   for $d \in |D|$ **do**   ▷ E step
      Compute $p(l|d)$, $\forall l$ with P_k
      $C[l] \leftarrow C[l] + p(l|d)$, $\forall l$
   $\hat{P} \leftarrow C/Z$ ▷ M step
   $P_{k+1} \leftarrow \eta\hat{P} + (1 - \eta)P_k$

Algorithm 2. Stepwise EM (sEM)

$P_1 \leftarrow 1/|L|$, $k \leftarrow 1$, $C_1 \leftarrow P_1 \cdot |D|$
for iteration $n \leftarrow 1 \ldots N$ **do**
   for $B \subset |D|$, $|B| = m$ **do**
      $\hat{C} \leftarrow \mathbf{0}$
      for $d \in B$ **do**   ▷ E step
         Compute $p(l|d)$, $\forall l$ with P_{n-1}
         $\hat{C}[l] \leftarrow \hat{C}[l] + p(l|d)$, $\forall l$
      $C_{k+1} \leftarrow \eta_k\hat{C} + (1 - \eta_k)C_k$ ▷ M step
      $P_{k+1} \leftarrow C_{k+1}/Z$, $k \leftarrow k + 1$

---

counts for each language are generated using the current priors P_k, and in the M step, the priors for iteration $k + 1$ are computed from these estimates.

In traditional batch EM, we perform the E and M steps over all the data, once per iteration. In an online setting, the driving assumption is that we get to see each data item only once. A number of online EM approaches have been proposed, including two related techniques styled *Incremental EM* by Neal and Hinton [8] and *Stepwise EM*, presented in a general form by Cappé and Moulines [2] and studied in the context of NLP tasks by Liang and Klein [4].

The key difference between batch and online EM is that for online variants, the E and M steps (parameter updates) occur every time an example is observed rather than once per iteration over the entire corpus. True online EM would then consist of single iteration over the data. The algorithms in [4] relax this assumption by running multiple iterations over the data but performing the E and M steps in an online manner. A standard alternative both we and Liang and Klein employ, analogous to gradient descent approaches, is to process a mini-batch of m examples rather than one example at a time.

We consider three EM variants: traditional batch EM; *Stepwise EM* based on [4], with and without mini-batches; and a hybrid *Streaming EM* approach which performs multiple iterations over each mini-batch but does not visit each batch more than once. We present pseudocode for the three approaches as applied to the language distribution estimation task respectively as Algorithms 1, 2, and 3.

For a set of languages L we denote as C the count vector of sufficient statistics computed from soft counts of classifier posteriors $p(l|d)$ over the current document set D. The current prior estimate at step k is an $|L|$-dimension distribution P_k and the rate parameter is denoted η_k. An appropriate normalization constant Z is maintained to ensure the current estimate $\hat{P}$ is a proper distribution.

Algorithm 3. Streaming EM (stEM)

$P_1 \leftarrow 1/|L|,\ k \leftarrow 1,\ C_1 \leftarrow P_1 \cdot |D|$
for batch $i \leftarrow 1 \ldots X$ **do**
    Sample batch $B_i \subset D,\ |B_i| = m$
    for iteration $n \leftarrow 1 \ldots N$ **do**
        $\hat{C} \leftarrow \mathbf{0}$
        for $d \in B_i$ **do** $\triangleright$ E step
            Compute $p(l|d),\ \forall l$ with P_k
            $\hat{C}[l] \leftarrow \hat{C}[l] + p(l|d),\ \forall l$
        $C_{k+1} \leftarrow \eta_k \hat{C} + (1 - \eta_k)C_k$ $\triangleright$ M step
        $P_{k+1} \leftarrow C_{k+1}/Z,\ k \leftarrow k + 1$

---

4   Data and Experiments

To examine the related aspects of identification performance and accuracy and efficiency in distribution estimation, we use Twitter's published Language ID evaluation corpus [10]. We use the uniformly sampled corpus, and at the time of our experiments, 71119 tweets in 80 languages were still available for download. For classification, as previously mentioned, we use the `langid.py` package from Liu and Baldwin [5] with default models trained on 97 languages, but not directly on Twitter.

We remove 'undefined' languages and restrict ourselves to an 80-language closed- set task. From this set we also selected 10 random subsets each of size $\{2, 5, 10, 20, 40\}$ to perform the Language ID and prior estimation tasks over an increasing number of language classes. Except for the full set, results are averaged over the 10 runs per subset size.

For the identification task we report the error rate, defined as the fraction of documents incorrectly labeled. For distribution estimation, we report RMS (root mean squared) error (Eq. 2) between the true distribution P_t and estimate P_k at step k. We also considered KL divergence between the two distributions, but as the trends were roughly equivalent to RMS error we report only the latter for clarity and brevity.

$$RMSe = \sqrt{\frac{\sum_{l \in L}(P_t(l) - P_k l)^2}{|L|}} \tag{2}$$

For both Batch EM, Stepwise EM, and Streaming EM, we must consider choices for the rate parameter η, and mini-batch size m for the latter two methods. Note that as m increases to the corpus size, Stepwise EM becomes Batch EM.

Although Liang and Klein [4] allow for decaying η_k, we found that in this task it offered no benefit, converging much more slowly compared to a fixed η.

As an illustration, Fig. 1 shows the ID error after 2 iterations on the full 80-language set for both Batch and Stepwise EM given varied η and m. For this task, Batch EM was more affected by the rate parameter, but mostly in terms of convergence rate, not absolute performance. We show this more clearly for the online EM algorithms' performance on the distribution estimation task in the Sect. 5.2 (cf. Figs. 4 and 5). The hyperparameters affect the rate of convergence, not the final value.

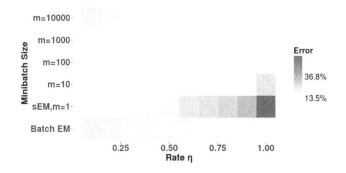

Fig. 1. ID Error for choices of η and m, Batch EM and Stepwise EM.

5   Results

5.1   Identification

Our first set of results illustrates the impact of estimated priors on the identification task (cf. Fig. 2). In the uniform prior condition, assuming no knowledge of the true distribution and no prior estimation, the error ranges from 2.2% to 21.8%. The 'Default' condition, using potentially mismatched priors based on the langid.py's default model, performs nearly as poorly as using uniform priors, with only 21.4% error on the 80 language condition. By contrast, the ideal scenario, with target priors known in advance, the error ranges from 1.8% to 11%.

Prior re-estimation using any of the previously described algorithms, Batch, Stepwise (sEM), or Streaming (stEM), when converged, gives ID error rates between 1.9% to 13.1%. The online approaches improve over the batch approach by roughly 1% to 2% absolute for the largest subset sizes, and as we discuss in the next section, they can achieve this with significantly fewer iterations over the data. While we cannot quite match the ideal condition, particularly as the number of classes increases, we can remove 75% or more of the gap in performance due to mismatched priors.

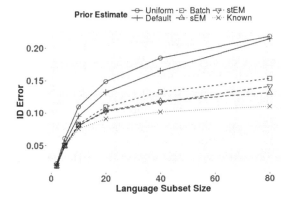

Fig. 2. ID Error for each EM method.

Regarding hyperparameter settings, these results reflect performance after 2 iterations over the data, given optimal settings from η and m. Batch EM achieved additional improvements from 15% to 14% on the 80 language set but required up to 10 iterations in total, whereas Fig. 2 reflects the performance achievable by an equivalent amount of processing between the EM approaches.

5.2 Distribution Estimation

Our second task is language distribution estimation, characterizing the overall data stream in addition to individual messages. For this task, a reasonable baseline is the Maximum Likelihood (ML) estimate from the uniform prior system (one iteration of Batch EM with $\eta = 1$). Figure 3 shows significant improvements over the ML baseline for all three EM variants, including up to a 75% relative

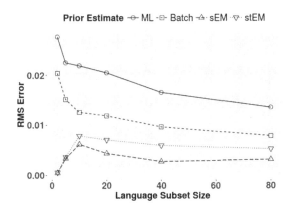

Fig. 3. Minimal RMS error per subset size.

reduction in the RMS error on the full 80-language test. These results present
the best observed performance over all 10 iterations.

The online approaches outperform Batch EM for all language subsets, more
significantly so for smaller subset sizes. When we consider the convergence of
Streaming versus Stepwise EM (cf. Fig. 5), however, the volatility once convergence is more or less achieved may account for differences between the minimally
observed RMS error of the two online approaches. But for a high volume environment the absolute error reduction at convergence is only part of the story;
the rate of convergence is the other.

Looking at the estimation error as a function of the data processed by each
algorithm, we can see in Figs. 4 and 5 the efficiency of the online approaches
vis-a-vis the batch method. Focusing on the full 80-language set, in Fig. 4 we
can see the effect of hyperparameters on convergence more clearly. Decreasing
the batch size m and increasing the rate parameter η both speed up convergence
to the point at which the observed minimum occurs after the algorithm touches

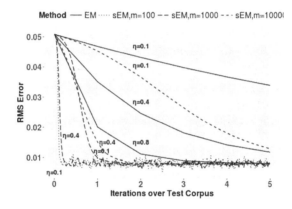

Fig. 4. RMSe by data observed, Batch EM and Stepwise EM (sEM).

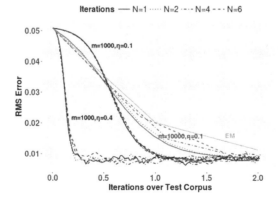

Fig. 5. RMSe by data observed, Stepwise EM (N = 1) and Streaming EM.

at most 25% of the data. With batch sizes of $m <= 100$, increasing η beyond 0.1 induces significant volatility.

When we look at the Streaming EM variant, we note that with iterations $N = 1$ this is equivalent to Stepwise EM. Increasing the number of iterations on each mini-batch has little effect on the overall estimation performance. It is just as good to update the estimate and process a new mini-batch. That being the case, we can say that when compared to a standard batch approach, the optimal estimation results can be achieved either Stepwise and Streaming EM with an order of magnitude less data.

6   Conclusion

We have presented a study of the positive impact of online EM methods for both estimating language distributions and improving per-document language identification from those estimates. Unlike a traditional batch approach, which as we have shown requires multiple passes over the data to achieve both its optimal prior estimate and associated identification improvement, online approaches quickly converge to maximal performance on both tasks. We can achieve converged prior estimates with at most 25% of the data needed by one pass of a batch approach, and with that estimate we can reduce the identification error rate by up to 40% relative to a uniform prior (unkonwn target environment) baseline.

Although we note the impact of mini-batch selection and rate parameter η, we recognize the need for a more principled stopping criteria or adjustment to the rate η. For the task described in this paper, we also assume the underlying language distribution is static. In subsequent work we hope to restructure the task to consider how to best adapt these online approaches to non-static distributions.

References

1. Bergsma, S., McNamee, P., Bagdouri, M., Fink, C., Wilson, T.: Language identification for creating language-specific twitter collections. In: Proceedings of the Second Workshop on Language in Social Media, pp. 65–74. Association for Computational Linguistics (2012)
2. Cappé, O., Moulines, E.: On-line expectation-maximization algorithm for latent data models. J. Royal Stat. Soc. Ser. B (Stat. Methodol.) 71(3), 593–613 (2009)
3. Carter, S., Weerkamp, W., Tsagkias, M.: Microblog language identification: overcoming the limitations of short, unedited and idiomatic text. Lang. Resour. Eval. **47**(1), 195–215 (2013)
4. Liang, P., Klein, D.: Online EM for unsupervised models. In: Proceedings of Human Language Technologies: The 2009 Annual Conference of the North American Chapter of the Association for Computational Linguistics, pp. 611–619. Association for Computational Linguistics (2009)
5. Lui, M., Baldwin, T.: langid.py: an off-the-shelf language identification tool. In: Proceedings of the ACL 2012 System Demonstrations, pp. 25–30. Association for Computational Linguistics (2012)

6. Mathur, P., Misra, A., Budur, E.: Language Identification from Text Documents (2015). http://cs229.stanford.edu/proj2015/324_report.pdf. Accessed 01 Feb 2017
7. McCree, A.: Estimating and exploiting language distributions of unlabeled data. In: Proceedings of Odyssey, pp. 210–214 (2010)
8. Neal, R., Hinton, G.: A view of the EM algorithm that justifies incremental, sparse, and other variants. In: Learning in Graphical Models, pp. 355–368. Springer (1998)
9. Dick Sites. Compact Language Detector 2 (2014). https://github.com/CLD2Owners/cld2. Accessed 01 Feb 2017
10. Trampus, M.: Evaluating Language Identification Performance (2015). https://blog.twitter.com/2015/evaluating-language-identification-performance. Accessed 01 Feb 2017

3rd International Workshop
on Mining the Social Web

Preface

Spiros Sirmakessis, Technological Institution of Western Greece, Greece;Maria Rigou, University of Patras, Greece; Evanthia Faliagka, Technological Institution of Western Greece, Greece, Olfa Nasraoui, University of Louisville, USA

The last decade the Social Web is rapidly becoming an important part of our digital lives with shared information in formats that range from text to rich multimedia. Social web networks help to improve the sense of connectedness with real and/or online communities and can be effective communication tools for corporations and groups.

Modeling and mining the vast volume of data dynamically produced and maintained in social web environments is a great challenge in an effort to extract, represent and discover meaningful knowledge. Social web mining is a type of data mining, a set of techniques for analyzing social web data to detect patterns. It combines data mining with social computing with the purpose of developing novel algorithms and tools ranging from text and multimedia content mining to web structure mining and community detection.

Social web mining is applied in domains such as user modeling, recommendations, personalization, e-learning, e-recruitment, opinion mining, sentiment analysis, visualization, folksonomies, multimedia searching and so on. These trends raise the need for mining big data comprising heterogeneous, dynamic data trails, as well as the critical need for privacy, security and ethical considerations.

This workshop aimed at studying (and even going beyond) the state of the art in social web mining, a field that merges the topics of social network applications and web mining, which are both major topics of interest for ICWE. The basic scope is to create a forum for professionals and researchers in the fields of personalization, web search, text mining etc to discuss the application of their techniques and methodologies in this new and very promising research area.

The workshop tried to encourage the discussion on new emergent issues related to current trends derived from the creation and use of modern Web applications.

Five very interesting presentations took place in two sessions, followed by a constructive discussion in new research issues and collaborations

- "Measuring personal branding in Social Media: Towards an Influence Indication score" by Evanthia Faliagka, Kostas Ramantas, Maria Rigou, and Spiros Sirmakessis, Technological Educational Institution of Western Greece, University of Patras, Hellenic Open University, Greece and Iquadrat Informatica, Barcelona, Spain.
  The exploding use of social media sites has allowed everyday people to build their own online personal brand, exploiting the social web to promote their strengths and unique qualities. Such passionate individuals make great fits for certain roles in a company as well as in leadership positions. Moreover, for certain positions the ability of candidates to build a strong personal brand and attract a high number of followers is a robust success predictor. In this direction, authors propose a new module for assessing candidates' personal brand strength, based on their social web activity. This module is then integrated in a company-oriented e-recruitment system which automates the candidate pre-screening process and evaluated as part of a pilot scenario.
- "Harvesting Knowledge from Social Networks: Extracting Typed Relationships among Entities." by Andrea Caielli, Marco Brambilla, Stefano Ceri and Florian Daniel, Politecnico di Milano, Italy.

Knowledge bases like DBpedia, Yago or Google's Knowledge Graph contain huge amounts of ontological knowledge harvested from (semi-)structured, curated data sources, such as relational databases or XML and HTML documents. Yet, the Web is full of knowledge that is not curated and/or structured and, hence, not easily indexed, for example social data. Most work so far in this context has been dedicated to the extraction of entities, i.e., people, things or concepts. The paper describes authors' work toward the extraction of relationships among entities. The objective is reconstructing a typed graph of entities and relationships to represent the knowledge contained in social data, without the need for a-priori domain knowledge. The experiments with real datasets show promising performance across a variety of domains.

- "Novel Comment Spam Filtering Method on Youtube: Sentiment Analysis and Personality Recognition" by Enaitz Ezpeleta, Inaki Garitano, Ignacio Arenaza-Nuno, Urko Zurutuza and Jose Maria Gomez Hidalgo, Electronics and Computing Department, Mondragon University and Pragsis Technologies, Spain

  The deeply entrenched use of Online Social Networks (OSNs), where millions of users share unconsciously any kind of personal data, offers a very attractive channel to attackers. They provide the possibility of sending spam messages through different channels (wall posts, comments, private messages). In this paper authors propose a novel spam filtering method focused on social media spam. It aims to demonstrate that using sentiment analysis and personality recognition techniques, in order to analyze the content of the texts, the improvement of spam filtering results is possible. They add these features to each OSN spam both independently and jointly, and then we compare Bayesian spam filters with and without the new features in terms of the number of false positive and accuracy. At the end, the results of the top ten filtering classifiers have been improved, reducing also the number of false positives (26.69% on average), reaching an 82.55% of accuracy.

- "Mining Communication Data in a Music Community: A Preliminary Analysis", by Fabio Calefato, Giuseppe Iaffaldano, Filippo Lanubile, Antonio Lategano and Nicole Novielli, University of Bari, Dip. Informatica, Bari, Italy.

  Comments play an important role within online creative communities because they make it possible to foster the production and improvement of authors' artifacts. Authors investigate how comment-based communication help shape members' behavior within online creative communities. In this paper, they report the results of a preliminary study aimed at mining the communication network of a music community for collaborative songwriting, where users collaborate online by first uploading new songs and then by adding new tracks and providing feedback in forms of comments.

- "Analyzing Museums and Key Influential Users on Twitter during the 'European Night of Museums 2016'", by Brigitte Juanals and Jean-Luc Minel, IRSIC, Aix Marseille University and University Paris Nanterre - CNRS, France

  In this paper, authors start by presenting a representation of message flows and their lexical and topic contents on Twitter, then an instrumented methodology to describe and analyze these flows and their distribution among the various stakeholders. The aim is to explore the engagement and interactions between different types of stakeholders and to identify key influential users. They apply their methodology and tools to the 12th edition of the cultural event "European Night of Museums" (NDM16).

June 2017

Spiros Sirmakessis
Maria Rigou
Evanthia Faliagka
Olfa Nasraoui

Organization

Program Committee

Evanthia Faliagka	Technological Educational Institution of Western Greece, Greece
John Garofalakis	University of Patras, Greece
Koutheair Khribi	ALECSO Organization, Tunisia
Maja Pivec	University of Applied Sciences FH JOANNEUM, Austria
Maria Rigou	University of Patras, Greece
Muhammet Demirbilek	Suleyman Demirel University, Turkey
Michalis Xenos	University of Patras, Greece
Olfa Nasraoui	University of Louisville, USA
Paolo Crippa	Università Politecnica delle Marche, Italy
Spiros Sioutas	Ionian University, Greece
Spiros Sirmakessis	Technological Educational Institution of Western, Greece
Zanifa Omary	The Institute of Finance Management, Tanzania

Analysing Cultural Events on Twitter

Brigitte Juanals[1] and Jean-Luc Minel[2(✉)]

[1] IRSIC, Aix Marseille University, Marseille, France
Brigitte.Juanals@univ-amu.fr
[2] MoDyCo, University Paris Nanterre - CNRS, Nanterre, France
jean-luc.minel@u-paris10.fr

Abstract. In this paper, we first present a model to represent message flows and their contents on Twitter, then a model and an instrumented methodology to describe and analyze these flows and their distribution among the various stakeholders. The aim is to explore the engagement and interactions between different types of stakeholders. We apply our methodology and tools to the 12th edition of the cultural event "European Night of Museums" (NDM16).

Keywords: Circulation of information · Influence
Instrumented methodology · Social network · Twitter
European Night of Museums

1 Introduction

Since the 2000s social networks owned by American companies (Facebook, Twitter, Instagram, YouTube, etc.) have become very popular in the cultural field. As these social networks attract the general Internet audience, cultural institutions have incorporated into their communication strategies a strong presence in these digital spaces through the dissemination of contents (news, practical or cultural information, representations of works and associated information, etc.) and the development of interaction with their public. These evolutions go hand in hand with the development of cultural marketing. Lastly, the "eventualization" of culture, following the explosion of temporary exhibitions, has amplified a "shift of patrimonial institutions to the logic of working like streaming media". It is a fact that in France and in Europe, over the last decade, temporary cultural events have multiplied, in the form of public events or festivals - such as the "European Heritage Days", "European Night of Museums", "La Nuit de l'Archéologie", "Passeurs d'images". These events have now become recurrent, generating initiatives that contribute to cultural outreach in society as well as to the development of cultural tourism.

Our methodology is based on the analysis of these events and checked on the 12th edition of the cultural event 'European Night of Museums' (NDM16), which took place in the heritage institutions that were partners in the event and was extended to digital media on the website dedicated to the operation as

I. Garrigós and M. Wimmer (Eds.): ICWE 2017, LNCS 10544, pp. 213–222, 2018.
https://doi.org/10.1007/978-3-319-74433-9_19

well as on social networks (Twitter, Facebook, Instagram). The outline of this paper is the following. First, in Sect. 2, we will present the specificities and the contribution of our approach and our methodology to collect and analyze flows of tweets. In Sect. 3, we describe the model designed then in Sect. 4 we discuss the results from quantitative and lexical analysis. Finally, we conclude in Sect. 5.

2   Related Work

Nowadays, museums and cultural institutions use social media as a means to communicate and promote their cultural activities, as well as to interact and engage with their visitors, the main use of social media by museums remaining information and promotion of activities such as exhibition openings or events [6]. A qualitative study on the ways that museums use Twitter in this perspective shows that they choose to link resources, engage the public with new social media tools and favor a two-way form of communication [14]. Villaespesa Cantalapiedra [17] carried out fieldwork including a series of interviews with museum professionals which showed that the term 'engagement', 'can be interpreted in a variety of ways (. . .): From fostering inspiration and creativity in the user, originating a change of behavior, increasing the user's knowledge, receiving interaction from the user in the form of a like or a comment,' [17]. In particular, when Langa [10] studied the building of a relationship that forty-eight museums engaged on Twitter with online users, she showed that its primary use was as a marketing tool (public relations, events announcements, fact of the day, etc.) and that it led to a lesser engagement and a low audience participation. As mentioned in [7], tweet analysis has led to a large number of studies in many do-mains such as ideology prediction in Information Sciences [4], natural disaster anticipation in Emergency [15] and tracking epidemic [13] while work in Social Sciences and Digital Humanities has developed tweet classifications [16]. However, few studies aim at classifying tweets according to communication classes. An exception worth mentioning is the work presented in Lovejoy and Saxton [11] in which the authors (Twitter users) analyze the global behavior of nonprofit organizations on Twitter based on three communication classes: Information, Community and Action classes. Recently, several studies on tweet classification have been carried out in NLP [1,9] but to the best of our knowledge, only [3] has classified cultural institutional tweets in communication categories based on NLP techniques.

3   Designing a Methodology

3.1   Designing a Model

So far, scientific studies on the forms of digital communication engaged in by cultural institutions and audiences have analyzed the practices of institutions and audiences as well as their uses of digital platforms. Our contribution aims to design a model for the circulation of message flows on a social network platform, taking the case of Twitter. We chose an inter-institution space that corresponds both to a social network platform widely used by institutions and to a growing communication situation in the cultural field at the present time. This choice led us to focus on the category of cultural event programmed on a national scale. This enables us to explore how information circulates and is exchanged as well as the communication relations established between the different stakeholders present in an inter-institution space. Based on the analysis of message flows on the scale of the cultural event studied, we attempt to answer questions concerning the communicative practices of the stakeholders, such as for example, what is the current strategic usage of social media conducted by different types of stakeholders (not only museums or cultural institutions) during cultural events? We expect marketing and promotional messages to be present but we also inquire into initiatives fostering audience participation, providing cultural contents and favoring interaction with users. We will specifically examine the communication policies of cultural institutions during a cultural event on Twitter in order to assess whether they are part of their mission to democratize culture for a wide audience on this platform or whether it is rather a marketing campaign to promote a place or an event. A second question concerns the identification of passing accounts (see below). Finally, two periods of time were distinguished. A period before the event and a period during the event. This distinction is an empirical consequence of our studies on Museum Week 2014 et 2015 [3].

Terminology and Attributes. Our analysis focuses on Twitter messages (called tweets) sent by accounts of cultural institutions and by other institutional or non-institutional stakeholders who participated in a cultural event. A first step was to build a terminology to describe the objects studied according to three dimensions: the message, the stakeholders, and the forms of stakeholder participation. Concerning messages, we will call a message sent by a twitter account an "original tweet" and an original message sent by an account different from the issuing account a "retweet". The current Twitter API gives access to the original tweet (and its sending account) of a retweet. The generic term tweet includes "original tweet" and "retweet". Regarding stakeholder qualification, we distinguished Twitter accounts, accounts managed by institutions (called "organizational account", OA), and accounts managed by individuals (called "private account", PA). This distinction is based both on the official list of museums in France provided by the French open data website, and the description on the Twitter account provided by the Twitter API. The analysis of the description field is necessary because non-museum institutions such as the City of Paris (@Paris) participated in the Night of Museums. Analysis of the flows during the MuseumWeek 2014 and 2015, European Night of Museums 2016, Europeans Days Heritage 2016 events, led us to identify six attributes used to qualify accounts according to their modes of participation and one computed score was associated at each attribute (cf. Table 1). We used the terms "participant", "producer", "relayed", "relaying", "mentioned" and "passing". The attribute "participant" was assigned to an account if it produced at least one original tweet or retweet during of the two temporal periods of the event (before and during the event). The attribute "producer" was assigned to an account if it produced at least one original tweet. The attribute "relayed" was assigned to an account if at least one of its tweets was retweeted or quoted. The "relaying" attribute was assigned to an account if the account retweeted or quoted at least one tweet. The "mentioned" attribute was assigned to an account if its Twitter account name was mentioned at least once in a tweet. The attribute "passing" was assigned to an account if it was both "relayed" and "relaying". Our hypothesis is that an account with a high passing score is a key influential user who actively participates at the circulation of information. Consequently, we computed for each account a passing score that is the product between the number of accounts that this account retweeted and the number of accounts that retweeted it. The value of this index is not significant in itself; it simply provides a means of comparing accounts. Note that these attributes were calculated irrespective of the number of followers. From these six attributes, it is possible, to compare the behavior of several accounts (see Sect. 4.2). Several quantitative analyses can be carried out. Quantitative analyses focus on the observation of flows and aim to identify accounts that contribute to the circulation of information during the cultural event. For each attribute (see above) a ranking of the accounts is computed, keeping only the first 10 or 15 accounts in this ranking. This make it possible to order the accounts that produce the largest number of original tweets, which are the most retweeted, and so on. In order to build a classifier, a classification analysis of the contents of the messages was carried out in three stages. First, a team composed of two linguists and 10 community managers of cultural institutions designed a model, that is to say, determined the classes in which to categorize the tweets, and the features used to assign a tweet to a class. Four classes were identified (Encouraging participation, Interacting with the community, Promoting the event and informing about it, Sharing experience). The features selected were semio-linguistic (mostly lexical, but also including punctuation marks, emoticons), tweet-specific features (for example, the presence/absence of hashtags in tweets) as well as metadata such as the identity of the account. In the second stage, a classifier was built based on a corpus of 1000 tweets annotated by hand by cultural experts according to the categories defined in the previous step [3]. The classifier is based on the Naive Bayes and SVM models, with unanimous vote. In a third stage, the classifier was applied to the corpus of tweets to categorize all the tweets. Results of the thorough evaluation of the quality of the classifier carried out on the MuseumWeek 2015 campaign are detailed in [7]; the F-measure $F_{0.5}$ coefficient is 0.696.

3.2   Implementing the Methodology

We implemented our methodology by building a workflow (cf. Fig. 1) based on the one hand, on open access tools like R^1 (statistical), TXM^2 (text mining),

---

[1] https://www.r-project.org/.
[2] http://textometrie.ens-lyon.fr/.

Table 1. Score calculation method

Participant	0 (no participation in the considered period of time) or 1
Producer	Total amount of tweets and retweets
Relayed	Total number of accounts which relayed his/her original tweets
Relaying	Total number of accounts she/he relayed
Mentioned	Total number of mentions of the account in text tweets
Passing	Product of relayed score by relaying score

Gephi[3] (graphs visualization), Neo4j[4] (graphs mining), Scikit-learn[5] (machine learning), and Sphynx (faceted search engine)[6], and on the other hand, we developed some scripts python. All data are stored in a NoSql database and the scripts are used to query this database and compute specific attributes.

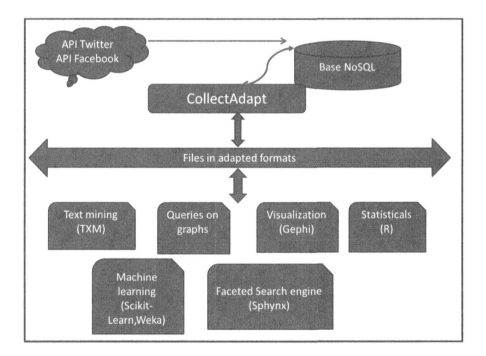

Fig. 1. Workflow and tools

---

[3] https://gephi.org/.

[4] https://neo4j.com/.

[5] http://scikit-learn.org/stable/.

[6] http://sphinxsearch.com/.

4 Applying the Methodology on the European Night of Museums Event

The analyses of the European Night of Museums (NDM16) were carried in the structuring content of the organizational and media framework in order to understand what happened during this cultural event, going beyond the display of quantitative data communicated at the time of its closure, i.e. 3000 events organized in France and in Europe, more than 2 million visitors who participated in the European Night of Museums in France.

The data acquisition stage consisted in harvesting tweets with only one hashtag, the official event hashtag #NDM16. We developed a script Python, based on Twarc (http://github.com/docnow/twarc) module proposed by Ed Summers using the streaming option of Twitter Application Programming Interface (API). In this paper, we limit the analysis to tweets in French sent during the week preceding the event and the day of the event, that is to say from 14 May to 21 May 2016 midnight. The main figures are the following: 11 264 tweets of which 3 301 original tweets (29%), 7 963 retweets (71%) sent by 4 012 participants.

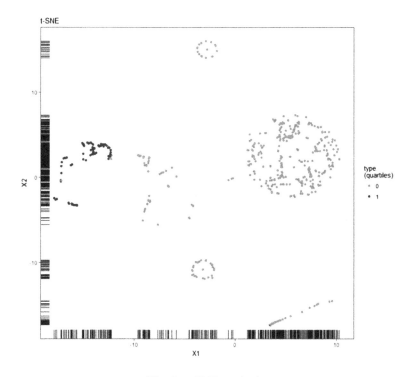

Fig. 2. t-SNE analysis

The specific figures are the following: more than half (56%) of organizational accounts and only 25% of private accounts produced original tweets.

Participation in this event was largely limited to the action of retweeting (75% of tweets) the messages sent by the institutional partners. The findings of the supervised classification of original tweets sent during the event are shown in Table 2. It should be noted that some tweets have been categorized twice (that is why the sum of the total percentages is greater than 100%). This table shows that the organizational accounts tweets mainly (93%) serve to promote and inform about local events planned for the occasion. This result is consistent with the organizational framework of the cultural event, the success of which is partly linked to its attendance. There is also some interaction with the public but messages of engagement are very sparse. We applied the t-SNE algorithm [12] to get a global cartography of the networks (Fig. 1). Several communities are well distinguished. One community (in green) composed mainly of organizational accounts, which is more productive and interactive, and others, composed entirely of private accounts (in pink) which produced few tweets (see Sect. 4.3).

Table 2. Supervised classification

Classes	Percentage
Encouraging participation	4%
Interacting with the community	19%
Promoting the event and informing about it	93%
Sharing experience	0%
Not classified	2%

4.1 Key Influential Users

Passing Accounts. We analysed the top ten passing accounts (see Sect. 3). A remarkable point is the non-correlation between their passing score and their number of followers. The Pearson-correlation computed on the these passing accounts (NuitdesMusées excluded) is equal to 0.15875, that is very low. Consequently, while the growth of followers of museums Twitter accounts is considered as a marketing target, the circulation of information during a cultural event is depending of key influential accounts which are not necessarily what is called 'big players' [5]. Some characteristics of these passing accounts must be pointed out. They are all organizational accounts with the exception of the account '@Mariette Escalier'. The owner of this private account is a professional in the field of cultural mediation. Ranked second after the organizational account of the event although she has less than 2 000 followers. In 5th place, the presence of the account of Alain Juppé, a French politician, mayor of the city of Bordeaux and former prime minister, shows that culture has become a political issue and plays an important role in marketing Cities and territories.

Great diversity was observed in the communicative practices of museum accounts. Some museums relay exclusively organizational accounts, while others relay only private accounts. We also noted that the passing accounts during the event are not the same as the passing accounts of the period preceding the event. Only the '@NuitdesMusées' and '@MinistèreCultureCom' accounts are common to both these periods (see [8] for more details).

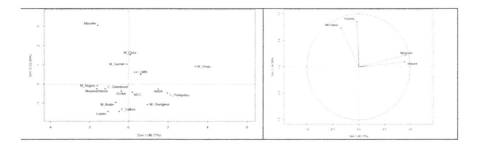

Fig. 3. Principal component analysis

In order to compare the 15 most active accounts, we performed a principal component analysis with 4 variables for each account: number of original tweets, mentioned score, relayed score and passing score (see Sect. 2). We did not take into account the official account of the event (@NuitdesMusees) which due to its official position, presents specific characteristics. This analysis shows the positions occupied by the 15 most active stakeholders in the 2016 NDM (Fig. 1). Among them, the Musée d'Orsay is in a remarkable position, far on the right; it was mentioned and relayed many times because it organized an event (a jazz concert in the museum) which was very well attended. The success of this in situ event was relayed on Twitter which worked in this respect as a soundboard whereas the Louvre Museum, which organized conferences, was seldom mentioned or relayed despite its reputation. Similarly, the position of the private account Mariette Escalier (cultural mediator) occupies another remarkable position, in the left top corner; she is a passing account and she sent a lot of tweets, unlike most private accounts.

Integration Score. The aggregated communities around the passing account are represented in Fig. 2. This spatial representation realized by applying the Louvain algorithm [2] makes possible to highlight several points. The private account of the politician Alain Juppé who sought to enhance his cultural program was largely relayed by the collective who supports him (Fig. 3), but Alain Juppé account (bottom right) is very isolated from the rest of the network. In order to support this, we calculated a score called integration score. This score is equal to the ratio between the cardinality of the set of accounts that have retweeted the passing account, among others, and the cardinality of the set of accounts that have only retweeted the passing account. Thus, if a collective of a passing account is totally isolated from the graph of all accounts, its integration score will be equal to zero; Conversely, if a passing account is well integrated, in other words, the members of this group retweets other accounts, its integration score will be

Fig. 4. Main communities (Color figure online)

equal to 1. For example, Alain Juppé integration score is equal to 0.36 while the score of Mariette Escalier is equal to 0.8. Other communities are grouped around museum accounts (on the top left) and are partially connected to the rest of the network. Nevertheless, it must pointed out that different communities did not interact. In other words, the Musée d'Orsay and the Center Pompidou, two Parisian museums share few common accounts, at least for the Night of Museums event. On the contrary, the community of the private account @Mariette Escalier (on the top right) is much more immersed in the network (Fig. 4).

5   Conclusion

We designed and implemented a methodology to analyze forms of engagement, participation and relationship between cultural institutions, organizations and audiences. Checking this methodology on the cultural event "European Night of Museums" 2016, we first applied the t-SNE algorithm to get a global cartography of the networks. We performed a correspondence analysis that shows the specificity of one private account and the role of two museums in Paris, the Musée d'Orsay and the Centre Pompidou, which played a major role in disseminating information. We intend to dig deeper into the instrumented methodology: more specifically, we are working on the extension of our method in order to take into account an incremental analysis of graphs. This conceptual work brings together research issues on the production and circulation of information with data mining and visualization software. Data mining is seen as an heuristic iterative and incremental process.

References

1. Lin, S.-D., et al. (eds.) 2nd Workshop on Natural Language Processing for Social Media. Association for Computational Linguistics and Dublin City University (2014)
2. Blondel, V., Guillaume, J.L., Lambiotte, R., Lefebvre, E.: Fast unfolding of communities in large networks. J. Stat. Mech. **2008**(10), P10008 (2008)
3. Courtin, A., Juanals, B., Minel, J.-L., de Saint Léger, M.: A tool-based methodology to analyze social network interactions in cultural fields: the use case "MuseumWeek". In: Aiello, L.M., McFarland, D. (eds.) SocInfo 2014. LNCS, vol. 8852, pp. 144–156. Springer, Cham (2015). https://doi.org/10.1007/978-3-319-15168-7_19
4. Djemili, S., Longhi, J., Marinica, C., Kotzinos, D., Sarfat, G.E.: What does twitter have to say about ideology? In: NLP 4 CMC: Natural Language Processing for Computer-Mediated Communication, pp. 16–25 (2014)
5. Espinos, A.: Museums on social media: analyzing growth through case studies. In: Museums and the Web (2016)
6. Fletcher, A., Lee, M.: Current social media uses and evaluations in American museums. Mus. Manag. Curator. **27**, 505–521 (2012)
7. Foucault, N., Courtin, A.: Automatic classification of tweets for analyzing communication behavior museums. In: LREC 2016, pp. 3006–3013 (2017)
8. Juanals, B., Minel, J.: Information flow on digital social networks during a cultural event: methodology and analysis of the European night of museums 2016 on twitter. In: SMS+Society Special Issue (2017)
9. Kothari, A., Magdy, W., Darwish, K., Mourad, A., Taei, A.: Detecting comments on news articles in microblogs. In: Kiciman, E., et al. (eds.) 7th International Conference on Web and Social Media (ICWSM). The AAAI Press (2013)
10. Langa, L.: Does twitter help museums engage with visitors? In: iSchools IDEALS, pp. 484–495. University of Illinois, Aix-les-Thermes (2014)
11. Lovejoy, K., Saxton, G.D.: Information, community, and action: how nonprofit organizations use social media. J. Comput. Mediat. Commun. **17**(3), 337–353 (2012)
12. Van der Maaten, L., Hinton, G.: Visualizing high-dimensional data using t-SNE. J. Mach. Learn. Res. **9**, 2579–2605 (2008)
13. Missier, P., Romanovsky, A., Miu, T., Pal, A., Daniilakis, M., Garcia, A., Cedrim, D., da Silva Sousa, L.: Tracking dengue epidemics using twitter content classification and topic modelling. In: Casteleyn, S., Dolog, P., Pautasso, C. (eds.) ICWE 2016. LNCS, vol. 9881, pp. 80–92. Springer, Cham (2016). https://doi.org/10.1007/978-3-319-46963-8_7
14. Osterman, M., Thirunarayanan, M., Ferris, E., Pabon, L., Paul, N., Berger, R.: Museums and twitter: an exploratory qualitative study of how museums use twitter for audience development and engagement. J. Educ. Multimed. Hypermedia **21**(3), 241–255 (2012)
15. Sakaki, T., Okazaki, M., Matsuo, Y.: Tweet analysis for real-time event detection and earthquake, reporting system development. IEEE Trans. Knowl. Data Eng. **25**(4), 919–931 (2013)
16. Shiri, A., Rathi, D.: Twitter content categorisation: a public library perspective. J. Inf. Knowl. Manag. **12**(4), 1350035 (2013)
17. Villaespesa Cantalapiedra, H.: Measuring social media success: the value of the balanced scorecard as a tool for evaluation and strategic management in museum. Ph.D. thesis, University of Leicester (2015)

Harvesting Knowledge from Social Networks: Extracting Typed Relationships Among Entities

Andrea Caielli, Marco Brambilla, Stefano Ceri, and Florian Daniel[(✉)]

Politecnico di Milano, DEIB, Via Ponzio 34/5, 20133 Milan, Italy
andrea.caielli@mail.polimi.it,
{marco.brambilla,stefano.ceri,florian.daniel}@polimi.it

Abstract. Knowledge bases like DBpedia, Yago or Google's Knowledge Graph contain huge amounts of ontological knowledge harvested from (semi-)structured, curated data sources, such as relational databases or XML and HTML documents. Yet, the Web is full of knowledge that is not curated and/or structured and, hence, not easily indexed, for example social data. Most work so far in this context has been dedicated to the extraction of entities, i.e., people, things or concepts. This paper describes our work toward the extraction of relationships among entities. The objective is reconstructing a typed graph of entities and relationships to represent the knowledge contained in social data, without the need for a-priori domain knowledge. The experiments with real datasets show promising performance across a variety of domains.

Keywords: Social networks · Relationship extraction · Domain graph

1 Introduction

In [3], we outlined a roadmap of work toward the identification and capturing of knowledge that is not yet contained in any well formalized knowledge base but only emerges from the observation of *social data* (data collected from social networks, such as Facebook, Twitter, Instagram). The problem is relevant, as understanding large volumes of social data is complex, and tools able to aid this understanding are still missing. The problem is timely, as it is no longer enough to describe a document only by the sentiment it expresses; it is important to also put that sentiment into context and to move toward comprehensive Social Media Analytics [7]. Finally, the problem is hard, as data in social networks is unstructured, ephemeral, and constantly changing.

In [4], we concentrated on the first building block, i.e., the semi-supervised extraction of *entities* from social data. In this paper we complement that work and report on our first experience with the extraction of *relationships*, able to put entities into context and to give meaning to the co-occurrence of entities inside a document. For instance, if we analyze the tweet in Fig. 1, we are able to

© Springer International Publishing AG, part of Springer Nature 2018
I. Garrigós and M. Wimmer (Eds.): ICWE 2017, LNCS 10544, pp. 223–227, 2018.
https://doi.org/10.1007/978-3-319-74433-9_20

identify two entities and one relationship that allow us to draw a typed triple. If we do so for a set of documents, we are able to draw a complete *domain graph*, producing the desired output.

Fig. 1. Analysis of a tweet on the Vikings TV series

With this paper, we contribute to the state of the art with (i) an integrated social data processing pipeline able to extract typed entities and relationships from Facebook posts and tweets, and (ii) a set of experiments with real datasets that demonstrate the practical viability of the approach. The key distinguishing feature of the work is its focus on highly unstructured social data (tweets and Facebook posts) without reliable grammar structures. Traditional relation extraction approaches – supervised [6], semi-supervised [1] or unsupervised – [5], commonly assume the availability of grammatically correct language corpora.

2   Extraction of Relationships

We approach the extraction of relationships as follows: Social data is extracted from social networks using their APIs or scraping content from their HTML pages (in this work, we specifically concentrate on Twitter and Facebook). Collected data is analyzed for entities and for relationships using different techniques in parallel to increase quality. Once entities and relationships are available, they are consolidated so as to eliminate duplicates and errors and to form correct tuples with consistent entity and relationship types. After analyzing all documents, a dedicated graph viewer enables the user to interactively inspect the obtained graph and to drill down into details.

Before executing this process, we prepare the content so that it becomes most similar to correct natural language, by substituting special symbols with natural language tokens. Social data heavily leverage on # *hashtags* (for topics) and @ *handles* (for identities); we substitute them with their corresponding entities. We also drop *URLs* from the documents, as we don't analyse them (although they are heavily used in social media). Known *acronyms* are written in their full texts and *author names* are added.

Extracting Entities. The extraction of entities leverages on Dandelion (https://dandelion.eu) and the Named Entity Recognizer (NER) of the Stanford coreNLP library (http://nlp.stanford.edu/software/CRF-NER.shtml). The former is based on DBpedia and enables the identification of entities contained in DBpedia. The latter is able to identify entities by analyzing the grammar structure of sentences. Both instruments are fed with the pre-processed data, and outputs are consolidated into one set of entities. After integration, entities are identified with good precision (see below).

Extracting Relationships. The extraction of relationships leverages on coreNLP OpenIE (http://nlp.stanford.edu/software/openie.html) and a purposefully designed extension (heuristic) inspired by the work of Bird et al. [2]: subjects and objects in subject–relationship–object triples identified by OpenIE are associated with an abstract "thing" type if OpenIE fails to identify a proper type. This enables identifying triples for cases where OpenIE would fail and deciding which triple is best if OpenIE extracts multiple conflicting triples for a given document. In addition, using the linguistic tokenization of coreNLP we extract noun-predicate-noun triples by applying pre-defined templates. The relationships identified by the two methods are again combined to avoid repetitions. The integration is based on relationship similarity and containment and analyzes the verbs, subjects and objects, giving preference to the most expressive relationships (containing the others).

Integrating and Typing Relationships. A good domain graph requires typed relationships. This is achieved by means of two complementary techniques: First, all identified verbs are clustered into synonym classes using wordnet-magic (https://www.npmjs.com/package/wordnet-magic), a node.js module for WordNet (https://wordnet.princeton.edu). Second, verbs are categorized linguistically using VerbNet (https://verbs.colorado.edu/verb-index/) and by looking for the membership in classes of the verb describing a relationship. We use both techniques and consolidate identified types.

3   Evaluation and Lessons

We ran the described relationship extraction process on five different datasets with documents retrieved from Facebook and Twitter (see the used Twitter/Facebook handles and hashtags between parentheses): *Black Sails* (#BlackSails, @BlkSails_ STARZ, @blacksails.starz), *Teen Wolf* (#TeenWolf, @MTVteenwolf, @Teen-Wolf), *Vikings* (#Vikings, @Vikings, @Vikings), the *Milan Fashion Week 2016* (#MFW, Twitter only), and *Rugby* (#AsOne, #RBS6nations, @rbs_6 _nations, @rbs6nations). Table 1 reports some statistics about the

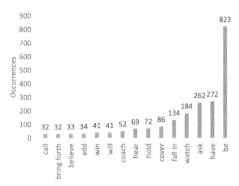

Fig. 2. Relationship types identified for the Rugby dataset

datasets: *# docs* tells the number of documents extracted per domain, *# entities* and *# rels* the number of entities and relationships extracted, and *# verb* *rels* the number of relationships for which meaningful descriptive verbs could be identified (types of relationships). Figure 2 exemplifies the types of relationships extracted for the Rugby dataset using synonym classes: besides the predominance of "bc" and "have," the identified verbs provide effective insight into the typical terminology of the domain.

Table 1. Description of datasets with P/R of algorithm

	Dataset				
	Black Sails	Teen Wolf	Vikings	Milan Fashion Week	Rugby
# docs	2495	2346	1969	1136	1796
# entities	1243	1045	978	1157	1558
# rels	2025	1549	1378	2311	5356
# verb rels	66	81	146	288	437
P(entities)	83.7%	76.0%	78.8%	67.3%	73.1%
R(entities)	79.9%	72.9%	76.3%	59.4%	74.1%
P(rel)	73.8%	75.8%	71.4%	54.7%	71.4%
R(rel)	92.1%	90.2%	82.1%	82.7%	95.2%

In order to assess the precision ($P = \frac{TP}{TP+FP}$) and recall ($R = \frac{TP}{TP+FN}$) of the extraction process, we randomly picked 100 samples from each domain, manually created a ground truth of relationships, and manually labeled the automatically extracted relations as true positive (TP), false positive (FP) or false negative (FN). The second part of Table 1 plots the results for the five datasets, distinguishing P and R for entities only and for complete relationships.

The results show that the joint use of syntactic techniques (that identify subject-predicate-object triples) and semantic techniques (that also require that entities and relationships be typed) produces good precision and recall. Precision is above 70% in all the use cases except the "Milano Fashion Week" – where however we miss social data from Facebook. Recall is in all cases above 80% and goes up to 95% in the case of Rugby; therefore, in our method false negatives are very few: all tokens which are labeled as relationships indeed correspond to relationships. Note that we obtain higher recall on relationships that on entities (therefore, we may miss some entities, but once they are understood then relationships are normally understood).

If we look at the quality of extracted relations, we found stronger results in the case of Rugby, due to the higher quality of tweets and posts, which commented aspects of the game and made statements about reality; in the case of TV series, with comparatively lower precision and recall, many tweets and posts expressed just comments or sentiments unrelated to the actual content of the series.

References

1. Banko, M., Cafarella, M.J., Soderland, S., Broadhead, M., Etzioni, O.: Open information extraction from the web. In: IJCAI 2007, pp. 2670–2676 (2007)
2. Bird, S., Klein, E., Loper, E.: Natural Language Processing with Python. O'Reilly Media Inc., Sebastopol (2009)
3. Brambilla, M., Ceri, S., Daniel, F., Della Valle, E.: On the quest for changing knowledge. In: 2016 Proceedings of the International Workshop on Data-Driven Innovation on the Web, Co-located with Web Science, pp. 3:1–3:5 (2016)
4. Brambilla, M., Ceri, S., Della Valle, E., Volonterio, R., Acero Salazar, F.: Extracting emerging knowledge from social media. In: WWW 2017 (2017, in print)
5. Poon, H., Domingos, P.: Unsupervised ontology induction from text. In: ACL 2010, pp. 296–305 (2010)
6. Soderland, S.: Learning information extraction rules for semi-structured and free text. Mach. Learn. **34**(1–3), 233–272 (1999)
7. Stieglitz, S., Dang-Xuan, L., Bruns, A., Neuberger, C.: Social media analytics. Bus. Inf. Syst. Eng. **6**(2), 89–96 (2014)

Novel Comment Spam Filtering Method on Youtube: Sentiment Analysis and Personality Recognition

Enaitz Ezpeleta[1(✉)] ⓘ, Iñaki Garitano[1], Ignacio Arenaza-Nuño[1],
José María Gómez Hidalgo[2], and Urko Zurutuza[1]

[1] Electronics and Computing Department, Mondragon University,
Goiru Kalea, 2, 20500 Arrasate-Mondragón, Spain
{eezpeleta,igaritano,iarenaza,uzurutuza}@mondragon.edu
[2] Pragsis Technologies, Manuel Tovar, 43-53, Fuencarral, 28034 Madrid, Spain
jmgomez@pragsis.com

Abstract. The deeply entrenched use of Online Social Networks (OSNs), where millions of users share unconsciously any kind of personal data, offers a very attractive channel to attackers. They provide the possibility of sending spam messages through different channels (wall posts, comments, private messages). In this paper we propose a novel spam filtering method focused on social media spam. It aims to demonstrate that using sentiment analysis and personality recognition techniques, in order to analyze the content of the texts, the improvement of spam filtering results is possible. We add these features to each OSN spam both independently and jointly, and then we compare Bayesian spam filters with and without the new features in terms of the number of false positive and accuracy. At the end, the results of the top ten filtering classifiers have been improved, reducing also the number of false positives (26.69% on average), reaching an 82.55% of accuracy.

Keywords: Spam · Social spam · Youtube · Polarity · Security
Personality

1 Introduction

The current massive publication of private information in Online Social Networks (OSNs), give the attackers the possibility of using every single information against the users. Those sites are also becoming an attractive segment to act inside them. This is a significant risk if we take into account the amount of users that the most popular OSNs have: Facebook reached 1.86 billion monthly active users as of December 31, 2016 [1]; Youtube has counted over a billion users in 2017 [2]; and Twitter has 313 million monthly active users as of June 30, 2016[3].

---

[1] http://newsroom.fb.com/company-info/.
[2] https://www.youtube.com/yt/press/statistics.html.
[3] https://about.twitter.com/company.

© Springer International Publishing AG, part of Springer Nature 2018
I. Garrigós and M. Wimmer (Eds.): ICWE 2017, LNCS 10544, pp. 228–240, 2018.
https://doi.org/10.1007/978-3-319-74433-9_21

As an example, in [1], Gao et al. carried out a study to quantify and characterize spam campaigns launched from accounts on OSNs. Their results clearly showed that OSNs are now a major delivery platform targeted for spam.

Being selling products, creating social alarm, creating public awareness campaigns, generating traffic with viral contents, fooling users with suspicious attachments, etc. the main purpose of spam messages, those type of communications have a specific writing style that spam filtering can take advantage of. In this study we focus on the possibility of using Natural Language Processing (NLP) techniques in order to improve results obtained with current spam filtering classifiers. On the one hand, as authors demonstrate in [2], sentiment analysis of the content can help to improve email spam detection. On the other hand, in [3] results validate the possibility of using personality recognition techniques in order to obtain better results. Taking as a baseline these two methods, the main objective of this paper is to demonstrate that sentiment analysis and personality recognition techniques help to improve current spam filtering results.

First, several spam filtering classifiers and different settings are applied to a known dataset in order to identify the best ones. After that, the different sentiment analyzers and a personality recognition model are applied to create new datasets adding this features. In the next step, a combined dataset is created adding the two features together. Once, the datasets are created, the best ten classifier are applied to the different datasets to obtain all the results. Finally, a comparison and an analysis of the results is carried out.

The remainder of this paper is organized as follows. Section 2 describes the previous work conducted in the area of social media spam filtering, and sentiment and personality recognition techniques. Section 3 describes the process of the aforementioned experiments, regarding Bayesian spam filtering and spam filtering using the polarity and the personality of the texts. In Sect. 4, the obtained results are described, and finally, we summarize our findings and give conclusions in Sect. 5.

2   Related Work

2.1   Online Social Network Spam

Numerous research related with spam and OSNs has been carried out [4]. In [5] authors demonstrate that it is possible to automatically identify accounts on three large social networking sites (Facebook, Twitter and MySpace) used by spammers, and block these spam profiles. Further, a framework for spam detection which is able to run across OSNs is proposed in [6]. An equally important study is presented in [7]. The authors developed a tool that detects compromised accounts based on anomalies detected in user behaviour. Finally, in [8] authors used classification and clustering techniques to detect spam campaigns inside different OSNs such as Facebook and Twitter. Ezpeleta et al. [9] showed that personalizing spam messages using publicly available OSN profile information lead to a significantly higher success rate than conventional, non-personalized spam.

In terms of spam inside OSNs, it is important to mention that a huge amount of studies about spam in Twitter have been performed. Authors explain in [10] how criminal accounts mix into and survive in the whole Twitter space. Moreover, Song ct al. [11] demonstrate how spammer detection is possible using the distance and connectivity between receiver and recipient, which are hard to manipulate by spammers.

The main problem is that although a lot of techniques has been published [12,13], spam messages are still a significant problem in OSNs.

2.2   Sentiment Analysis

As explained in [14], the area of SA has had a huge burst of research activity during these last years, but there has been a continued interest for a while. Currently there are several research topics on opinion mining and the most important ones are explained in [15]. Among those topics we identified the document sentiment classification as a possible option for spam filtering.

The main objective of this area is classifying the positive or negative character of a document [14]. In order to classify such sentiment, some researchers use supervised learning techniques, where three classes are previously defined (positive, negative and neutral) [16]. Some other authors propose the use of unsupervised learning. In unsupervised learning techniques, opinion words or phrases are the dominating indicators for sentiment classification [17].

Moreover, authors in [18] demonstrate the possibility of using tweets sentiment analysis in order to improve spam filtering results in Twitter.

2.3   Personality Recognition

Personality is a psychological construct aimed at explaining the wide variety of human behaviors in terms of a few, stable and measurable individual characteristics [19]. As authors explain in [20], two main models to formalize personality have been defined: Myers-Briggs personality model [21], which defines the personality using four dimensions: Extroversion or Introversion, Thinking or Felling, Judging or Perceiving and Sensing or iNtuition; and the Big Five model [22] which divides the personality in 5 traits: Openness to experience, Conscientiousness, Extroversion, Agreeableness and Neuroticism.

As it is shown in [23] every text contains a lot of information about the personality of the authors, being this the reason that personality recognition became a potential tool for Natural Language Processing. During the last years, different research in personality recognition in blogs [24], offline texts [23] or online social networks [25,26] have been published.

In [27] authors prove that personality prediction is feasible, and their email feature set can predict personality with reasonable accuracies. This work shows that it is possible to predict the personality of a writer using email messages.

Moreover, personality recognition is used in order to detect opinion spam in social media [28], and other researchers present the relationship between personality traits and deceptive communication [29].

3   Design and Implementation

As we mentioned in Sect. 1 first of all, the best spam filtering classifiers identified in the literature and several settings are applied to dataset composed of social media spam in order to identify the best ten. After that, original dataset is fed with sentiment, and personality features in a way that four datasets are kept for comparison: the original one, the original with a polarity feature, the original with the personality feature, and finally the aggregation of both polarity and personality features to the original dataset. Next, the ten classifiers that better discriminate the original are applied to all the datasets in order to compare the results. All the process is presented in the Fig. 1.

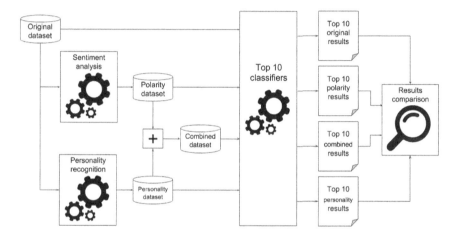

Fig. 1. Novel social media comments filtering method.

During those experiments 10-fold cross-validation technique is used, and the results are analyzed in terms the number of false positive and the accuracy. Accuracy is the percentage of testing set examples correctly classified by the classifier. And legitimate messages classified as spam are considered false positives.

3.1   Datasets

During this work a publicly available dataset is used:

- *Youtube Comments Dataset*[4]: Presented in [30]. This dataset contains multilingual 6,431,471 comments from a popular social media website, Youtube[5]. Among all the comments, 481,334 are marked as spam.
  In order to use similar number of texts to the experiments presented in [2,3]

---

[4] http://mlg.ucd.ie/yt/.
[5] www.youtube.com.

we created a new subset composed of 1,000 spam and 3,000 ham comments. Those texts have been selected randomly and only taking into account comments written in English.

3.2 Social Media Spam Filtering

With the objective of identifying the best spam classifiers, several spam classifiers using different settings are applied to the Youtube Comments dataset.

Following the strategy presented in [2], 7 different classifiers and 56 settings combinations per each classifiers are applied (392 combinations in total), and the best ten results are presented in Table 1.

Table 1. Results of the best ten classifiers

#	Spam classifier	TP	TN	FP	FN	Accuracy (Acc)
1	NBM.c.stwv.go.ngtok	389	2911	89	611	82.50
2	NBMU.c.stwv.go.ngtok	389	2911	89	611	82.50
3	NBM.stwv.go.ngtok	370	2929	71	630	82.48
4	NBMU.stwv.go.ngtok	370	2929	71	630	82.48
5	NBM.c.stwv.go.ngtok.stemmer	379	2919	81	621	82.45
6	NBMU.c.stwv.go.ngtok.stemmer	379	2919	81	621	82.45
7	NBM.stwv.go.ngtok.stemmer	358	2936	64	642	82.35
8	NBMU.stwv.go.ngtok.stemmer	358	2936	64	642	82.35
9	CNB.stwv.go.ngtok	417	2875	125	583	82.30
10	CNB.stwv.go.ngtok.stemmer	400	2891	109	600	82.28

During this study different nomenclatures and acronyms, which are explained in Table 2, are used. We use the same nomenclatures in this paper.

Once the best classifiers and the best results are identified using the original dataset, in the following steps the objective is to improve these results. To do that, the same classifiers are applied to the new datasets, which are created adding personality and polarity features to the original dataset.

3.3 Using Sentiment Analysis to Improve Social Media Spam Filtering

The main objective of this part is to add the polarity of each message to the original dataset. To do that, we analyze the procedure shown in [2] where the best sentiment classifiers were identified to carry out the experiments.

Based on the accuracies presented in the mentioned paper, where several sentiment classifiers were applied to the Movies Review dataset[6], the best four

---

[6] http://www.cs.cornell.edu/People/pabo/movie-review-data/.

Table 2. Nomenclatures

	Meaning		Meaning
CNB	Complement Naive Bayes	.stwv	String to Word Vector
NBM	Naive Bayes Multinomial	.go	General options
NBMU	Naive Bayes Multinomial Updatable	.wtok	Word Tokenizer
.c	idft F, tft F, outwc T[a]	.ngtok	NGram Tokenizer 1-3
.i.c	idft T, tft F, outwc T[a]	.stemmer	Stemmer
.i.t.c	idft T, tft T, outwc T[a]	.igain	Attribute selection using InfoGainAttributeEval

[a]idft means Inverse Document Frequency (IDF) Transformation; tft means Term Frequency score (TF) Transformation; outwc counts the words occurrences.

classifiers are selected (*Adjective*, *Adjective+*, *TextBlob 0.05* and *TextBlob 0.1*). Those ones are used to annotate the text included in Youtube comments dataset which has not been annotated for sentiment. As a result, we obtain four new datasets (one per each classifier). The original one and the new four are used in the experiments.

3.4 Using Personality Recognition to Improve Social Media Spam Filtering

The next phase in our study aims to apply personality recognition techniques to each Youtube comment in order to create a new dataset, adding this feature to the original dataset.

Like in [3], in this study we use one of the most trusted personality model: Myers-Briggs personality model. This model is composed by four different dimensions (Extroversion or Introversion, Thinking or Feeling, Judging or Perceiving and Sensing or iNtuition), which are mandatory in order to determine the personality of each message. To calculate them, we use publicly available machine learning web services for text classification hosted in *uClassify*[7]. Among all the possibilities offered in this website, we focus on the Myers-Briggs functions developed by Mattias Östmar.

As the author explains, each function determines a certain dimension of the personality type according to Myers-Briggs personality model. The analysis is based on the writing style and should not be confused with the Myers-Briggs Type Indicator (MBTI) which determines personality type based on self-assessment questionnaires. Training texts are manually selected based on personality and writing style according to [31].

Those are the used functions:

– *Myers-Briggs Attitude:* Analyzes the Extroversion or Introversion dimension.
– *Myers-Briggs Judging Function:* Determines the Thinking or Feeling dimension.

---

[7] https://www.uclassify.com.

– *Myers-Briggs Lifestyle:* Determines the Judging or Perceiving dimension.
– *Myers-Briggs Perceiving Function:* Determines the Sensing or iNtuition dimension.

Each function returns a float within the range [0.0, 1.0] per each pair of characteristics of the dimension. For example, if we test a certain text and we obtain X value for Extroversion, the value for Introversion is 1-X. Thus, we only record one value per each function: Extroversion, Sensing, Thinking and Judging.

Those four values of each comment are added to the original dataset in order to create a new dataset. During the experiments, this new dataset is used in order to see the influence of the personality during the social media spam filtering. To do that, we apply the top ten classifiers mentioned previously to the original dataset and to the new one, and we compare the results.

3.5   Combining Sentiment Analysis and Personality Recognition

Finally, in order to demonstrate that the combination of different features can help in OSN spam filtering, we create a new dataset adding the polarity and the personality of each comment to the original dataset.

4   Experimental Results

4.1   Using Sentiment Analysis to Improve Social Media Spam Filtering

Descriptive Experiment. To perform this experiment the sentiment analyzers identified in Sect. 3.3 are applied to the Youtube comments dataset in order to analyze the distribution of the comments in terms of polarity. The average of the obtained results are shown in the Fig. 2.

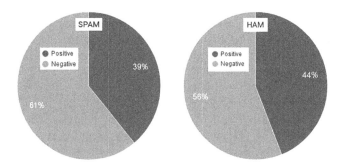

Fig. 2. Sentiment analysis of the original dataset.

Figure 2 shows that while in the previous studies such as [2,3], spam messages are more positive than legitimate messages, in this case, spam comments are more negative than legitimate comments.

Predictive Experiments and Comparison. In order to analyze the influence of the sentiment analysis in spam filtering, predictive experiments are carried out.

Then, we apply the best ten classifiers to the labeled datasets and we compare the obtained results with those obtained without polarity feature. The comparison between different results is presented in Tables 3. Tables show that sentiment analysis of the texts can help to improve the filtering results using an OSN dataset too. For instance, the best accuracy of the original dataset is improved from an 82.50% to an 82.53% using the polarity feature. Furthermore, the number of false positive are reduced in all the cases, reducing by 10% the original number in some cases (for example, from 89 to 70).

Table 3. Comparing original results with the results obtained using different sentiment classifiers.

Classifier #	Sentiment analyzer									
	None		*Adjective*		*Adjective+*		*TextBlob005*		*TextBlob01*	
	FP	Acc	FP	Acc	FP	Acc	FP	Acc	FP	Acc
1	89	82.50	70	82.23	71	82.03	82	82.33	83	82.30
2	89	82.50	70	82.23	71	82.03	82	82.33	83	82.30
3	71	82.48	56	82.18	55	82.03	66	82.35	67	82.33
4	71	82.48	56	82.18	55	82.03	66	82.35	67	82.33
5	81	82.45	60	82.50	60	82.43	74	82.48	74	82.53
6	81	82.45	60	82.50	60	82.43	74	82.48	74	82.53
7	64	82.35	54	82.10	52	81.98	59	82.23	59	82.20
8	64	82.35	54	82.10	52	81.98	59	82.23	59	82.20
9	125	82.30	88	82.43	79	82.43	104	82.40	104	82.40
10	109	82.28	75	82.43	68	82.48	94	82.35	94	82.35

4.2 Using Personality Recognition to Improve Social Media Spam Filtering

Descriptive Experiment. Taking into account the personality recognition functions presented in Sect. 3.4, a descriptive analysis of the dataset is done. During this experiment, the different dimensions of the personality model are added to the original dataset, and a new dataset is created. The obtained results are shown in the Fig. 3.

Although the differences between ham and spam comments are not significant, Fig. 3 shows that the biggest difference is in terms of *thinking* feature. So in the next step, first of all a experiment using all the dimensions is carried out and after that, another test is also done adding only the *thinking* feature to the original dataset to analyze the difference.

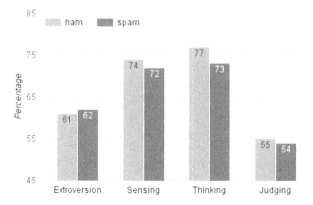

Fig. 3. Descriptive analysis in terms of personality recognition of the dataset.

Predictive Experiment and Comparison. To analyze if personality recognition techniques help in OSNs spam filtering, on the one hand the best ten classifiers identified in Sect. 3.2 are applied to the labeled dataset. On the other hand, taking into account the results obtained in the descriptive experiment, where we can see that the main difference between ham and spam comments is the *thinking* feature, the same experiment is carried out adding only this dimension to the original dataset. The results obtained during this experiment are presented also in Table 4.

Table 4. Comparison of the best ten classifiers

Classifier #	Original		Personality		Thinking	
	FP	Acc	FP	Acc	FP	Acc
1	89	82.50	51	82.15	76	82.38
2	89	82.50	43	81.98	70	82.43
3	71	82.48	42	81.98	61	82.35
4	71	82.48	32	81.73	56	82.35
5	81	82.45	46	82.23	69	82.48
6	81	82.45	37	82.00	65	82.48
7	64	82.35	39	81.83	56	82.40
8	64	82.35	29	81.60	52	82.28
9	125	82.30	60	82.35	100	82.30
10	109	82.28	54	82.40	87	82.45

In the first scenario (personality column), results show that while the number of false positive is reduced in every case, the accuracy is only improved in two out of ten cases.

Using only the most representative dimension (Thinking column), the accuracy is improved in more classifiers than in the previous column. The number of false positives is also reduced compared to the original dataset. Moreover, the best accuracy (82.50%) is not improved but the same percentage is obtained. The significant reduction of the number of false positive give means to validate that personality recognition techniques help in OSNs spam filtering.

4.3   Combining Sentiment Analysis and Personality Recognition

Finally, to analyze if this new detection method could improve OSN spam filtering results, a new experiment is performed. The best ten classifiers are applied to the combined dataset, and a comparison of all the results is presented in Table 5.

Table 5. Comparison of the best classifiers using the dataset of Youtube comments

Classifier #	Used technique								FP reduction (%)
	None		Polarity		Personality		Comb		
	FP	Acc	FP	Acc	FP	Acc	FP	Acc	
1	89	**82.50**	83	82.30	76	82.38	**71**	82.30	20.22
2	89	**82.50**	83	82.30	70	82.43	**66**	82.30	25.84
3	71	**82.48**	67	82.33	61	82.35	**57**	82.20	19.72
4	71	**82.48**	67	82.33	56	82.35	**51**	82.23	28.17
5	81	82.45	74	**82.53**	69	82.48	**60**	82.48	25.93
6	81	82.45	74	82.53	65	82.48	**53**	**82.55**	34.57
7	64	82.35	59	82.20	56	**82.40**	51	82.18	20.31
8	64	**82.35**	59	82.20	52	82.28	**46**	82.13	28.13
9	125	82.30	104	82.40	100	82.30	**84**	**82.50**	32.80
10	109	82.28	94	82.35	87	**82.45**	**75**	82.43	31.19

Results demonstrate that the combination of different techniques improves spam filtering in both terms: accuracy and the number of false positive. The number of false positive is reduced in every case, and the best accuracy is obtained using the combined dataset (82.55%). The number of false positives is reduced to 26.69% on average.

5   Conclusions

This paper presents a new filtering method that gives the research community the opportunity of detecting non evident intent in spam. This new method consists of using polarity and personality features of each text and the combination of both. We added the features to an original dataset, and we carried out different experiments with and without the features.

As results reveal these techniques reduce the number of false positives in 26.69% (on average) and the best accuracy is improved (82.50% vs 82.55%). Despite the difference in percentage does not seem to be relevant, from 82.50% to 82.55%, if we take into account the amount of real spam traffic in OSNs, the improvement is significant. Results provided means to validate our hypothesis that it is possible to identify some insights of the intention of the texts using those techniques, and more spam texts are correctly classified.

Acknowledgments. This work has been developed by the intelligent systems for industrial systems group supported by the Department of Education, Language policy and Culture of the Basque Government. It has been partially funded by the Basque Department of Education, Language policy and Culture under the project SocialSPAM (PI 2014 1 102).

We thank Mattias Östmar for the valuable tools developed and published. And we thank Jon Kågström (Founder of uClassify (https://www.uclassify.com)) for the opportunity to use their API for research purposes.

References

1. Gao, H., Hu, J., Wilson, C., Li, Z., Chen, Y., Zhao, B.Y.: Detecting and characterizing social spam campaigns. In: Proceedings of the 17th ACM Conference on Computer and Communications Security, CCS 2010, pp. 681–683. ACM, New York (2010)
2. Ezpeleta, E., Zurutuza, U., Gómez Hidalgo, J.M.: Does sentiment analysis help in Bayesian spam filtering? In: Martínez-Álvarez, F., Troncoso, A., Quintián, H., Corchado, E. (eds.) HAIS 2016. LNCS (LNAI), vol. 9648, pp. 79–90. Springer, Cham (2016). https://doi.org/10.1007/978-3-319-32034-2_7
3. Ezpeleta, E., Zurutuza, U., Gómez Hidalgo, J.M.: Using personality recognition techniques to improve Bayesian spam filtering. Journal Procesamiento del Lenguaje Natural **57**, 125–132 (2016)
4. Almaatouq, A., Shmueli, E., Nouh, M., Alabdulkareem, A., Singh, V.K., Alsaleh, M., Alarifi, A., Alfaris, A., Pentland, A.S.: If it looks like a spammer and behaves like a spammer, it must be a spammer: analysis and detection of microblogging spam accounts. Int. J. Inf. Secur. **15**(5), 475–491 (2016)
5. Stringhini, G., Kruegel, C., Vigna, G.: Detecting spammers on social networks. In: Proceedings of the 26th Annual Computer Security Applications Conference, ACSAC 2010, pp. 1–9. ACM, New York (2010)
6. Wang, D., Irani, D., Pu, C.: A social-spam detection framework. In: Proceedings of the 8th Annual Collaboration, Electronic Messaging, Anti-abuse and Spam Conference, pp. 46–54. ACM (2011)
7. Egele, M., Stringhini, G., Kruegel, C., Vigna, G.: COMPA: detecting compromised accounts on social networks. In: NDSS. The Internet Society (2013)
8. Gao, H., Chen, Y., Lee, K., Palsetia, D., Choudhary, A.N.: Towards online spam filtering in social networks. In: NDSS. The Internet Society (2012)
9. Ezpeleta, E., Zurutuza, U., Hidalgo, J.M.G.: A study of the personalization of spam content using facebook public information. Log. J. IGPL **25**(1), 30–41 (2017)

10. Yang, C., Harkreader, R., Zhang, J., Shin, S., Gu, G.: Analyzing spammers' social networks for fun and profit: a case study of cyber criminal ecosystem on twitter. In: Proceedings of the 21st International Conference on World Wide Web, pp. 71–80. ACM (2012)

11. Song, J., Lee, S., Kim, J.: Spam filtering in twitter using sender-receiver relationship. In: Sommer, R., Balzarotti, D., Maier, G. (eds.) RAID 2011. LNCS, vol. 6961, pp. 301–317. Springer, Heidelberg (2011). https://doi.org/10.1007/978-3-642-23644-0_16

12. Wang, A.H.: Don't follow me: spam detection in twitter. In: Proceedings of the 2010 International Conference on Security and Cryptography (SECRYPT), pp. 1–10. IEEE (2010)

13. Zheng, X., Zeng, Z., Chen, Z., Yu, Y., Rong, C.: Detecting spammers on social networks. Neurocomputing **159**, 27–34 (2015)

14. Pang, B., Lee, L.: Opinion mining and sentiment analysis. Found. Trends Inf. Retr. **2**(1–2), 1–135 (2008)

15. Liu, B., Zhang, L.: A survey of opinion mining and sentiment analysis. In: Aggarwal, C., Zhai, C. (eds.) Mining Text Data, pp. 415–463. Springer, Boston (2012). https://doi.org/10.1007/978-1-4614-3223-4_13

16. Pang, B., Lee, L., Vaithyanathan, S.: Thumbs up?: Sentiment classification using machine learning techniques. In: Proceedings of the ACL-02 Conference on Empirical Methods in Natural Language Processing, EMNLP 2002, vol. 10, pp. 79–86. Association for Computational Linguistics, Stroudsburg (2002)

17. Turney, P.D.: Thumbs up or thumbs down?: Semantic orientation applied to unsupervised classification of reviews. In: Proceedings of the 40th Annual Meeting on Association for Computational Linguistics, ACL 2002, pp. 417–424. Association for Computational Linguistics, Stroudsburg (2002)

18. Perveen, N., Missen, M.M.S., Rasool, Q., Akhtar, N.: Sentiment based twitter spam detection. Int. J. Adv. Comput. Sci. Appl. (IJACSA) **7**(7), 568–573 (2016)

19. Vinciarelli, A., Mohammadi, G.: A survey of personality computing. IEEE Trans. Affect. Comput. **5**(3), 273–291 (2014)

20. Celli, F., Poesio, M.: PR2: a language independent unsupervised tool for personality recognition from text. CoRR abs/1402.2796 (2014)

21. Myers, I.B., Myers, P.B.: Gifts Differing: Understanding Personality Type. CPP Inc., Palo Alto (1980)

22. Costa, P.T., McCrae, R.R.: Normal personality assessment in clinical practice: the neo personality inventory. Psychol. Assess. **4**(1), 5 (1992)

23. Mairesse, F., Walker, M.A., Mehl, M.R., Moore, R.K.: Using linguistic cues for the automatic recognition of personality in conversation and text. J. Artif. Int. Res. **30**(1), 457–500 (2007)

24. Oberlander, J., Nowson, S.: Whose thumb is it anyway?: Classifying author personality from weblog text. In: Proceedings of the COLING/ACL on Main Conference Poster Sessions, COLING-ACL 2006, pp. 627–634. Association for Computational Linguistics, Stroudsburg (2006)

25. Bai, S., Zhu, T., Cheng, L.: Big-five personality prediction based on user behaviors at social network sites. CoRR abs/1204.4809 (2012)

26. Rangel, F., Celli, F., Rosso, P., Potthast, M., Stein, B., Daelemans, W.: Overview of the 3rd author profiling task at PAN 2015. In: Working Notes Papers of the CLEF 2015 Evaluation Labs. CEUR Workshop Proceedings, CLEF and CEUR-WS.org, September 2015

27. Shen, J., Brdiczka, O., Liu, J.: Understanding email writers: personality prediction from email messages. In: Carberry, S., Weibelzahl, S., Micarelli, A., Semeraro, G. (eds.) UMAP 2013. LNCS, vol. 7899, pp. 318–330. Springer, Heidelberg (2013). https://doi.org/10.1007/978-3-642-38844-6_29
28. Hernández Fusilier, D., Montes-y-Gómez, M., Rosso, P., Guzmán Cabrera, R.: Detecting positive and negative deceptive opinions using PU-learning. Inf. Process. Manag. **51**(4), 433–443 (2015)
29. Fornaciari, T., Celli, F., Poesio, M.: The effect of personality type on deceptive communication style. In: 2013 European Intelligence and Security Informatics Conference (EISIC), pp. 1–6, August 2013
30. O'Callaghan, D., Harrigan, M., Carthy, J., Cunningham, P.: Network analysis of recurring youtube spam campaigns. CoRR abs/1201.3783 (2012)
31. Jensen, G.H., DiTiberio, J.K.: Personality and the Teaching of Composition. Ablex, Norwood (1989)

Mining Communication Data in a Music Community: A Preliminary Analysis

Fabio Calefato, Giuseppe Iaffaldano$^{(\boxtimes)}$, Filippo Lanubile, Antonio Lategano, and Nicole Novielli

Dip. Informatica, University of Bari, Bari, Italy
{fabio.calefato,giuseppe.iaffaldano,filippo.lanubile,
antonio.lategano,nicole.novielli}@uniba.it

Abstract. Comments play an important role within online creative communities because they make it possible to foster the production and improvement of authors' artifacts. We investigate how comment-based communication help shape members' behavior within online creative communities. In this paper, we report the results of a preliminary study aimed at mining the communication network of a music community for collaborative songwriting, where users collaborate online by first uploading new songs and then by adding new tracks and providing feedback in forms of comments.

Keywords: Computer-mediated communication · Online creative communities
Social networks · SNA

1 Introduction

Online creative communities are virtual groups whose members volunteer to collaborate over the Internet to produce music, movies, games, and other cultural products [6]. Active feedback actions, such as commenting, are fundamental to the success of creative communities [5]. Comments encourage members to produce new artifacts or provide advice for improving existing content. Over time, comments also help build trust between the authors of posts and commenters, facilitate the formation of groups of users who share content and provide support [2, 3].

There has been a considerable amount of studies on social behavior in online communities of software developers. For example, Xu et al. [8] consider two developers socially related if they participate in the same project. Instead, Bird et al. [1] consider developers related if there is evidence of email communication – an arguably more direct evidence of an existing social link.

Although social networks of software developers have been comprehensively studied from different perspectives, how communication help shape members' behavior within online artistic communities is relatively unexplored in previous research. Accordingly, we conducted an empirical study to investigate communication in a music community where users collaborate online by first uploading new songs and then by adding new tracks (e.g., sing over them, play another instrument, add audio effects), as an extension of previous creative work. As the music community includes both authors,

© Springer International Publishing AG, part of Springer Nature 2018
I. Garrigós and M. Wimmer (Eds.): ICWE 2017, LNCS 10544, pp. 241–251, 2018.
https://doi.org/10.1007/978-3-319-74433-9_22

who write songs, and music lovers, who play songs and give feedback to authors through comments, we are interested in understanding how the communication activity relates to (*i*) the songwriting activity and (*ii*) the establishment of links between authors and commenters in the underlying social network.

Accordingly, we define the following research questions:

RQ1 - What are the properties of the community communication network?

RQ2 - Do authors and non-authors play different roles in the community communication network?

RQ3 – Is there a relationship between the communication and the songwriting activity?

We address these research questions using a combination of social network analysis, correlation analysis, and descriptive statistics of the activity traces left by community members.

The remainder of this paper is organized as follows. In Sect. 2, we portray the music community and build the underlying communication network. The results of the analysis are reported in Sect. 3. Finally, we draw conclusions and outline future work directions in Sect. 4.

2   Communication Within the Community

Songtree[1] is a social platform for the collaborative creation and sharing of music founded in 2015. It relies on a growing community of over 100,000 music enthusiasts and musicians who contributed more than 37,000 songs. The platform is available both on the web and as a mobile app. Musicians create their songs through an incremental, collaborative process that starts with the sharing of a new song, which represents the root of a song tree to be built collaboratively. Both the author of a new song as well as other musicians in the community may contribute to collaborative creation by *overdubbing*, that is, recording new tracks over a baseline song, e.g., by playing new instruments or adding voice, thus originating a new branch of the song tree (see Fig. 1).

.

---

[1] http://songtr.ee

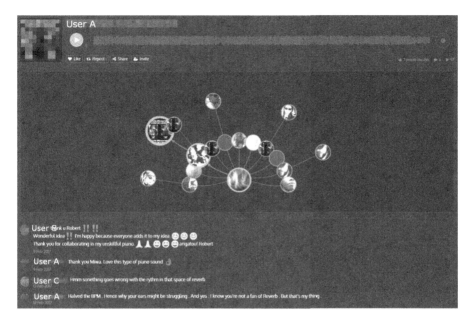

Fig. 1. An example of a song tree with root and derived songs/nodes.

In Songtree, we can distinguish two member profiles, namely authors and non-authors. Authors contribute to the community by writing and sharing songs, either new ones or overdubs. Every song in Songtree may originate a thread of discussions composed of comments contributed by community members. Non-authors are users who do not share any song but nonetheless enjoy listening to music. Non-authors may be 'lurkers', who do not leave any sign of appreciation, or 'active'. The latter, in turn, are divided into 'mute' who contribute to the community activities only by providing non-written signals (e.g. liking, reposting), and 'commenters' who contribute by giving a written feedback on others' songs (see Fig. 2).

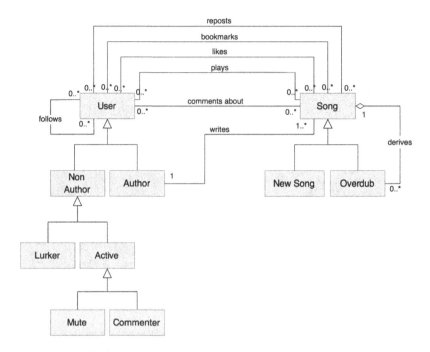

Fig. 2. A conceptual model of the Songtree community.

Since the focus of the study is on the communication activity, we build a communication network based on the commenting activity of users, whether authors or just commenters.

To understand the nature of comments on a song, we performed a preliminary, qualitative investigation based on a sample of comments from the Songtree database. More specifically, we extracted and manually analyzed the content of the discussion originated by 50 commented songs, randomly extracted from the dataset (described next). We observed that in 92% of the cases comments were appreciations for the song; in 6% of the comments we found a message directed to another commenter; the remaining 2% were other types of comments. Based on this evidence, we can assume that comments in Songtree are usually employed to provide feedback to the author of the song and, therefore, we can represent communication within the community as a *feedback network*.

Thus, we built the feedback network as a directed weighted graph where a link from node B to A represents the action of user B commenting on one or more songs authored by user A.

We focus on two social network analysis measures, that is, *in-degree* and *out-degree*, which are indicators of the importance of an individual in a network [7]. The number of incoming edges (in-degree) is a function of the number of different users an author has received comments from, while the number of outcoming edges (out-degree) is the number of different authors a user has provided comments to.

We built the dataset used for the current study from the entire SQL dump of Songtree up to December 2016. We queried the database to extract some statistics concerning the registered users and their songwriting and commenting activities. A breakdown of the extracted data is reported in Table 1.

Table 1. Data extracted from the Songtree dump.

Concept	Instances	Association	Instances
Song	37,300	Comment	28,827
New song	16,769	Repost	817
Overdub	20,531	Like	38,787
User	111,276	Bookmark	4,714
Author	5,520	Play	566,103
Non-author	105,756		
Lurker	102,470		
Active	3,286		
Mute	2,496		
Commenter	790		

We retained in the final dataset only those songs with at least one comment (6,214 out of 20,531). Furthermore, comment threads related to a song often include replies from the same author expressing gratitude towards other commenters. As such, self-comments were removed from our final dataset, obtaining 18,154 out of 28,827 comments. We also excluded from the final dataset those authors who commented only on their own songs, totaling 1,051 (out of 5,520) authors who received comments from other members, and 562 authors who commented on others' songs.

Finally, the data extracted from the final dataset were exported into TSV (Tab Separated Value), a compatible format for the Gephi[2] tool, used for network graph building and social network analysis. Figure 3 shows the feedback network diagram of Songtree in which the node size is proportional to the in-degree while the edge width is proportional to the number of received comments.

---

[2] https://gephi.org

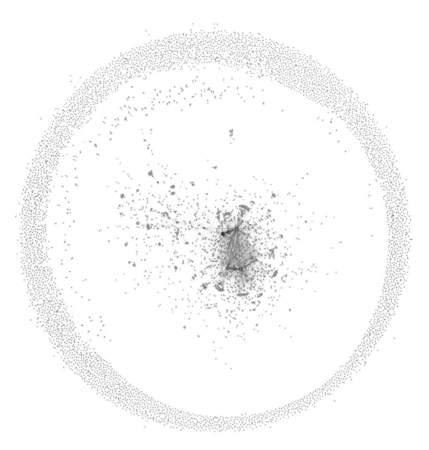

Fig. 3. Feedback network diagram (nodes = 6,310, edges = 4,366).

3 Results

In this section, we report the results of our empirical analysis, grouped by research question.

3.1 Properties of the Feedback Network

Results in Fig. 4a and b show different types of users' behavior, according to a typical power-law distribution. For the sake of completeness, we also report the distribution of comments made and received by users in the network (see Fig. 4c and d, respectively). As common for online communities [4], the majority of community members send only a few comments while there is a small group of members very active in commenting other people's songs. Similarly, the great majority of members only receive a few comments, while there is a small group of members who receive more than 500 comments. This evidence suggests that the in-degree of a member is an indication of higher status in the community, i.e., authors of popular songs receive more comments on the artifact they share.

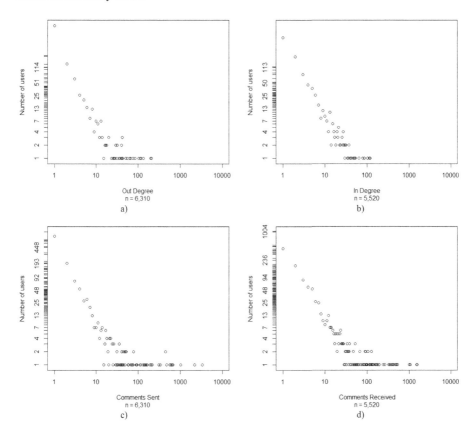

Fig. 4. Communication behavior in the Songtree community. Charts represent the distribution of (a) out-degree, (b) in-degree, (c) comments sent, and (d) comments received.

Next, we examine the relationship between the number of comments sent by an author (i.e., a member that has posted at least one song) and her related in-degree. Considering those authors who both commented and received at least one comment ($n = 405$), we observe a moderate positive association between the two metrics, as depicted in Fig. 5 and further confirmed by the Spearman's rank coefficient equal to 0.6. This evidence suggests that the commenting activity may contribute to increasing the visibility of an author's artifacts in the network.

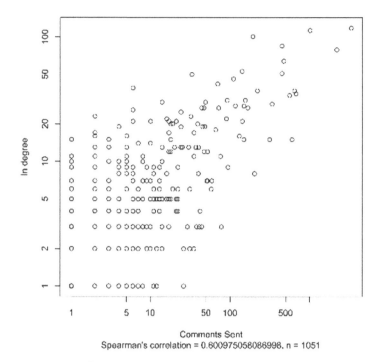

Fig. 5. How in-degree grows with number of comments sent by an author

3.2 Roles Played by Authors and Non-authors in the Feedback Network

First, we analyzed whether there are differences in the commenting behavior of authors and non-authors (see Table 2). Looking at the table, we observe that a higher percentage of non-authors (94.3%) do not provide any comment. To assess the extent of such percentages, we performed a chi-square test of independence, which reveals a relationship between authorship and commenting activity ($\chi^2 = 3{,}890.3$, p < 2.2e-16).

Table 2. Commenting activity: authors vs. non-authors.

Frequency percent	No comments	One or more comments	Tot.
Authors	4,958	562	*5,520*
	4.5%	0.5%	*5.0%*
Non-authors	104,966	790	*105,756*
	94.3%	0.7%	*95.0%*
Tot.	*109,924*	*1,352*	*111,276*
	98.8%	*1.2%*	*100.0%*

We refine our analysis by comparing the commenting behavior of authors against *active* users, thus excluding lurkers who may only be registered for curiosity without ever returning a visit. From Table 3, we note that a higher percentage of authors (56.3%)

do not provide any comment compared to active users (28.3%). Also in this case, the chi-square test of independence revealed a significant relationship between the categories in Table 3 ($\chi^2 = 304.48$, p < 2.2e-16), indicating that active users are more inclined to leave comments than authors.

Table 3. Commenting activity: authors vs. active users.

Frequency percent	No comments	One or more comments	Tot.
Authors	4,958	562	5,520
	56.3%	6.4%	62.7%
Active	2,496	790	3,286
	28.3%	9.0%	37.3%
Tot.	7,454	1,352	8,806
	84.6%	15.4%	100.0%

3.3   Relationship Between Communication and Songwriting Activities

Since we analyze here the relationship between the commenting and songwriting activities, we run a correlation analysis restricted to authors only. We observe a weak Spearman's rank correlation (r = 0.36, n = 5,520) between the number of comments sent by a Songtree user and number of songs recorded (Fig. 6). Similar correlation values are

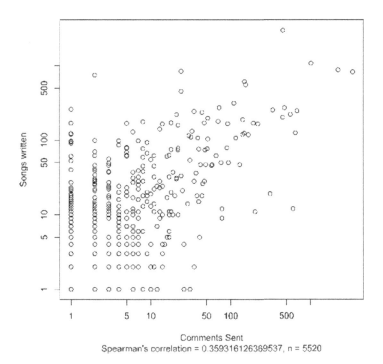

Fig. 6. Correlation between authors' commenting activity and songwriting activity.

observed if we distinguish between new songs (r = 0.33, n = 4,756) and overdubs (r = 0.43, n = 1,405), as shown respectively in Fig. 7a and b.

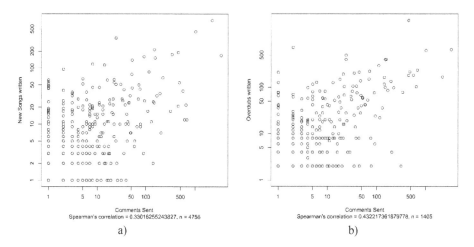

Fig. 7. Correlation between (a) authors' commenting activity and new-song writing activity; (b) authors' commenting activity and overdubbing activity.

4   Conclusions and Future Work

In this paper, we described a preliminary study aimed at mining the communication activity of a music community for collaborative songwriting.

We found that the in-degree and out-degree measures of the feedback network exhibit typical long-tailed, power-law distribution, meaning that a few members account for the bulk of the comments sent and received. We also observed a moderate relationship between the number of comments sent by an author and the number of different people who commented to her songs (i.e., in-degree), meaning that comments may positively contribute to the visibility of author's creations. Besides, we analyzed the relation between communication and songwriting activity and found that active users, thus excluding lurkers, are more inclined to provide feedback than authors.

Considering the variety of genres and people in the community, we intend to replicate this analysis to study the relations among the different sub-communities built around music genres (e.g., rock, hip-hop, classical). Besides, we will further investigate the songwriting activity, specifically how collaborations take form and which are the factors that increment the attractiveness of a song.

Acknowledgements. We thank Songtree for contributing their data. This work has been partially supported by the project EmoQuest, funded by MIUR under the SIR program.

References

1. Bird, C., Gourley, A., Devanbu, P., Gertz, M., Swaminathan, A.: Mining email social networks. In: Proceedings of the 2006 International Workshop on Mining Software Repositories, NY, USA, pp. 137–143. ACM, New York (2006)
2. Blau, P.M.: Exchange and Power in Social Life. Transaction Publishers, Emerson (1964)
3. Burke, M., Settles, B.: Plugged in to the community: social motivators in online goal-setting groups. In: Proceedings of the 5th International Conference on Communities Technologies, NY, USA, pp. 1–10. ACM, New York (2011)
4. Newman, M.E.J.: The structure and function of complex networks. SIAM Rev. **45**, 167–256 (2003). https://doi.org/10.1137/S003614450342480
5. Schultheiss, D., Blieske, A., Solf, A., Staeudtner, S.: How to encourage the crowd? a study about user typologies and motivations on crowdsourcing platforms. In: Proceedings of the 2013 IEEE/ACM 6th International Conference on Utility and Cloud Computing. IEEE Computer Society, Washington, DC, USA, pp. 506–509 (2013)
6. Settles, B., Dow, S.: Let's get together: the formation and success of online creative collaborations. In: Proceedings of SIGCHI Conference on Human Factors in Computing Systems, NY, USA, pp. 2009–2018. ACM, New York (2013)
7. Wasserman, S., Faust, K.: Social Network Analysis: Methods and Applications. Cambridge University Press, Cambridge (1994). Sociology The Journal of the British Sociol. assoc. 8: xxxi, 825
8. Xu, J., Gao, Y., Christley, S., Madey, G.: A topological analysis of the open source software development community. In: Proceedings of the 38th Annual Hawaii International Conference System Science (2005)

Measuring Personal Branding in Social Media: Towards an Influence Indication Score

Evanthia Faliagka[1], Kostas Ramantas[2], Maria Rigou[3,4],
and Spiros Sirmakessis[1,4(✉)]

[1] Department of Computer and Informatics Engineering,
Technological Institution of Western Greece,
National Road Antirrio-Ioannina, 30020 Antirrio, Greece
syrma@teiwest.gr
[2] Iquadrat Informatica, Barcelona, Spain
[3] Department of Computer Engineering and Informatics,
University of Patras, Rion Campus, 26500 Patras, Greece
[4] Hellenic Open University, Parodos Aristotelous 18, 26335 Patras, Greece

Abstract. The exploding use of social media sites has allowed everyday people to build their own online personal brand, exploiting the social web to promote their strengths and unique qualities. Such passionate individuals make great fits for certain roles in a company as well as in leadership positions. Moreover, for certain positions the ability of candidates to build a strong personal brand and attract a high number of followers is a robust success predictor. In this direction, we propose a new module for assessing candidates' personal brand strength, based on their social web activity. This module is then integrated in a company-oriented e-recruitment system which automates the candidate pre-screening process and evaluated as part of a pilot scenario.

Keywords: Personal branding · Social web mining · e-recruitment

1 Introduction

In the era of Web 2.0, a lot of people use the WWW as a tool for career development and job search [1–3] and at the same time companies also rely on automated web-based e-recruitment tools for their hiring process. Modern e-recruitment systems typically include some form of automation, analyzing the applicant profiles to determine the ones that fit the position's specifications and increasing efficiency. For example, SAT telecom reported 44% cost savings and a drop in the average time needed to fill a vacancy from 70 to 37 days [4] after deploying an e-recruitment system. But in practice the required skills of the applicant are not the only factor that determines the final decision about hiring, as subjective criteria such as personality or perceived match to the corporate culture are equally important. Such subjective criteria could previously only be assessed by human recruiters at the interview stage. However, the exploding use of social media sites means that recruiters can often get a glimpse of a candidates' personality from their online behavior at a very early stage of the recruitment process [5]. It is an established fact that HR offices exploit social media sites to assess potential

© Springer International Publishing AG, part of Springer Nature 2018
I. Garrigós and M. Wimmer (Eds.): ICWE 2017, LNCS 10544, pp. 252–261, 2018.
https://doi.org/10.1007/978-3-319-74433-9_23

employees. Career Builder reported that 60% of employers have admitted to leverage information posted to social networking sites in the hiring process [6]. This information could affect their perception of their candidate in either a positive way (e.g., attesting to skills, qualifications, and ability to fit in the organization) or in a negative way (e.g., if inappropriate photos, alcohol and drug abuse or discriminatory comments are involved).

As users become educated regarding the risks of social media use, carefully managing their online identity and making use of the platforms' privacy controls is gradually becoming the norm. However, a minority of passionate candidates take this approach one step further, evolving their online identity in their own unique *personal brand* [7]. Personal branding is similar to the product branding, in that it involves promoting an individuals' strengths and unique qualities to a target audience [8]. Such passionate individuals make great fits for certain roles in a company, as well as in leadership positions. Thus, it would make sense companies' e-recruitment systems to identify and promote individuals with strong personal brands. In this direction in [9] an integrated company oriented e-recruitment system is proposed. The system automates the candidate pre screening process providing an overall candidate ranking based on a combination of supervised learning and semantic skills matching. Applicant evaluation is based on a predefined set of objective criteria evaluated on the basis of applicant's skills that are directly extracted from his LinkedIn profile, as well as his personality traits extracted by textually analyzing blog posts.

In this work, we propose a new e-recruitment module which infers a candidate's "personal brand" strength by combining measurements of social activity relevance and social influence. Candidates can then be short-listed for consideration in appropriate job positions. To showcase the effectiveness of the proposed scheme, a prototype has been implemented. The produced candidates' listing combining personal branding scores automatically extracted from each candidate's social media activity and has been assessed against actual scores manually assigned by human recruiters. The next sections provide details regarding the implementation of the new module. The discussion moves to the pilot recruitment scenario that was used to evaluate the effectiveness of the proposed approach and the paper ends with the main conclusions reached.

2 Personal Branding Strategies and Tools

The concept of Personal Branding, proposed by Tom Peters in [10] and initially assumed to only be relevant to celebrities, is increasingly becoming important for everyday people. Developing a personal brand is a similar process to product branding [11, 12], in that individuals are promoting their strengths and uniqueness. Personal branding in the digital space is associated primarily with social media activity, where one consciously strives to differentiate oneself and create a unique online identity, for attaining some specific objectives. In this work we will only focus on personal branding in the professional setting, where the key objective is career development. In this context, a common personal branding strategy is sharing ones knowledge and experiences through social media sites, thus creating a narrative or sharing one's professional story [14]. Moreover, sharing recent developments and advice in one's field of expertise corroborates their experience and skills. Personal branding requires **consistency**, and engaging the **right audience**.

Individuals that are interested in building their own personal brand have a wide range of social media tools in their arsenal:

- LinkedIn is the premier tool of career development and networking, allowing users to showcase their skills, experience, and also includes some interesting social networking functionalities. Users are free to share "status updates" with their network, or people that "follow" them.
- Twitter also has high potential to build one's personal brand, as twitter users can appeal to a very wide audience, which is not typically limited to their social circle. Although not strictly a professional development tool, it can be employed as one if users specifically target an audience in a specific domain and keep focus on sharing relevant information.
- Question-and-Answer sites such as Quora or StackOverflow help users establish themselves as an authority in their domain, by answering questions and proposing solutions to problems. These sites also typically keep track of answered questions, and users can gain reputation points which attest their contribution and overall rank.
- Blogs are usually a complementary means of personal branding, as they require a very high time commitment and it is hard to keep a consistent posting schedule. Moreover, keeping track of readers and engaging them is not as straightforward as in micro-blogging platforms. However, they are ideal for posting longer form texts to thoroughly expand on a topic, explain a complex technical subject, etc.
- Facebook is definitely not ideal in its use as a personal branding tool, but it is still useful due to the strong networking effects. Although it is uncommon a personal Facebook account to be exclusively work-related, it has the benefit of engaging audiences that have no presence in other social media sites.

3   A New Module for Assessing Personal Brand Strength

A strong personal brand is considered highly desired in certain job positions as it could act as a strong success predictor (see Table 1). Currently, identification of such highly-sought individuals can only be performed by a human recruiter, as part of an unofficial background check on applicants, based on their (social) web presence. Automated recruitment systems typically rely on formal qualifications and keyword searches. Only candidates that have passed the pre-screening phase are typically assessed by hiring managers, who are able to see beyond skill-sets, and assess how a candidate would fit in the corporate culture. This approach has limitations, as it is still a time consuming process and does not work well when the applicants use pseudonymous accounts or have a very common name and surname. Moreover, there is a high risk that exceptionally talented candidates with strong personal brands could be filtered-out by automated tools for trivial causes (e.g. having been fired from a previous job could exclude a strongly-branded candidate). A better approach would be to automate this background check, so that it is performed directly by the e-recruitment system, which both increases efficiency and prevents the aforementioned risk. In [15]

Table 1. Positions where a strong personal brand is highly sought after

Marketing	Since personal branding and product branding are closely related, a success on the former predicts success on the latter
Leadership positions	Leaders inherently have a strong personal brand, being the mentors and influencers that offer their thoughts and perspective to their community. A strong social presence clearly defines the value that a leader can deliver
Junior position	Investing in personal branding indicates passion and commitment, which are strong predictors of success for candidates without relevant experience that typically apply for starter/intern positions
Technology evangelist	Technology evangelists are actively pushing a new product or technology via networking effects and a strong personal brand proves their ability to influence their community

the authors proposed a first approach to such a system that relies on users' social web activities to automate the candidate evaluation and pre-screening process.

In this section, a new approach is proposed for automatically assessing a candidates' personal branding, that has been implemented as an e-recruitment module for the aforementioned system. The proposed system is able to make inferences on the applicants' brand strength based on his social media use. Specifically, asking the applicant to log-in to the system with his Facebook or Twitter credentials, provides access to a large amount of information, such as status updates, interaction with other users and interests ("likes"). This allows the system to automatically assess whether the candidate has a clear personal branding strategy, and the level of influence the candidate is perceived to have in his domain of expertise. An influential candidate with a personal branding strategy in the position domain is considered a crucial asset for certain positions. In the following table (Table 1) we summarize positions where a strong personal brand is a highly sought-after characteristic.

Although this is out of scope of this work, as can be seen in Fig. 1 a fully functional e-recruitment system is expected to also implement a ranking function that will assess the candidates' overall relevance to a specific job position, based on the scores of individual selection criteria [5]. Numerous ranking functions based on AHP [16] or Machine Learning techniques [17] can be found in the literature.

To assess the strength of a candidates' personal brand we define the following criteria and can be mapped to real numbers in the interval [0, 1]. Their values can be calculated with web mining techniques, exploiting the candidates' social presence:

- *relevance*: refers to candidates that have a social media presence that is relevant to the position offered. This indicates that the candidate has a personal branding strategy in the specific domain.
- *influence*: candidates that others tend to use as a source of information or arguments. They typically receive a high number of social interactions (e.g., shares, re-tweets, comments, etc.).

We will therefore define a candidate with a strong personal brand as one with a social media presence focused on the domain of the position ("relevance") and a high degree of influence. In the following sections, we detail the method employed to derive these two metrics.

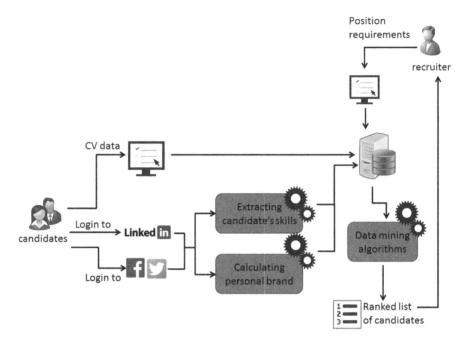

Fig. 1. Personal branding component in a general e-recruitment context

3.1   Measuring User Relevance

The first step required to calculate the "relevance" metric is to define the set of domains related to the offered position(s) that are supported by the system. In the case of our system related domains are selected from the categories of the Open Directory Project (ODP) [18]. In this work, a selection of high-level domains was made, that includes the thematic categories in Table 2.

Table 2. DMOZ domains & sub-domains

1. Sales & Marketing	2. Computer security
5. Computer software	4. Finance
7. Healthcare	6. News
9. Management	8. Science

The second step is to create a corpus of words which are representative for each selected category. To create the corpus we used the Open Directory Project predetermined hierarchy of categories so as to access websites on the specific topics that respond to related information needs. Then, we parsed these websites to make a corpus of words for each topic. Specifically, we used features extracted from the HTML code of the site's webpages including the pure text contained in it and the text of specific tag values as headings (<title>, <h1>) and meta information (<meta>). By discarding terms that appear with a frequency less than a user-defined threshold (for our pilot testing we used the value of 100 times, and we processed only adjectives, verbs and nouns) we form a vocabulary that represents each category (domain).

To find which categories are mentioned by the candidate often we analyze not only the hashtags that can directly give the information we need, but also the raw text of tweets and Facebook posts. We process the text in the tweets and Facebook posts and compute daily unigram frequencies. By discarding terms that appear less than the specified threshold, we form a vocabulary of size $|V| = 71,555$. We then form a user term-frequency matrix with the mean term frequencies per user during the time interval Δt. All term frequencies are normalized with the total number of tweets and Facebook posts posted by the user. The final step is to compute a topic score for each user-topic pair to assign the DMOZ categories to the candidates. For that reason, we used the Jaccard index, also known as the Jaccard similarity coefficient [19]. The Jaccard coefficient measures similarity between finite sample sets and is defined as the size of the intersection divided by the size of the union of the sample sets:

$$J(A, B) = \frac{|A \cap B|}{|A \cup B|} \qquad (1)$$

Clearly,

$$0 \leq J(A, B) \leq 1 \qquad (2)$$

To calculate the "relevance" metric we calculate the Jaccard coefficient for every pair of {DMOZ domain word, candidate word} and the score is the greatest of the calculated values.

3.2 Measuring User Influence

A set of metrics should be defined in order to investigate candidates' branding activity. The goal is to identify which candidates are so passionate about work-related topics that can influence others. In this context we propose a set of social web activity metrics (note: all metrics that count social activity such as posts/tweets, likes, etc., take into account only relatively recent activities that were recorded in the period of the last 12 months and filter out older activities):

- $Fb_{friends}$, $Twitter_{followers}$, $Blog_{subscribers}$: the size of a user's network (friends, followers, subscribers) in each social platform.
- $Twitter_{ff\_rate}$: the number of a user's followers divided by the number of user's this user follows.
- Fb_{share_rate}: the number of a user's Fb posts that have been shared by one or more of his friends divided by the total number of user posts.
- Fb_{react_rate}: the number of posts that received some kind of reaction (like/love/haha etc. or comment) by at least 10% of a user's friends divided by the total number of user's posts.
- $Twitter_{retweet\_rate}$: the number of a user's tweets that have been retweeted by one or more of his followers divided by the total number of user tweets.

- $Blog_{react\_rate}$: the number of blog posts that received some kind of reaction by subscribers or users (i.e. were posted in social media or were commented) divided by the total number of blog posts.
- Fb_{indiv_react}: the number of individual friends who share user posts or tag the user divided by the total number user's friends.
- $Twitter_{indiv\_react}$: the number of individual followers who retweet content or mention the user divided by the total number user's followers.

Especially in Twitter we will also use the Follower/Following Ratio. It compares the amount of users who have subscribed to a user to the number of users that he follows. A higher Follower/Following Ratio denotes that the user has more people following him that those that he follows and this is an indication of an influential user. Ratio values less than 1 indicate that the users follows more users than the users that follow him and this is not an indication of an influential user (rather the user might be considered a mass-follower). This ratio however, as well as the amount of friends/followers are not reliable metrics for determining a user's degree of influence [20] and must be viewed in context with the interaction ratios.

On the other hand, interactions (and especially shares and retweets) are much clearer indications of a user that attracts interest and is considered by others as a source of reliable or interesting information. In order to quantify a user's interactions, we measure the number of a candidate's retweets and mentions in a time period of 1 year (or similarly shares and interactions on Facebook). We also calculate the number of individual users who retweet or mention a particular user divided by the total amount of his followers.

To calculate the previous metrics we only take into account posts (status updates or tweets) that their content relates to one of the position related domains (such as the ones illustrated in Table 2). The methodology detailed in Sect. 3.1 is employed to filter-out status updates or tweets that are not relevant to the qualifications required by the job position (i.e. the related domains). The rationale is that we are not interested in the candidates' general social web impact, but rather on how successful they are in disseminating information about work-related topics.

4   Pilot Scenario

In this section we present an experiment that was conducted in order to identify the importance of each one of the metrics mentioned above in someone's brand. We set up a pilot scenario with a lead SW engineer position opening and a sample of 30 candidates ranging in age from 24 to 40. We used young participants because they are most likely to take into consideration their brand due to the often career transitions. Each one of these participants used our system, which scanned their Facebook, Twitter and blog account and calculated the metrics defined in Sect. 3.

Then we asked a human resources (HR) professional at the university to evaluate the same participants and assign a score on a scale from 1 = limited brand strategy to 5 = strong brand strategy. The complete interview process thus lasted from 45 to 90 min. During the interview the HR professional asked questions about the candidate's branding strategy, what he wanted to achieve with it and other open type questions. Then he asked each participant to show the pages of their social accounts so as to evaluate their real online presence. A part of the results is shown in the following table (Table 3).

Table 3. Calculated metrics and recruiter's overall evaluation

candidates	Fb$_{friends}$	Blog$_{subscribers}$	Twit-ter$_{fr\_rate}$	Fb $_{share\_rate}$	Fb$_{react\_rate}$	Twitter$_{in-div\_reac}$	recruiter
1	953	1587	1,69	0,62	0,03	0,15	4
3	1768	0	1,92	0,67	0,09	0,11	3
4	1635	991	1,38	0,73	0,09	0,12	5
8	1428	0	1,28	0,59	0,03	0,09	5
9	1684	1027	1,22	0,35	0,04	0,08	3
10	742	1350	1,24	0,39	0,03	0,07	4
11	1358	975	1,15	0,34	0,07	0,11	3
12	942	1124	1,23	0,29	0,06	0,09	3
13	3108	0	0	1,28	0,08	0	4
14	0	0	1,27	0	0	0,12	4
18	941	1151	1,15	0,37	0,03	0,06	5
19	1032	964	1,35	0,32	0,03	0,04	3
20	948	734	1,22	0,35	0,04	0,08	4
21	862	873	1,14	0,29	0,03	0,05	3
22	2908	0	0	1,17	0,06	0	2
23	0	0	1,19	0	0	0,14	3
24	0	845	1,12	0	0	0,07	4
25	539	0	1,09	0,35	0,02	0,05	3
26	985	1013	0	0,29	0,03	0	3
27	911	1052	1,09	0,31	0,02	0,05	4
29	239	0	0,92	0,15	0,02	0,02	3
30	422	814	0,83	0,17	0,02	0,03	4

We used Weka to evaluate the learning-to-rank models. We wanted to find the correlation of the scores output from the system with the actual scores assigned by the recruiter.

Table 4 shows the correlation coefficients for 4 different machine learning models, namely: Linear Regression (LR), M5' model tree (M5'), REP Tree decision tree (REP), and Regression (SVR). It must be noted here that all values are averages, obtained with the 10-fold cross validation technique. The correlation coefficient of the Linear Regression performs very well suggesting that the selection criteria are linearly separable.

Table 4. Correlation coefficient of our method

	LR	M5'	REP	SVR
Correlation coefficient	0.7628	0,67	0,57	0.7703

$$Influence\ Indication = 0.3413 * Fb_{friends} + 0.2859 * Twitter_{followers}$$
$$- 0.0423 * Blog_{subscribers} + 0.056 * Twitter_{ff_{rate}}$$
$$+ 0.1217 * Fb_{share_{rate}} + 0.0299 * Fb_{react_{rate}}$$
$$+ 0.3093 * Twitter_{retweet\_rate} + 0.4392 * Blog_{react\_rate}$$
$$+ 0.0493 * Fb_{indiv\_react} + 0.3796 * Twitter_{indiv\_react}$$
$$- 0.1337$$

5 Conclusions

In this work we proposed an e-recruitment module that infers a candidate's "personal brand" strength by combining measurements of social activity relevance and social influence. Social influence is measured in terms of an influence indication score based on a proposed set of linearly separable social activity metrics. Personal branding is similar to product branding, in that it involves promoting an individual's strengths and unique qualities to a target audience. A common personal branding strategy is sharing one's knowledge and experiences through social media sites, thus creating a narrative or sharing one's professional story. Strongly-branded candidates can be great fits for certain roles in a company (marketing, leadership, junior positions, technology evangelists, etc.) and this assessment can be crucial in the recruitment process. To showcase the effectiveness of the proposed scheme, the produced candidates' listing has been assessed against actual scores manually assigned by a human recruiter.

We plan to experiment with the system in full scale for better fine-tuning the influence indication score formula. Moreover, the system will be expanded to also integrate LinkedIn branding metrics in the influence indication score. It would also be useful to provide visualization of the metrics and the overall branding strength to enable intuitive understanding of a candidate's network and social networking activity that relates to professional content.

References

1. Jansen, B., Jansen, K., Spink, A.: Using the web to look for work: implications for online job seeking and recruiting. Internet Res. **15**, 49–66 (2005)
2. Bizer, C., Heese, R., Mochol, M., Oldakowski, R., Tolksdorf, R., Eckstein, R.: The impact of semantic web technologies on job recruitment processes. In: Ferstl, O.K., Sinz, E.J., Eckert, S., Isselhorst, T. (eds.) Wirtschaftsinformatik 2005, pp. 1367–1381. Springer, Heidelberg (2005). https://doi.org/10.1007/3-7908-1624-8_72

3. Ho, L., Kuo, T., Lin, B.: Influence of online learning skills in cyberspace. Internet Res. **20**, 55–71 (2010)
4. Pande, S.: E-recruitment creates order out of chaos at SAT telecom: system cuts costs and improves efficiency. Hum. Res. Manag. Int. Digest **19**, 21–23 (2011)
5. Faliagka, E., Rigou, M., Sirmakessis, S.: An e-recruitment system exploiting candidates' social presence. Current Trends in Web Engineering. LNCS, vol. 9396, pp. 153–162. Springer, Cham (2015). https://doi.org/10.1007/978-3-319-24800-4_13
6. Career Builder. http://www.careerbuilder.com/share/aboutus/pressreleasesdetail.aspx?ed=12/31/2016&id=pr945&sd=4/28/2016. Accessed 22 June 2017
7. Johnson, K: The importance of personal branding in social media: educating students to create and manage their personal brand. Int. J. Educ. Soc. Sci. **4**(1) (2017)
8. Labrecque, L., Markos, E., Milne, G.: Online personal branding: processes, challenges, and implications. J. Interact. Mark. **25**(2011), 37–50 (2010)
9. Faliagka, E., Iliadis, L., Karydis, I., Rigou, M., Sioutas, S., Tsakalidis, A., Tzimas, G.: On-line consistent ranking on e-recruitment: seeking the truth behind a well-formed CV. Artif. Intell. Rev. **42**, 515–528 (2014)
10. Fast Company. https://www.fastcompany.com/28905/brand-called-you. Accessed 22 June 2017
11. Kaputa, C.: UR a Brand! How Smart People Brand Themselves for Business Success. Davies-Black Publishing, Mountain View (2005)
12. Schwabel, D.: Me 2.0: A Powerful Way to Achieve Brand Success. Kaplan Publishers, NewYork (2009)
13. LEVO. https://www.levo.com/posts/7-ways-to-build-an-unstoppable-personal-brand-in-2017. Accessed 22 June 2017
14. Brooks, A.K., Anumudu, C.: Identity development in personal branding instruction. Adult Learn. **27**(1), 23–29 (2016)
15. Faliagka, E., Tsakalidis, A., Tzimas, G.: An integrated e-recruitment system for automated personality mining and applicant ranking. Internet Res. **22**(5), 551–568 (2012)
16. Saaty, T.L.: How to make a decision: the analytic hierarchy process. Eur. J. Oper. Res. **48**, 9–26 (1990)
17. Basak, D., Srimanta, P., Dipak, C.P.: Support vector regression. Neural Inf. Process. Lett. Rev. **10**, 203–224 (2007)
18. DMOZ (n.d.). http://dmoztools.net/. Accessed 6 Sept 2016
19. Suphakit, N., Jatsada, S., Ekkachai, N., Supachanun, W.: Using of Jaccard coefficient for keywords similarity. In: Proceedings of the International Multi Conference of Engineers and Computer Scientists (2013)
20. Cha, M., Haddadi, H., Benevenuto, F., Gummadi, P.K.: Measuring user influence in Twitter: the million follower fallacy. ICWSM **10**, 10–17 (2010)

ICWE 2017 Tutorials

Big Web Data: Warehousing and Analytics

Recent Trends and Future Challenges

Alfredo Cuzzocrea[✉]

University of Trieste and ICAR-CNR, Trieste, Italy
alfredo.cuzzocrea@dia.units.it

Abstract. *Big Web Data* are gaining momentum for a widespread family of applications, ranging from Web advertisement to Web recommendation systems, from Semantic Web to Social Web systems, and so forth. In all these contexts, *big data methodologies and paradigms* play a leading role. *Big Web data warehousing and analytics* are two fortunate approaches to this end, as they are effectively able to extract actionable knowledge from massive big Web data repositories. In line with this emerging research trend, this paper explores state-of-the-art big Web data warehousing and analytics proposals, and future challenges in this scientific area.

Keywords: Big data · Big web data · Big web data warehousing
Big web data analytics

1 Introduction

Supporting *warehousing and analytics over Big Web Data* is more and more important at now (e.g., [1, 2]). This emerging trend is stirred-up by recent advances of big data methodologies and technologies (e.g., [3, 4]) that are pervading challenging Web application scenarios such as Web recommendation systems, Web advertisement systems, Deep Web, Wisdom Web, Social Web and, not last for relevance, social networks.

In each of these application scenarios, big Web data play a critical role in order to support decision-making processes that can become relevant for a wide family of society sectors, ranging from social scenarios to e-government scenarios, from e-procurement scenarios to smart city scenarios, and so forth. To this end, big Web data must be collected, cleaned, stored, periodically-integrated with recent updates, aggregated and queried as to fully-support truly big data analytics processes over them.

In this scenario, *OLAP methodologies* over big Web data plays a critical role, as, thanks to fortunate *multidimensional abstractions*, OLAP allows us to extract actionable knowledge from such class of big data repertories, and it can reasonably considered as a first-class kind of big Web data analytics methodologies. In order to provide OLAP over big Web data, first appropriate warehousing methodologies must be considered. Indeed, before aggregation, big Web data must be processed according to consolidate data warehousing methodologies, as to keep advantage from authoritative results deriving from decades of research in the field. In line with these considerations, this

© Springer International Publishing AG, part of Springer Nature 2018
I. Garrigós and M. Wimmer (Eds.): ICWE 2017, LNCS 10544, pp. 265–266, 2018.
https://doi.org/10.1007/978-3-319-74433-9_24

paper explores state-of-the-art big Web data warehousing and analytics proposals, and future challenges in this scientific area.

2   State-of-the-Art Big Web Data Warehousing and Analytics Proposals

Among the wide literature available on big Web data warehousing and analytics, some relevant are: [1, 2]. [1] proposes *Kvasir*, a semantic recommendation system, on top of *latent semantic analysis* and other state-of-the-art big data technologies to seamlessly integrate an automated and proactive content provision service into Web browsing. [2] describes an *architecture-centric methodology*, called *Architecture-centric Agile Big data Analytics* (AABA), to address the technical, organizational, and rapid technology change challenges of both big data system development and agile delivery of big data analytics for Web-based Systems.

3   Big Web Data Warehousing and Analytics: Future Challenges

A plethora of research challenges in the context of big Web data warehousing and analytics arise at now. Among others, our attention was captured by the following ones:

- *Big Web Data Integration Issues*: here the main problem consists in devising models, techniques and algorithms for integrating big Web data, which are usually highly-heterogeneous in nature;
- *Big Web Data ETL Processes*: supporting ETL processes over big Web data opens the door to a wide collection of emerging challenges in the field, such as: *data alimentation methods, event-based vs time-based ETL*, and so forth;
- *OLAP over Big Web Data*: computing aggregates over big Web data, e.g. those defined by recent SPARQL queries, is an exciting challenge for the future.

4   Conclusions

Starting from emerging research trends, this paper has explored state-of-the-art big Web data warehousing and analytics proposals, and future challenges in this scientific area.

References

1. Wang, L., Tasoulis, S.K., Roos, T., Kangasharju, J.: Kvasir: scalable provision of semantically relevant web content on big data framework. IEEE Trans. Big Data **2**(3), 219–233 (2016)
2. Chen, H.-M., Kazman, R., Haziyev, S.: Agile big data analytics for web-based systems: an architecture-centric approach. IEEE Trans. Big Data **2**(3), 234–248 (2016)
3. Cuzzocrea, A., Saccà, D., Ullman, J.D.: Big data: a research agenda. In: IDEAS 2013, pp. 198–203 (2013)
4. Cuzzocrea, A., Song, I.-Y., Davis, K.C.: Analytics over large-scale multidimensional data: the big data revolution! In: DOLAP 2011, pp. 101–104 (2011)

Model-Based Development of JavaScript Web Applications

Gerd Wagner$^{(\boxtimes)}$ ⓘ

Department of Informatics,
Brandenburg University of Technology, Cottbus, Germany
G.Wagner@b-tu.de

Abstract. This tutorial presents a model-based approach to developing plain JavaScript web applications with responsive constraint validation, enumeration attributes, uni- and bi-directional associations, and inheritance in class hierarchies. It also shows how to implement the discussed information management concepts and techniques in a generic way in the form of three model-based development libraries: cLASSjs, mODELcLASSjs and mODELvIEWjs.

1 Model-Based Development

In model-based development, there is a basic distinction between three kinds of models as engineering artifacts resulting from corresponding modeling activities in the analysis, design and implementation phases: (1) solution-independent *domain models*, also called *conceptual models*, (2) platform-independent *design models*, (3) platform-specific *implementation models*, as described in the following diagram.

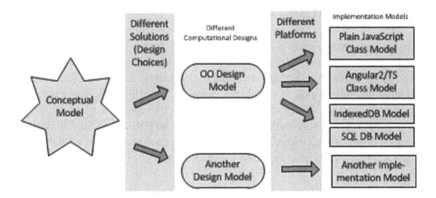

In the case of JavaScript web apps, it is natural to combine model-based development with the *Model-View-Controller (MVC)* architecture paradigm such that the app's *Model*, in the form of a set of *model classes*, is obtained by coding the JavaScript class model derived from the information design model. Depending on the choice of data storage technology (local storage, IndexedDB or cloud storage), a corresponding

© Springer International Publishing AG, part of Springer Nature 2018
I. Garrigós and M. Wimmer (Eds.): ICWE 2017, LNCS 10544, pp. 267–268, 2018.
https://doi.org/10.1007/978-3-319-74433-9_25

data model is, along with the JavaScript class model, derived from the information design model. The data model is the basis for coding a database schema for the chosen data storage technology.

2   Validation, Enumerations, Associations and Class Hierarchies in Class Models and JavaScript Code

We present a model-based approach to four fundamental issues in app development: constraint validation, enumeration attributes, uni- and bi-directional associations, and inheritance in class hierarchies. The proposed approach supports responsive constraint validation by defining integrity constraints in model classes and performing data validation both in model classes (before save/commit) and in the user interface (on input and before submit).

Many apps need to deal with attributes that have special datatypes, called enumerations, as their range. We present a model-based approach to enumeration attributes and show how to make up for JavaScript's lack of a built-in enumeration element.

Whenever an app has to manage the data of more than one object type, it is very common that there are associations between some of them. We present a model-based approach to dealing with uni- and bi-directional associations both in model classes and in the user interface code.

Subtypes and inheritance are important elements of information models. We present a model-based approach to dealing with class hierarchies in JavaScript web apps.

All of these issues are discussed in [1].

3   Creating Rich Model Classes with cLASSjs/mODELcLASSjs

JavaScript's meta-programming capabilities allow defining meta-classes for creating (1) enumerations, (2) rich model classes with (a) expressive property declarations that may include all kinds of constraint definitions, (b) generic data conversion functions, and (c) multiple inheritance. The tutorial presents three libraries that exploit these meta-programming capabilities of JavaScript for model-based development. cLASSjs [2] allows creating constructor-based model classes. mODELcLASSjs [3] allows creating factory-based model classes with multiple inheritance. Finally, mODELvIEWjs [3] supports model-based user interface programming.

References

1. Wagner, G., Diaconescu, I.M.: Web Applications with JavaScript or Java. De Gruyter (2017). http://web-engineering.info/WebAppBook
2. cLASSjs code repo. https://github.com/gwagner57/cLASSjs
3. oNTOjs code repo. https://bitbucket.org/gwagner57/ontojs

Liquid Web Applications: ICWE2017 Tutorial

Andrea Gallidabino[1], Tommi Mikkonen[2], Niko Mäkitalo[2(✉)],
Cesare Pautasso[1], Kari Systä[3], Antero Taivalsaari[4], and Jari Voutilainen[5]

[1] Faculty of Informatics, University of Lugano (USI), Lugano, Switzerland
`andrea.gallidabino@usi.ch, c.pautasso@ieee.org`
[2] Department of Computer Science, University of Helsinki, Helsinki, Finland
`{tommi.mikkonen,niko.makitalo}@helsinki.fi`
[3] Department of Pervasive Computing, Tampere University of Technology,
Tampere, Finland
`kari.systa@tut.fi`
[4] Nokia Technologies, Tampere, Finland
`antero.taivalsaari@nokia.com`
[5] Gofore, Tampere, Finland
`jari.voutilainen@iki.fi`

Abstract. As the users possess a growing number of personal computers, smart phones, tablets, and other connected computing devices, the architecture of Web applications needs to be redesigned to enable truly seamless cross-device and multi-device use. In this tutorial, we address the *Liquid Software* concept in the context of Web applications. Liquid Web applications not only can take full advantage of the computing, storage and communication resources available on all devices owned by the end user, but also can seamlessly and dynamically migrate from one device to another, continuously following the user's attention and context. We survey how and to which extent Web technologies can support the novel requirements of Liquid Software, showing technology demonstrations that will be discussed hands-on, at the level of source code.

1 Introduction

Today, the average consumer in the U.S. or Europe has two primary computing devices – a personal computer (usually a laptop) and a smartphone. Device shipment trends indicate that number of additional Web-enabled devices is growing rapidly. Users expect to be provided with computation and storage that is constantly available, capable of delivering value even in few moments, without requiring active attention and effort from the user's part to manage the devices used to deliver it. The architecture of current Web applications does not live up to these expectations. While content is increasingly available on the Web and the users have many ways to access it, the users are unnecessarily burdened and exposed to the complexity and additional setup and maintenance hassles caused by the large number of devices at their disposal.

© Springer International Publishing AG, part of Springer Nature 2018
I. Garrigós and M. Wimmer (Eds.): ICWE 2017, LNCS 10544, pp. 269–271, 2018.
https://doi.org/10.1007/978-3-319-74433-9_26

To create software that truly supports seamless, casual and effortless multi-device use, the architecture of Web applications needs to be redesigned to enable what we call *Liquid Software*. From the end user's perspective, liquid software means that the software has a built-in ability to perform adaptive, live migration across devices. The role of the Web is to act as a platform-independent execution environment and medium that provides suitable abstractions for serialization, migration, relocation, and adaptation that are needed to develop such applications in a platform-independent fashion.

In this tutorial, we address the *Liquid Software* concept in the context of Web applications. We discuss the design space of Liquid Software, and survey how and to which extent current Web technologies can support the novel requirements in this area. Furthermore, we show concrete technology demonstrations of the Liquid.js for Polymer [1] and Liquid.js for DOM frameworks [2].

2   Tutorial Contents

There are three key parts to the tutorial, as listed below:

Motivation and use cases. This part covers the fundamentals of liquid software in terms of practical use cases, such as *Sequential Screening* and *Simultaneous Screening*. This part of the tutorial is elaborated further in [3].

Design space for liquid software. This part of the tutorial takes a look at the design space of Liquid Software, covering numerous existing approaches and their characteristics. The goal is to demonstrate how the different aspects of Liquid Software have evolved, and how they fit in the broader scope of computer systems. This part of the tutorial is based on [4].

Technology demonstrators. The final part of the tutorial presents a number of hands-on demonstrators to Liquid Software. The required software will be made available to participants, and we aim to enable every participant to create a Liquid Web App of their own. This part of the tutorial is based on [1,2].

3   Expected Audience and Equipment

The target audience of the workshop consists of researchers and practitioners who are interested in understanding Liquid Software concepts and technology. In order to participate in the hands-on parts of the technology demonstrators, a laptop with a modern web browser is required.

References

1. Gallidabino, A., Pautasso, C.: The liquid.js framework for migrating and cloning stateful web components across multiple devices. In: Proceedings of the 25th International Conference on the World Wide Web (WWW), Demonstrations, pp. 183–186 (2016)
2. Voutilainen, J.-P., Mikkonen, T., Systä, K.: Synchronizing application state using virtual DOM trees. In: Casteleyn, S., Dolog, P., Pautasso, C. (eds.) ICWE 2016. LNCS, vol. 9881, pp. 142–154. Springer, Cham (2016). https://doi.org/10.1007/978-3-319-46963-8_12
3. Mikkonen, T., Systä, K., Pautasso, C.: Towards liquid web applications. In: Cimiano, P., Frasincar, F., Houben, G.-J., Schwabe, D. (eds.) ICWE 2015. LNCS, vol. 9114, pp. 134–143. Springer, Cham (2015). https://doi.org/10.1007/978-3-319-19890-3_10
4. Gallidabino, A., Pautasso, C., Mikkonen, T., Systä, K., Voutilainen, J., Taivalsaari, A.: Architecting liquid software. J. Web Eng. **16**, 433–470 (2017)

Author Index